# RUDE WORDS

# RUDE WORDS

A Discursive History of the
London Library

## John Wells

MACMILLAN
LONDON

Copyright © John Wells 1991

The right of John Wells to be identified
as author of this work has been
asserted by him in accordance with
the Copyright, Designs and Patents Act 1988.

First published 1991 by
MACMILLAN LONDON LIMITED
Cavaye Place London SW10 9PG
and Basingstoke

Associated companies in Auckland, Delhi, Dublin, Gaborone,
Hamburg, Harare, Hong Kong, Johannesburg, Kuala Lumpur,
Lagos, Manzini, Melbourne, Mexico City, Nairobi, New York,
Singapore and Tokyo

ISBN 0-333-47519-4

A CIP catalogue record for this book is available from
the British Library

Typeset by Florencetype Ltd, Kewstoke, Avon
Printed and bound in Great Britain by
Billings Bookplan, Worcester

*For Joan Bailey,*
*who has loved the London Library*
*all her life.*

The accomplished and distinguished,
the beautiful, the wise, something
of what is best in England, have
listened patiently to my
rude words.

*Thomas Carlyle, 1840*

# Contents

# Acknowledgements

My thanks to Katie Owen, a terrifying but exhilarating editor; to John Grigg for suggesting the idea of the book in the first place, for his encouragement and help; to Joan Bailey, who though retired from the library has worked with amazing cheerfulness and enthusiasm, checking references, photocopying hundreds of pages of minutes and reports and telling me endless funny stories, only a few of which I have been able to print. Also, of course, to Douglas Matthews, Michael Higgins, Peter Halsey and all the staff, without whom it would not be the London Library.

For their help and suggestions I am also grateful, among many others, to Robyn Airlie, Lord and Lady Annan, Dr Rosemary Ashton, the Hon. Mrs Michael Astor, Duncan Back, Andrew Barrow, Professor Quentin Bell, Anne Olivier Bell, Professor Sir Isaiah Berlin OM, Andrew Best, Lord Bonham Carter, Lord Briggs of Lewes, Miss Bolton, Christopher Booker, Philip Bovey, Mrs Christopher Brocklebank, Professor Dorothea Bynon, Mirabel Cecil, Lady Chancellor, Diana Chardin, Richard Chopping, Anne Crosse, Lord Dacre, Christopher Date, Dr Fram Dinshaw, Ruth Edwardes, Judith Eagle, Valerie Eliot, Lady Elton FSA, Norman Entract, Roy Fuller, Bamber Gascoigne, Stanley Gillam, Lewis Golden, Lord Goodman, John Gornall, Jennifer Greenwell, Miron Grindea, Denis Hart, Christopher Hawtree, Lady Dorothy Heber Percy, Sir Nicholas Henderson, Marie Hersch, Dr David Hill, Brian Inglis, Tony Inglis, Richard Ingrams, Louis Jebb, Lord Jenkins of Hillhead, Mervyn Jones, Alison Kenny, Peter Langdon-Davis, Patrick Leigh Fermor, Barbara Leigh-Hunt, Laura Lindsay, Christopher Logue, Elizabeth Longford, Nesta Macdonald, M. M. Mahood, John Murray, George Newkey-Burden, Lord Norwich, Simon Nowell-Smith, Patrick O'Connor, Dr Nicholas Orme, Bruce Page, Frances Partridge, Dr Donald Parry, Tanya Pollunen, Sir Victor Pritchett, Roger Purnell, Mrs Cyril Ray, Miss Robertshaw, Sir Steven Runciman, Richard Russeil CVO, Charles Seaton, Patrick Streeter, Gunnvor Stallybrass, Ian Thomson, Kathleen Tillotson, C. R. Vinycomb, Professor Martha S. Vogeler, Ashley White and Stephen Winkworth.

ACKNOWLEDGEMENTS

Finally, for their help and patience, on what has often turned out to be a wild goose chase, to the staff of Balliol College Library, the BBC Written Archives, the British Museum, the British Library, the *Daily Telegraph*, Harrow School, the Imperial War Museum, the National Library of Ireland, the National Portrait Gallery, Nuffield College, Oxford, the Philological Society, the Portico Library Manchester, the Royal Belfast Academic Institution, the Royal Literary Fund, the *Spectator*, the Royal Statistical Society, Trinity College, Cambridge, the Victoria and Albert Museum Library and the Westminster Public Libraries.

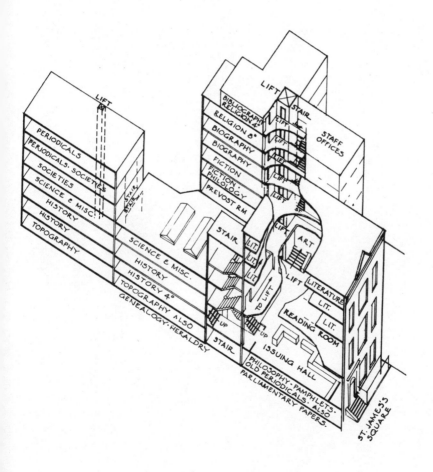

The London Library: an isometric plan

# The Golden Age

*The world is full of bores: what it needs is a good accountant*

Genet

T.S. Eliot's briefcase, black leather and stamped in gold with the initials T.S.E., was propped against the next chair. It was full of papers belonging to his widow Valerie, who was looking very much as she looked in pictures taken with the Great Man in the fifties. The summer sun was streaming in through the high, round-topped window of the Prevost Room, highlighting the soft pink dome of the chairman, John Grigg, glinting and flashing in the water jugs, picking up dazzling white on the papers scattered on the long polished table. I could for a moment understand the awe felt by the friend of a Canadian boasting about being on the committee of the London Library who said, 'My God, that's superior to the Order of Merit!'

We were debating the nature of the library in the way theologians might debate the nature of paradise. Even Frances Partridge, last survivor of godless Bloomsbury, admits that there is 'something religious' about the place: 'a kind of "I believe in the London Library, maker of Heaven and Earth" '.

The meeting began ordinarily enough with a flurry of interest in the design of next year's Christmas cards, and there was a moment of mild alarm on the part of library fundamentalists when a publisher, rather in the manner of a bishop producing a pair of frilly bloomers, held up a plastic London Library carrier bag for discreet sale on the premises. Then we moved on to talk about making changes to the building, and suddenly there was an unfamiliar sense of tension in the room.

The battle raged over a microscopic difference of opinion. Some years before, an earlier committee had embarked rather unwisely on a rebuilding scheme that had come to grief. A piece of property in Duke Street belonging to the library was leased to a cheerful Italian café, the Bonbonniere, the smell of whose cooking and remote cries of 'Due poach' eggs e bacon, due toast!' sometimes found their way into Topography. Even before the lease expired,

1

the committee wanted to develop part of the library adjoining it. This scheme having foundered, the committee was a bit windy. We were all agreed in principle that we should go ahead; the only quibble now was over whether or not to commission what was called a feasibility study. John Grigg, chairman of the committee, was in favour, the treasurer Lewis Golden was against it.

It was an appalling display. Mild-mannered Old Etonians talked of 'moving out of the existing building', and said they didn't give a damn about preserving the traditions of the library; the treasurer, supported by a marchioness and several other persons of title, threatened to resign; and someone, referring to the committee as a whole, used the word 'amateur'. John Grigg, a seasoned revolutionary from the days when as Lord Altrincham he was challenged to a duel by an Italian monarchist for allegedly insulting the Queen, did his best to remain calm when the feasibility study was crushed by a narrow majority. We had decided, or so I imagined at the time, that the library was flawless, perfect, the sum of all goodness, incapable of improvement. We liked it as it was.

I have purposely remained vague about precisely who said what that afternoon. To reveal anything spoken in confidence where no member of the press has ever been admitted would not be the act of a gentleman. The word Gentlemen is painted in large, elegant black letters on the door of both the upstairs and the downstairs Gents, and at the London Library you feel they mean it.

The only significant contribution I made during my time on the committee, suitably enough for a lavatory humorist, was to plead for the restoration of the upstairs Gents. That, like the library, is full of atmosphere, beyond a grained and varnished door halfway up the red-carpeted stairs from the Reading Room to English Literature. It is all cracked white tiles and glazed brick, with an old glass tumbler in a metal ring above the ancient washbasin, a worn piece of Imperial Leather soap, and an even more ancient hairbrush that might, who knows, have disciplined the thinning hair of Eliot himself. There is a high urinal of suitably antique design, and three spacious cubicles in panelled wood, any one of which could have accommodated Lytton Strachey, H. G. Wells, T. E. Lawrence, Rudyard Kipling, John Masefield, Hilaire Belloc and E. M. Forster, though probably not at the same time.

In 1976 it was threatened with demolition and I argued that it should be preserved; on being elected to the committee I urged successfully that the black plastic seats should be replaced with wooden ones.

The downstairs Gents also has its surprises, not least its authentic and original wooden seat: the surprise lies in its hidden counter-weight, again of archaic design, causing the seat as soon as it is put down to spring up again, catching the incautious a woody slap.

According to Joan Bailey, who began working at the library in 1941, the year of its centenary, one very odd gentleman strolled in once when she was working at the front desk. She did not recognise him, but this was understandable as he was wearing high heels, a frock and a pretty hat, and was carrying a large handbag. Joan reported the matter to her colleagues – 'I said to them, "That was a feller!" ' – convinced that her eyes had not deceived her. The visitor disappeared into the Ladies, shut himself in a cubicle, produced a brace and bit from his handbag and bored a small hole in the wooden partition. Through this he apparently peeped. What upset the librarian when the carpenters came to block the hole was that he turned out not to have been a member.

It is the Members Only notice at the door that makes the place so different. The London Library is still private, belonging to its members, and ruled by their elected committee: if they agitate about lavatory seats or having a particular periodical like *The Woman Journalist, Proceedings of the Huguenot Society* or *Stand To!* made available in the Reading Room, there is at least a chance that the committee or the librarian will do something about it, as they did when the library was founded by private subscription in 1841.

Frances Partridge, who has been a member for some seventy years, and whose father was Charles Darwin's architect, regrets now that she never asked him about the founders, all of whom he knew as a young man: 'I suppose I was just a little thing running about. He probably didn't think I'd have been interested.' She too has a lavatory anecdote, about the time Anne Olivier Bell was editing Virginia Woolf's diaries and got stuck in the Ladies in the basement. Mrs Bell was then in her seventies. 'She banged and banged, but nobody came. In the end she had to climb up through an airshaft, or it may have been a window.'

Even after seventy years, the library has lost none of its mystery for her. 'The extraordinary thing is that you always seem to get lost. Whatever you're looking for, you get lost somehow.' This is, of course, part of the library's charm. On the back wall of the Issue

Hall downstairs, near John Forster's clock and facing you as you come in from the street, there is a sectional plan of the building. Standing in front of it you might reasonably assume that the high oblong on the left of the plan represented the upper floors reached by the staircase on your left, the high oblong on the right of the plan the upper floors reached by the lift on your right, and the low section in the middle, marked 'You are here', the Issue Hall where you are standing. You would be wrong. The high section on the left of the plan represents the front of the building, behind you, and the high section on the right represents the back of the building, in front of you. The low section in the middle of the plan is also in front of you, but out of sight behind a wall. If, during the eighty or ninety years since the plan was commissioned by the great librarian Charles Hagberg Wright, someone had rehung it on the wall on the left of the stairs, it would have made perfect sense.

But the mystery is what the members love: in *The Book with Seven Seals* by Agnes Douton, there is a description of a childhood visit to the library some time in the 1870s. She and her friend Molly walk down from Jermyn Street into St James's Square to take their books back, and see Carlyle himself 'absorbed in the books he has called into being'. They have been reading 'Mr. Harrison Ainsworth's books' – historical novels like *Old St Paul's* – and the librarian, though I would prefer to think it was his assistant John Edward Jones, takes them through to the back of the building, where they look out of a window at workmen digging out old foundations in Duke Street. They have uncovered a plague pit, and the librarian shows them 'skulls and bones, necklaces, bracelets and rings . . .' Somehow, even today, you expect all of that whenever you go to the library.

I have known it for twenty years, and I have come to love everything about it, most of all the smell of dust and old leather in the stacks at the back, with the narrow, iron-grilled floors between the books. 'Looking upwards and downwards through the half-transparent floors of the book-stack,' Raymond Mortimer wrote, 'I feel inside the brain of mankind.' Less imaginative souls can look down into narrowing perspectives of more books, and more iron-grilled floors: glancing upwards, if they are lucky, they will find themselves looking up the skirt of a young researcher on the floor above.

There is, as in most libraries, a heavily charged erotic atmosphere in the Reading Room: a girl undoing a button of her cardigan lifts a head from every armchair. It is hard not to imagine urgent ecstasies in the more secluded areas of Biography, but the only story I was told was of two American research students meeting in the library who have since married. Joan Bailey was convinced that people used to jam the lift between floors in order to make love, though Christopher Logue thought the lift was so slow you wouldn't have needed to jam it.

The nearest I got to anything really scandalous was a report that there was a man in the French Pub in Soho who claimed to have made love to a girl among the Early Fathers. This is on the top floor, and would seem to be the safest place. Frances Partridge said she thought it was very likely. 'They'd have been over-excited by all those books on theology.'

Sir Nicholas Henderson certainly recalled picking up girls there just before the war, but most of all he remembered the wisdom and knowledge of books of old Mr Cox, who had joined the library in 1883, and remembered Gladstone coming in, Walter Pater in his yellow gloves, and George Gissing, 'Grey man: grey clothes, grey hair, grey face.'

Cox was by then a heavy, tortoise-like figure with a gruff cockney voice, a tobacco-stained white moustache and metal-framed glasses. He was a lifelong bachelor, but even he seems to have been susceptible to the underlying erotic mood. When Joan Bailey came in one very hot summer day without stockings and in sandals he surprised her by leaning back, peering under the desk, and saying, 'Ooh, Miss Bailey, I can see your *toes*!'

There is a less agreeable charge in the metal-framed bookcases in the stacks, which are famous for giving you electric shocks, but even that you learn to love in the end, like the soft pop and putter of the fluorescent tubes that light each passage as you pull a string with a little white button on the end. Most of all I love the possibility of browsing along the open shelves, finding books I'd never have had the patience to look up in the catalogue, and knowing that however obscure the subject, the library will have some kind of book about it, waiting to be found after a few moments' enjoyable search, pulled out of the shelves and taken home. There are, of course, cynics who would deny this, and a wag recently wrote in a book review, 'an element of the supernatural is introduced when a reader finds the book he is looking for in the London Library.'

But almost everybody believes in the way, on those open shelves, that books seem mysteriously to offer themselves when you are thinking about a particular subject, though not many have had the experience of one of the library's more eccentric members who claimed that a book literally leaped out of the shelves and hit her. It was by the notorious practitioner in the black arts, Aleister Crowley.

Virginia Woolf had very mixed feelings about the place. She particularly despised her husband, Leonard Woolf, and Desmond McCarthy for going in to look up 'the f--- word' in the 'Slang Dictionary', finding the page heavily thumbed, and coming out shaking their heads at the kind of people who used the library.

The book is still there, on the high shelves reached by a catwalk along the south wall of the Reading Room: *Slang and its Analogues* by Farmer and Henley, privately published in 1893. The thumb-marks, too, are still there; those looking up the f--- word itself are told it means 'an act of coition', and are directed to 'see GREENS'. 'To get one's greens' then leads on to a very colourful sequence of synonyms, including 'to dance the blanket hornpipe, the matri-monial polka, to work the dumb oracle, to have a grind, a hoist-in, a jottle, a jumble-guts, to Adam and Eve it, to blow the ground-sels, to do the divine work of fatherhood (Whitman), to go trom-boning, to enter the lists of love (Shakespeare), to take a turn in Bushey Park, Cock Alley, among the parsley, to whack it up or to wollop it in'.

Despite the fact that she had to share the library with people who enjoyed that kind of masculine filth, Virginia Woolf con-tinued to use it all her life. But she remained touchy. When E. M. Forster asked her if she would serve on the committee, she remem-bered him saying ten years before that they were 'sniffy about women', and turned him down. A fortnight before she committed suicide in 1941, she wrote in her diary, 'Last night I analysed my London Library complex to L[eonard]. That sudden terror has vanished.'

Frances Partridge, who worked in the Reading Room with her, also experienced something of the sudden terror when she was driven to the library by 'a very nice taxi man'. 'He said he was interested in libraries and he thought he might join. I wasn't too sure whether he'd really feel at home there.'

One person who would have made damn sure he would not was Mr Cox. Roy Fuller, who has his hero pursued through the stacks in his novel *The Second Curtain* by a sinister hit-man, was probably more terrified himself when he strolled in during the war in naval officer's uniform to apply for membership, absent-mindedly lit a cigarette, and Mr Cox shouted, 'No smokin'!' He seemed, as Fuller remembers, 'not displeased to score off a temporary naval officer sporting a walking stick.'

The library became a registered charity twenty years ago and it is now not necessary for anyone wanting to join to be proposed by an existing member, so that it is no longer exclusive in the literal sense of the word, but the awe-inspiring literary-snobbish reputation it has acquired somehow lingers on, with all the hidden taboos and old jokes attached to other exclusive clubs. A girl joining the library recently was being shown round by the librarian when a younger member of the staff ran up and told him someone had died in one of the armchairs in the Reading Room. He came back a few moments later and said it was all right, just someone who slept with his eyes open.

Democracy has to some extent broken in. Socially unambitious researchers use the Reading Room on the BBC's corporate sub-scription, and a few poorer students have their subscriptions paid by the London Library Trust, formerly the Carlyle Trust. There are, as there always have been, seedier semi-literary figures to be seen nosing among the stacks or waiting at the Issue Desk. In the last century they would have been popularising journalists; today they are television personalities. But there are, compared to other librar-ies, few Indian or West African faces: a Nigerian grandee with a passion for helicopters did, it is true, work for a while behind the porters' counter packing up books for country members. He told me he always made a point of saying good morning to Enoch Powell.

Mr Cox particularly enjoyed humiliating any writers he did not approve of, asking J. B. Priestley as he leant forward to sign a book out to repeat his name more loudly. He did so with great embar-rassment. 'Priestley!' Cox gave him a fishy stare, and asked 'Initial?'

Edith Sitwell he considered above herself, progressing as she did into the library in a grotesque Renaissance hat, followed by a chauffeur laden with books, and extending a clammy and beringed hand to all the staff behind the desk. J. W. Lambert, as a very young man, was aware that Cox was intentionally dawdling with his book in order to keep her waiting, watching out of the corner of his eye until she showed signs of impatience, and then bellowing, 'One moment, Miss Sitwell, *if* you please.'

But he was happiest with the conventional aristocracy, and shouting 'Tolstoy for the Countess'. One member returning books very late explained that he had been on a cruise. Cox glared, and the member added, 'with Lord Sowerby'. Cox's expression immediately softened into a charming smile. 'Ah! And was Lord Sowerby . . . affable?'

For seventy years, from the time he joined the staff as a boy, Cox was in a sense the library incarnate. He was a snob in his element, and the snobbery is somehow smoked into the library with the culture. If it were not so smoked it is possible the old Victorian institution would not have been preserved. Its books have been sent by post to every large country house in the British Isles, and without the support of the ruling class it could well have gone the way of many other private libraries, now in dissolution.

But the single individual who has managed its funds and been more than anyone else responsible for its preservation in recent years is the treasurer, Lewis Golden. I watched him at the end of that tempestuous committee meeting, a small, quiet man with high cheekbones and slightly hooded eyes, tucking his pen in his inside pocket, and wondered how he managed, even when the committee was more docile, to control the finances of so unworldly an institution.

Since the seventies, when he was first brought in by Michael Astor, he had by shrewd investment and the inspired purchase of shares turned the London Library from a business on its beam-ends to an efficient organisation with capital in the bank, more secure than it has ever been in its 150-year history. I knew very little about him. He told me he was not a member when he was asked to join the committee, though his wife was; and that he had had a serious illness in middle life, since when he had devoted himself to work he thought worthwhile: he also looked after Lambeth Palace Library.

As I went out through the Reading Room, lit by high windows looking out on St James's Square, the walls lined from floor to ceiling with dictionaries and encyclopedias, its iron spiral staircases leading up to the galleries under the yellowing plaster ceiling, the members our committee had been trying to represent working at their little tables or slumbering in their deep armchairs round the fireplace, I vaguely remembered that somewhere in the library there was a book of Lewis Golden's memoirs.

Downstairs in the hall I tried the card index. The drawer marked GOLD–GORD was full of tightly packed cards: *Golden Ages of the*

*Great Cities* 1952, See BOWRA C. M. and J. CARCOPINO etc.; *The Golden Apple*: a round of stories, songs, spells and riddles 1980, L. Serbo-Croatian; *The Golden Casket*, Chinese novelists of the Two Millennia, See BAUER W. and H. FRANKE ed; *The Golden Fleece*, wherein is related the riches of English wools in its manufacturies, W. S., Gent 1656; *The Golden Milestone*, 50 years of the A.A., See KEIR D. E. and B. MORGAN ed; *The Golden Peacock*, anthol. of Yiddish Poetry tr. 1944, See LEFTWICH J. ed; *The Golden Pomegranate*, sel. from the Poetry of the Mogul Empire in India 1526–1856, See BOWEN J. C. E. ed; *Der Goldene Schnitt*, grosse Erzähler der Neuen Rundschau 1890–1960, See SCHWERIN C. ed; *The Golden Treasury* rev. and enl., See PALGRAVE, Francis T., L. English Anthol.

I resisted all of these, since this was supposed to be the author catalogue, and was finally rewarded by finding authors rather than titles. *Golden, Grace Lydia*, 'Old Bankside' Topog. London; *Golden, Harry Lewis*, 'The Lynching of Leo Frank' S. Crime; *Golden, Herbert Herschel*, and S. O. Sinches, 'Modern French Literature and Language' Bibliog. Fr.; then *Golden, Morris*, 'Richardson's Characters' L. English Lit. I was stumped. I eventually ran him to ground in Later Accessions: *Golden, L.*, 'Echoes from Arnhem' H. European War II. I then began the familiar ritual of getting lost in the London Library.

Fortunately I was rescued by the librarian, Douglas Matthews, who muttered, 'Military History', smoothed his cockatoo-comb of crinkly red hair over his wide red librarian's forehead, and led me off down a little passage past an umbrella stand, up some clanging iron-grid stairs, patted an alphabetical list of unlikely subjects attached to the end of a bookstack to reorientate himself, and pulled one of the little strings with a white plastic button on the end without appearing to sustain any serious electric shock.

There was the usual wait while the fluorescent tube between the bookshelves puttered and popped, then the dim light flickered and came on. Douglas strode off down the clanging canyon, running his finger along the spines of a top shelf saying, 'Golden, Golden, Golden,' and I found it somewhere else entirely. A book bound in green cloth, published by William Kimber, with the library's familiar red label designed by Reynolds Stone on the front, and a bookplate inside saying it had been presented to the library by the author in 1984.

I thanked Douglas, pulled up one of the little wooden stools provided to help persons of restricted growth to reach the top shelf, and set about discovering Lewis Golden's secret. Rather surprisingly for an accountant, he was signals officer to the First Airborne Division at Arnhem. He joined up as a signalman, was commissioned, and volunteered at nineteen to join the paratroops. His commanding officer, one Ginger Moberley, told him that this was a hand-picked unit, and he hadn't picked Golden. But Golden persisted.

After advancing through North Africa, he was selected to parachute at night into German-occupied Sicily in the summer of 1943 with a green torch to direct Allied glider landings. He was flown in by a Chilean pilot in a Panama hat, who like others was discomfited by the German flak and dropped Lewis some miles from the target area by bright moonlight into the middle of a German position. He was shot at as he swung down, had hand grenades thrown at him when he landed, and managed shortly before dawn to find cover under a single bush, where he lay all day within earshot of the Germans in the intense heat, unable to move a muscle as the horseflies fed on his face.

When he eventually managed to rejoin what remained of the British invasion force he recognised a member of the Durham Light Infantry, and walked towards him, making as much noise as possible. 'When I was twenty yards from him the bugger fired at me.'

He then waited in England for months for the sadly scaled-down version of the airborne thrust Churchill had planned to deliver the death blow to the retreating *Wehrmacht*. Patiently, they rehearsed operations Tuxedo, Wastage, Wild Oats, Beneficiary, Swordhilt, Hands Up, Transfigure, Boxer, Axehead, Linnet, Linnet II, Infatuate, Comet, and one or two that never even got names. Each in turn was cancelled, until in a mood of crazed frustration in which anything seemed preferable to more rehearsals, they were dropped a bridge too far, for Operation Market Garden at Arnhem.

Despite the heavy wireless equipment, adverse reception conditions and the wilful use of the wrong radio channel by one senior officer, Golden had managed to maintain remarkably effective communications. In the end, unrelieved and outnumbered, pinned down by German snipers in the wreckage of a Dutch hotel, he and what was left of his unit were ordered to retreat. He swam across the Rhine at night, his driver drowning in his arms in midstream.

I realised I had misunderstood Lewis Golden's position at the committee meeting. He wasn't really opposed to progress, but his wartime experience had made him cautious. Nor was John Grigg being particularly rash in asking for a feasibility study. Grigg, as a historian, represented the literary-patrician element in the tradition of the library, providing the inspiration, in touch with writers and politicians, collecting ideas and patronage; Lewis Golden represented the tough, dogged line of undersung heroes, many of them lawyers, who saw it as a worthwhile cause and somehow kept the roof on.

\* \* \*

Three years later, in 1991, I was in the Librarian's Room, and Douglas Matthews was showing me a cardboard model of the library, a solid block from St James's Square through to the old Italian café in Duke Street. The new extension slotted in with a satisfying click, and it was difficult to see where it had gone in.

A new building fund was to be launched to pay for it, and the librarian, John Grigg and Lewis Golden were celebrating the fact that an anonymous English gentleman had given the library half a million pounds. I was about to ask them why anyone in their right mind would want to do such a thing. Then I thought about it; and I suppose the best way of answering that question is to go back to another afternoon in early summer, 150 years before, when the London Library did not exist.

# The Tree Igdrasil

*Carlyle, as so often, was only showing off.*

Robert Birley
*Footnotes*

It was nearly four o'clock in the afternoon of Friday, 22 May 1840, and on the tables at the back of the lecture hall there were stacks of freshly printed prospectuses for 'a new Subscription Library to be founded in the West-end of London'. Standing ready, on Carlyle's instructions, to 'thrust them into people's fists' as the lecture ended, were two young men: William Dougal Christie, a blue-eyed, boyish-looking lawyer recently down from Cambridge, and John Forster, in his late twenties, Dickens' friend and first biographer. Christie was the son of a doctor in the East India Company, Forster the son of a butcher from Newcastle, 'a big, burly man with a strong voice, a pleasant laugh and given to joking', a flamboyant literary journalist who would thump the table in moments of high emotion. He greeted Carlyle, when he came to dinner, as 'My Prophet!'

Carlyle had become a lot of people's prophet, and the London Library was born of a passionate love affair between the prophet Carlyle and literary London. In the early summer of 1840 he had already been preparing the ground for more than eighteen months. The great public gathering at the Freemasons' Tavern that would give the library shape and form was still four weeks away, and the library itself would not open its doors to lend books for another year. But that afternoon was the climax, the moment of ecstatic conception.

Carlyle referred to it later as 'the Glory of Portman Square'. In a big public room, every chair taken, the fashionable crowd listened in fascinated stillness as he stood on the low platform at the front, brawny hands gripping the lectern, conjuring language out of thin air, 'the wild Annandale voice growing high and earnest', until they broke into rounds of spontaneous applause and, at the end of some of his convoluted, elaborately decorated poetic phrases, actually stamped on the floor and cheered.

He was thirty-nine, lean, muscular and nearly six feet tall: a lanky, clean-shaven Scot with a big jaw and thick black hair. He had a ruddy, open-air complexion that made society ladies say he looked like a cowboy from the plains of North America, though when he was suffering from nervous indigestion he turned oddly pale. His large, expressive, mesmeric eyes were, according to various women who fell under their spell, either grey or violet-blue.

Carlyle had arrived in London in 1834 as the virtually unknown author of *Sartor Resartus*, the satirical life and opinions of Herr Teufelsrdröckh, or Mr Devilcrappe, in which forms and institutions are compared to clothes. *Fraser's Magazine* had been reluctant to print it, and it had not been well received. His career as a public speaker had begun in 1837, the year he published his highly coloured and imaginative *The French Revolution*, hailed by Thackeray and carried about by Dickens who read it aloud to his friends.

His lectures had been promoted from the beginning as a social event. Lecturing was an accepted way for writers to supplement their income, and ever since the story got out of John Stuart Mill's housemaid inadvertently lighting the fire with the original manuscript of *The French Revolution*, Carlyle had been thought of in the literary drawing rooms as a martyr, a long-suffering and otherworldly figure who lived on the breadline in unfashionable Chelsea.

His aristocratic admirers decided to launch him during the London Season, when Mayfair was jammed every night with carriages ferrying guests from one party to the next, and when Carlyle grumpily allowed himself to be lionised, always claiming that going out to dinner made him sick with nerves for days afterwards.

Handbills were distributed, and tickets costing a guinea were on sale at smart bookshops. James Spedding, a rising star at the Colonial Office who was to devote most of his life to his edition of Bacon, provoking predictable puns about 'slices of Bacon', alerted his old friend from Cambridge, Monckton Milnes. Milnes was a young MP who published poetry, collected French books about the history of flagellation and kindred topics, and as a tireless social butterfly could be relied on to spread the word.

I take the opportunity of writing to make you know, if you do not know already, that Carlyle will be lecturing on German literature next month. Of course you will be here to attend the said lectures, but I want you to come up a little before they begin, that you may assist in procuring the attendance of others. The list of subscribers is at present not large, and you are just the man to make it grow. As it is Carlyle's first essay in this kind, it is important that there should be a respectable number of hearers. Some name of decided piety is, I believe, rather wanted. Learning, taste and nobility are represented by Hallam, Rogers, and Lord Lansdowne.

Carlyle's first series of six lectures covered the whole history of German literature from 'the Teutonic people and the *Nibelungen Lied*' to the latest developments in nineteenth-century German poetry. They were to be delivered at Almack's elegant eighteenth-century plaster-and-gilt Assembly Rooms in King Street, St James's, where a few years later Charles Kemble gave his famous readings from Shakespeare.

Carlyle was very nervous: he wrote to his old mother in Craigenputtock suggesting that his opening lecture might run as follows: 'Good Christians, it has become entirely impossible for me to talk to you about German, or any literature, or terrestrial thing; one request only I have to make, that you would be kind enough to cover me under a tub for the next six weeks and to go your ways with all my blessing.'

Jane Welsh Carlyle had more practical anxieties: there was the problem of getting him to 'the place of execution' by three o'clock in the afternoon in time to start, and, worse, given Carlyle's incapacity to use one word when a thousand would do, of persuading him to stop at the end of an hour. Someone suggested laying a lighted cigar on the lectern as the clock struck four.

There was an audience of two hundred. Henry Hallam, historian and father of Tennyson's much-mourned friend Arthur, 'a broad, old, positive man with laughing eyes', was in the chair to introduce him. Carlyle got to his feet, looked down, picked at his notes, and having determined to speak extempore, began.

The first set of lectures was a great success: after all the expenses were paid Carlyle cleared £135. He always remembered the pleasure of coming home and giving his wife and his mother – who had come to London specially – a golden guinea each, 'like a medal struck to commemorate a triumph'.

The following year he announced twice as many lectures at double the price: a course of twelve on the History of Literature at two guineas a ticket. He began with the origins of language, of religion, of the gods. 'The Greeks recognised a destiny, a great dumb black power, ruling time, which knew nobody for its master and in its decrees was as inflexible as adamant, and every one knew it was there . . .' He ended, once again, on modern German literature.

This second course began in April 1838, the year of Queen Victoria's coronation, at the lecture rooms in Portman Square. *The Times* described 'the cultivated and intelligent aspect of the audience, of whom an unusually large proportion appeared to be of a high order, both as to station and to education, and in whom there was consequently a great number of pleasing and expressive countenances.'

The first members of the London Library were already assembling, and the Founder was leading them through the still unbuilt stacks, making associations that could only be made by browsing through its open shelves, or dreaming over its books by their own firesides.

Leigh Hunt, in the *Examiner*, noted with some amusement 'a union of what is usually called respectability with selectness of taste and understanding'. Carlyle himself was delighted. 'My audience was supposed to be the best for rank, beauty and intelligence, ever collected in London. I had Bonnie Braw Dames, Ladies this, Ladies that, though I dared not look at them lest they should put me out. I had old men of fourscore; men in middle-age, with fine, steel-grey beards; young men of the Universities, of the law profession, all sitting quite mum there, and the Annandale voice gollying at them.'

Jane Carlyle was equally impressed: 'Women so beautiful and intelligent that they looked like emanations from the moon; and men whose faces are histories, in which one may read with ever new interest.' F. D. Maurice, the radical clergyman, said he was more edified by the lectures than by anything he had heard for a long time.

Monckton Milnes, never taken quite seriously as Member of Parliament for Pontefract, but an arbiter of fashion in the drawing rooms, loved the way Carlyle spoke. 'His personality is most attractive. There he stands, simple as a child, and his happy thought dances on his lips and in his eyes, and takes word and goes away, and he bids it God speed, whatever it may be.'

This second series made Carlyle almost three hundred guineas. John Sterling, another fan from Cambridge, was very amused at some of the fashionable ladies Carlyle reduced to tears with the beauty of his words. He noticed they took the trouble to write down dates rather than ideas, and wrote them down wrong. Thackeray gave him a glowing notice in *The Times*.

Only Leigh Hunt, model for Dickens' feckless Mr Skimpole in *Bleak House*, behaved badly: according to Carlyle, though Leigh Hunt's descendants were still denying the story at the turn of the century, Hunt borrowed two guineas of the proceeds which he never returned, and devoted a large part of his review in the *Examiner* to quibbling with Carlyle's thoughts in praise of thrift.

In 1839, again in Portman Square, he gave a third course of six lectures on 'The Revolutions of Modern Europe'. The audience increased every week, and Carlyle was frequently interrupted by loud applause, and shouts of 'Splendid!' and 'Devilish fine!' In the second lecture, on 'Protestantism', Leigh Hunt noticed the stillness in the room, what he called the 'increased silence' when Carlyle was at his best: 'a noble homeliness, a passionate simplicity and familiarity of speech, which gives startling effect to his sincerity.' Even the ladies seemed to be concentrating: 'the pretty church-and-state bonnets seem to think through all their ribbons.'

Looking at the street outside afterwards, packed with carriages that had brought the audience across Oxford Street from Mayfair, with liveried servants gossiping as they waited for their employers, Jane Carlyle thought the English aristocracy, though there is always the possibility she was being ironic, were 'the most open to light of any class Carlyle had to do with'. She called him *Car*lyle, with the stress on the first syllable; they stressed the second, and thought he was 'a glorious fellow', 'a fine, wild, chaotic chap'.

Carlyle himself considered lecturing 'a mixture of sincerity and play-acting'. Believing as he did in sincerity, and hating the disagreeable nervous tension he experienced before the play-acting, he determined that the 1840 course of lectures should be his last.

His subject, he wrote to Emerson in Massachusetts, was 'Heroes – from Odin to Robert Burns'. That was the kind of shock juxtaposition that thrilled his listeners. They lived at a dangerous and alarming time, in an age of iron rivets and gigantic scars in the countryside where navvies excavated railway cuttings; of bustling commercial energy, and of threatening social unrest, when all kinds of old authority seemed in danger. The gloomier ideas of the eighteenth-century French *philosophes*, man as a machine in a godless mechanical universe – 'all the salon-philosophical lumber of the last century, the saddest spiritual paralysis and mere death-life of the souls of men' – seemed suddenly realised, and Carlyle was not alone in hating them.

James Spedding saw the conflict as being 'between the Steam Locomotive and the Philosopher's Stone', and by shackling together Odin and Robert Burns, a pagan deity and a poor Scots poet, Carlyle was proclaiming a new faith that would somehow reconcile the modern world with ancient awe, steam power with 'the snow-jokuls, roaring geysers, sulphur-pools and horrid volcanic chasms of Iceland, the wast chaotic battlefield of Frost and Fire'.

Unconsciously, of course, Carlyle was confronting gigantic images of himself: Odin, the wild man–god from the North, Luther and his 'rude, plebean face, with its huge crag-like brows and bones, the emblem of rugged energy', Burns the ploughboy, with the mud as it were still on his boots, 'handing down jewelled Duchesses to dinner', just as Carlyle did, often to his wife Jane's intense irritation.

But he was also asking his audience to confront their own ancient savage selves, and what must have thrilled the early Victorian ladies in their high-buttoned dresses, and even the early Victorian gentlemen in their stocks and high flyaway collars, double-breasted waistcoats and baggy-shouldered frockcoats, was Carlyle's rousing invitation, spiritually speaking, to take their clothes off and dance naked in the rain.

Carlyle's political ideas have had a bad press. It is no coincidence that he was singled out for praise by the Nazis, or that Goebbels read him aloud to Hitler during his last days in the Bunker: some of his instincts were bad and dangerous. He denounced the ballot box and democracy in favour of 'might', and 'the Strongest Man in England'. Constitutional monarchs were to be despised as wearing 'a piece of bent metal', when the original 'King' or 'Cunning Man' had earned his right to rule.

In his satirical pamphlet on *The Nigger Question*, where he was asking for less money to be spent in the colonies and more at home in Ireland, he imagined a kind of Aryan Great Chain of Being from 'the Wisest Man at the top of society, and the next wisest man next, and so on till we reached the Demarara Nigger (from whom downwards, through the horse etc.)'. He was also, like many outsiders, capable of cheap anti-Semitism.

But his lectures on 'Heroes and Hero-Worship' were not about politics in the accepted sense of the term; they were about rediscovering the wonder of existence, of being alive in a still mysterious universe, of recognising the 'sham' from the authentic, even in words.

He asked his listeners to imagine they were the first Pagan Thinker:

> To the wild, deep-hearted man all was yet new, not veiled under names or formulas; it stood naked, flashing-in on him there, beautiful, awful, unspeakable. This green flowery rock-built earth, the trees, the mountains, rivers, many-sounding seas – the great deep sea of azure that swims overhead, the winds sweeping through it; the black cloud fashioning itself together, now pouring out fire, now hail and rain; what *is* it? Ay, what? At bottom we do not yet know; we can never know at all. It is not by our superior insight that we escape the difficulty; it is by our superior levity, our inattention, our *want* of insight. It is by *not* thinking that we cease to wonder at it. Hardened round us, encasing every notion, is a wrapping of traditions, hearsays, mere words.

But somehow, when Carlyle used them, words were not 'mere words': like his beloved Germans, he clamped words together, sometimes shackled with a hyphen, banging them against each other until 'the poor undevout wrappages' shattered and released what he called the original *thing*: primitive and real, purged of the dust accumulated over centuries of unthinking use. Then, purified and consecrated, he used them to conjure with. Suddenly they were transformed into 'the word of truth' that would live and bear fruit in the minds of his hearers, just as seed-corn thrown into the earth would grow while the chaff and rubbish died.

At the back of his mind all the time, just below the surface of the text, is the idea of his new library, where such words would be stored and always available.

On the day he was due to deliver his first lecture, on 'The Hero as God', Carlyle had woken at half past four in the morning and felt terrible. He asked them to think about the meaning of hero-worship. 'Fancy your own generous heart's-love of some greatest man expanding till it *transcended* all bounds, till it filled and overflowed the whole field of your thought! Or what if this man Odin – since the great, deep soul is ever an enigma, a kind of terror and wonder to himself – should have felt that he *was* divine; that *he* was some effluence of the "Wuotan", *Movement*, Supreme Power and Divinity, of whom to his rapt vision all Nature was the awful Flame-image . . .'

In words and place names, at least, Odin was still alive in early Victorian England. 'Our own Wednesday, is it not still Odin's Day? Wednesbury, Wansborough, Wanstead, Wandsworth: Odin grew into England too, these are still leaves from that root!'

This led him on to a meditation on Icelandic literature, on the Tree Igdrasil: the pagan image of everything that is and ever was and ever shall be, alive and growing, uniting them in their lecture room in Portman Square in a terrifying sense of wonder at the dynamic interrelationship of all life.

All life is figured by them as a Tree. Igdrasil, the Ash-tree of Existence, has its roots deep-down in the kingdom of Hela or Death; its trunk reaches up heaven-high, spreads its boughs over the whole Universe: it is the Tree of Existence. At the foot of it, in the Death-kingdom, sit three *Normas*, Fates: the Past, Present, Future; watering its roots from the Sacred Well. Its 'boughs' with their buddings and disleafings – events, things suffered, things done, catastrophes – stretch through all lands and times. Is not every leaf a biography, every fibre there an act or word?

The 'beautiful people', he told his mother afterwards, seemed happy and sat listening to his words as if they had been the gospel. He thought his second lecture, on Mahomet, 'The Hero as Prophet', was the best he had ever delivered. In it he came as close as he dared to challenging what he called 'Christianism'.

When he quoted Coleridge: 'You do not believe, you only believe you believe!', he was not asking them to believe in Christianity. Off the record, in a letter to Jane, he described a painting of Christ by Correggio as 'a thing to be cut into pork sausages if found alive'. In the lecture on Mahomet he was more carefully ironic: 'As there is no danger of our becoming, any of us, Mahometans, I mean to say all the good of him I possibly can.' Christ was venerated as 'the highest voice ever heard on earth', and even got a kind word as an art critic for his observations about the lilies of the field.

But Christianism was only a phase. 'Odinism was Valour, Christianism was Humility, a nobler kind of Valour.' 'The thing a man does practically believe (and this is often enough *without* asserting it even to himself, much less to others) concerning his vital relations to this mysterious Universe, and his duty and destiny there, that is in all cases the primary thing for him, and creatively determines all the rest. That is his *religion*.' Behind the tree of Calvary, more awesome, infinitely vaster, splintering all the idols and images of painted wood and plaster, was the Tree Igdrasil.

Carlyle told his mother the lecture was attended by 'bishops and all kinds of people'. 'I vomited it forth on them like wild Annandale grapeshot; . . . they seemed greatly astonished and greatly pleased.' This was not entirely true: his old admirer F. D. Maurice had his reservations about his habit of falling into a 'wild pantheistic rant', but as a man uneasy in the Church of England, he still found Carlyle's ideas compelling.

The actor Macready had cut his afternoon rehearsal to be there, and was 'charmed and carried away . . . impressed most of all by Carlyle's conviction of truth'. Browning was also in the audience, and when Carlyle dismissed Bentham's view of mankind as 'beggarlier and falser' than that of Mahomet, John Stuart Mill was moved to rise to his feet and shout 'No!'

But Carlyle's new religion was not as primitive as it seemed. As a preacher he depended on a vast range of reading, and when he came to talk to his audience about books he treated them as something sacred. In the printed lectures he spells them always with a capital letter, as 'Books'.

> Certainly the Art of Writing is the most miraculous of all things man has devised. Odin's *Runes* were the first form of the work of a Hero; Books, written words, are still miraculous *Runes*, the latest form. In Books lies the *soul* of the whole Past Time; the articulate, audible voice of the Past, when the body and material substance of it has altogether vanished like a dream. All that Mankind has done, thought, gained or been; it is lying as in magic preservation in the pages of Books. They are the chosen possession of men.

Through Books living experience could be transmitted directly from the dead to the living. In Books, ancient civilisations were alive, dangerous with seed that could impregnate remote generations. 'Do not Books accomplish *miracles*, as *Runes* were fabled to do? They persuade men. Not the wretchedest circulating library novel, which foolish girls thumb and con in remote villages, but will help to regulate the actual practical weddings and households of those foolish girls . . .'

Following the chain of associations, he then linked books, or words, to building. 'What built St. Paul's Cathedral? Look at the heart of the matter, it was that divine Hebrew Book, the word partly' – Carlyle was still careful not to offend any Christian fundamentalists who believed the Bible to have been dictated by God down to the last comma – 'the word partly of the man Moses, an outlaw tending his Midianitish herds, four-thousand years ago, in the wildernesses of Sinai!'

Offstage the modern Moses was often extremely pessimistic about the power of his own word to summon either the books or the bricks and mortar of the London Library into existence. Sitting on the hearthrug at Cheyne Row, puffing on his clay pipe with the green mouthpiece and considerately blowing the smoke up the chimney – unlike Tennyson, who filled the room with pipe smoke – he confessed to grave doubts about the success of the forthcoming meeting to raise funds at the Freemasons' Tavern.

It was in his mind during the next lecture, on 'The Hero as Poet'. Talking of Dante and Shakespeare, he asked his audience rhetorically what it was that had brought 'Shakspeare', as he preferred to spell it, into being. It was, he told them, a free gift of nature. 'No dining at the Freemasons' Tavern, opening subscription lists, selling of shares, and infinite other jangling and true or false endeavouring!'

In the audience at the fifth lecture, on 'The Hero as Man of Letters', was Caroline Fox. She was twenty-one years old, a member of the rich Quaker family and a friend of John Sterling, and she immediately noticed the Mellors-Lady Chatterley relationship between the speaker and his audience. 'Carlyle soon appeared, and looked as if he felt a well-dressed London audience scarcely the arena for him to figure in as a popular lecturer.'

He is a tall, robust-looking man; rugged simplicity and indomitable strength are in his face, and such a glow of genius in it – flashing from his beautiful grey eyes, from the remoteness of their deep setting under that massive brow. His manner is very quiet, but he speaks like one tremendously convinced of what he utters, and who had much – very much – in him that was quite unutterable, quite unfit to be uttered to the uninitiated ear; and when the Englishman's sense of beauty or

21

truth exhibited itself in vociferous cheers, he would impatiently, almost contemptuously wave his hand, as if that were not the kind of homage which Truth demanded. He began in a rather low and nervous voice, with a broad Scotch accent, but it soon grew firm, and shrank not abashed from its great task.

In 'The Hero as Man of Letters' Carlyle praised Doctor Johnson as an independent man. A poor student at Oxford with holes in his shoes, Johnson found a new pair left on his doorstep by an anonymous gentleman commoner, and threw them out of the window rather than be dependent on any man's charity. Again there is an echo of the library, a place where the poor man of letters, a hero in his own right, guardian of the divine fire, could find material of the kind Carlyle had found: Icelandic sagas, the origin of *Hamlet* in the Norse myth of 'Amleth', the Black Stone of Mecca as an 'aerolite', the Pilgrim Fathers praying on the shore at Delft before they went aboard the *Mayflower*. It might, admittedly, mean the man of letters being dependent on literary-minded London Society, but that Carlyle seemed all too ready to accept.

The last lecture, on 'The Hero as King', was a natural finale, bringing together all the conscious and unconscious themes of the series. Arguing for belief, he recalled Napoleon on deck with his *philosophes* on the way to Egypt, after they had logically proved that there could be no God, when he waved a hand up at the stars and said, 'Very ingenious, gentlemen, but who made all that?'

Again, he unconsciously projected himself and his own weaknesses on the giant figure of Cromwell: 'working in such an element of boundless hypochondria, *un*formed black of darkness! And yet withal this hypochondria, what was it but the very greatness of the man?'

'After many other effective touches,' wrote Caroline Fox, 'which compelled you to side with Carlyle as to Cromwell's self-devotion and magnanimity, he gave the finishing stroke with an air of most innocent wonderment – "and yet I believe I am the first to say that Cromwell was an honest man!" '

Carlyle himself was amazed by the audience's response.

On the last day I went to speak of Cromwell with a head *full of air*; you know that wretched physical feeling; I had been concerned with drugs had awakened at five, etc. It is absolute

22

martyrdom. My tongue could hardly wag at all when I got done. Yet the good people sate breathless, or broke out into all kinds of testimonies of goodwill; seemed to like very much indeed the huge ragged image I gave them of a believing Calvinistic soldier and reformer. In a word, we got right handsomely through.

Concluding that last lecture, Carlyle thanked his audience: 'The accomplished and distinguished,' he told them, 'the beautiful, the wise, something of what is best in England, have listened patiently to my rude words.' The colossal mock modesty implicit in the term 'rude words' – rough, untutored, peasant language from the seer of Craigenputtock – provoked a slowly growing roar of laughter from the floor, to be followed a few seconds later, as he stepped down from the lectern, by a storm of deafening, foot-stamping cheering and applause. 'With many feelings', he concluded, 'I heartily thank you; and say, Good be with you all!'

Something of what was best in England was already behind him, and by changing one letter in his word of benediction, he was appealing to many politically confused semi-Christian philanthropists, desperate for a cause. As Forster and Christie set about thrusting the prospectuses into fists in the hubbub of congratulation, they had reason to hope that the new London Library, like St Paul's Cathedral, was capable of being summoned into existence by the creative word.

Like all miracles, it was going to take a great deal of very hard work.

# Angels and
# Ministers of Grace

*Would to God I had sought and suffered that carnal union,*
*which the world calls sin, but which leads, as I know well,*
*in frequent cases to brotherhood and mutual good services*
*through life.*

John Addington Symonds, *Memoirs*

Emerson, when he visited Carlyle at Craigenputtock, described 'the house amid desolate heathery hills, where the lonely scholar nourished his mighty heart'. Carlyle called it 'the Nithsdale peat-desert', and believed, like Jane, that there was more to nourish the mighty heart in London. But even in London a great deal of his spiritual sustenance still came from Books, and he still could not afford to buy them.

In a much-quoted note in his diary in Scotland in May 1832 Carlyle had written: 'What a sad way I am in for want of libraries, of books to gather facts from! Why is there not a Majesty's library in every county town? There is a Majesty's gaol and gallows in every one!'

'Majesty's libraries' were resisted by conservatives, who saw them either as arsenals of dissent or a prelude to free Punch and Judy shows on the rates. They were fostered by those who believed they would keep the working man out of the public house, but they did not exist until the time of William Ewart's Public Libraries Act in 1850. The first opened in Canterbury, and the London boroughs generally lagged behind the provinces. St Margaret's, Westminster, was one of the earliest, but the majority did not come into being until the end of the century.

In Edinburgh there were two private libraries, with an entrance fee and an annual subscription, the Signet and the Advocates' Library, both of which allowed books to be taken out, and Carlyle used both of them grumpily, complaining about the way the lawyers 'hied thither to lounge, to talk nonsense and read newspapers in the chief rooms'. Other provincial towns had their own subscription libraries, most of them with their own reading rooms and good stocks of history, geography, and reference books as well as the Classics and English and foreign literature. But there was nothing of the kind in London.

Carlyle could, certainly, have borrowed novels and a few serious books from one of the so-called circulating libraries, which we shall be considering in a later chapter, but otherwise there were only one or two small and specialised collections, like Dr Williams' Library, which still exists in Gordon Square, and the London Institution in Finsbury Circus. Neither allowed books to be taken home.

Had he arrived thirty years earlier it would have been a different story. He could have found most of the general books he needed on the open shelves of a subscription library within a stone's throw of St James's Square; he could have met all his literary friends – Coleridge often spent his mornings there – as well as dukes and generals and foreign ambassadors; he could have read the papers and periodicals by an open fire in the reading room until closing time, and then taken his books home with him to Chelsea. It was called the London Library.

It had been founded in 1785 by Dr Andrew Kippis, editor of *Biographia Britannica*. Dr Johnson had been asked to edit it and refused, though he told Boswell he wished 'the superintendence of this literary Temple of Fame had been assigned to a friend to the constitution of Church and State'. Kippis, in other words, did not subscribe to the Thirty-Nine Articles of Belief of the Church of England, and the library was intended for the benefit of Nonconformists, many of them clergymen, excluded from Oxford and Cambridge.

The first London Library opened at 10 Ludgate Street, near the bookshops of St Paul's Churchyard, with a membership of 121, of whom ten were women. As with the present library they could submit requests, and a committee of twelve decided what should be bought. It was used by friends of Tom Paine, active in France during the Revolution, by practical engineers like the author of a book on docks for the Port of London, and by an unfrocked monk shaken in his beliefs by the Lisbon earthquake of 1755. Nares, founder of the Royal Society of Literature, was a member, and so was Samuel Foot Simmons, one of those entrusted with the care of George III in his insanity.

By 1801 it was near bankrupt and all the books were moved to the home of one of its members, Charles Taylor, in Hatton Garden.

The house was crammed with books, upstairs, downstairs, in the hall and passages. The tables, the library-counters, the shelves and the floor (who shall say if the floor had carpet?) all heaped with books; books of all sizes and sorts – books in piles, that had slid down from chairs or stools and had rested unmoved until a deep deposit of dust had formed on them.

They had then amalgamated with the Westminster Literary Society, and by the time the combined library moved to 44 Jermyn Street the Poet Laureate, Henry James Pye, was a member of the committee, William Wilberforce was a vice-president, and the president was Francis Rawdon-Hastings, a distinguished soldier who was later governor-general of India. The librarian, Mr Price, lived on the premises and assured 'residents at the West-end of the town' that he was 'ever willing to afford such information as may be required respecting the nature of the Library mode of admission etc etc.' In 1820 there was another financial crisis, and after two more moves, to Charles Street and then to Air Street, the first London Library closed five years later with the death of its librarian.

Carlyle was therefore dependent for both general reading and for his study of original papers on the British Museum. He had been a reader there since 1831, when he was proposed by Basil Montagu. That in itself must have appealed to Carlyle's sense of self-esteem, as the museum's collection was then housed in Montagu House, a crumbling old mansion in a corner of the present museum site, with stuffed giraffes at the head of the stairs guarding what Cobbett dismissed as a 'cabinet of curiosities', and looked after by a part-time staff of elderly clergymen. It was literally collapsing under the weight of books, with pit-props shoring up its floors. He had obediently renewed his ticket seven times, the last occasion being on 15 December 1838.

Smirke's new building was by then half-finished – the famous domed Reading Room was not completed for another twenty years – and the minutes of the museum's trustees are full of deliveries of quartz, Greek statues and 'duplicate hippopotamuses'. New display cases were being hammered together all over the building, and most of the books had been moved into a square room at the back on the ground floor, known as the King's Library. From a description of the atmosphere there, written probably by Sterling after listening to

Carlyle in full flood, it cannot even at the best of times have been an easy place to work.

> Here will the whole tribe of extracters, bookmakers, borrowers and stealers of original thought, congregate – flower-drawers, insect-painters, curious [in the sense of pornographic] print and passage-hunters – snorers, snufflers, wheezers, spitters – exhalers of all fumes between the aromatic and the mephitic – the fidgety, the half-hour readers – those who spell to themselves, utter isolated *hems*!, stifled titters, and preternatural noises incident to the poring race, or betray their mortality by sounds still more disagreeable.

Carlyle could never find a seat and had to perch on ladders, and despite the motto on his own bookplate, *Humilitate* – by or with humility – he was not a man to suffer with the common herd. He said it gave him what he called his 'museum headache', and that one of his neighbours was a lunatic 'whose friends brought him there every day to puddle away the time' and who blew his nose very loudly on the stroke of every half hour.

He was also at daggers drawn with the recently appointed Keeper of Printed Books, Panizzi, a difficult figure to assess, particularly because of his legendary quarrels with Carlyle. He was a crucial influence in creating the library of the British Museum, and he had many friends, including Gladstone and Lord Clarendon, first president of the London Library. He also had many enemies, was blackballed from the Athenaeum, and was seen by his colleagues as 'a tortuous villain'. He had, too, a disagreeable habit in a librarian of barking at those who displeased him like an Italian sergeant-major.

A republican refugee from Modena, he settled first in Liverpool, where he was able to advise Brougham on Roman Law in a case involving a local schoolgirl who had been abducted and taken to France. He came to London under the protection of the Duke of Sussex, known as 'the only intelligent Royal Duke' and a Mason. Whether or not the Duke was in any way moved to intervene on his behalf by Panizzi's having been a member of the *Carbonaria*, a similar secret society in Italy, the 'Italian harlequin' with no academic experience and no interest in teaching became the first Professor of Italian at the newly founded London University. Having few pupils, he was introduced into the drawing rooms of

London by an old but influential blue-stocking, Lady Dacre, and made himself agreeable to Thomas Grenville, a rich collector of antiquarian books. In 1830 Grenville became a trustee of the British Museum, and Panizzi joined the staff.

With Carlyle he did have particularly bad luck. His initial task on arriving at the museum was to catalogue the pamphlets on the French Revolution, a job he knew he had not had time to do properly: Carlyle's first public criticism of the museum was to ridicule this catalogue. When Carlyle finished with the Revolution in France he immediately turned to the study of Oliver Cromwell and the Civil War in England, the papers relating to which had been sorted, while he was doing a great deal of other work, by Panizzi.

Carlyle told the Royal Commission on the British Museum Library that for all the use they were to the student, the Civil War papers might have been locked in a trunk and sunk on the Dogger Bank. If they had been edited, he said, they had been edited as a man might edit a load of old bricks, by tipping them off the back of a cart.

Even without such public criticism, Panizzi was not having an easy time. He had sacked all the old clergymen, appointed a full-time staff, and was now at loggerheads with the conservative-aristocratic trustees who consistently thwarted his plans to revise the general catalogue. Carlyle frequently criticised this too. It had been made in 1810: since then the museum had acquired 30,000 more books, and these had been 'interleaved'.

But the real trouble came when Panizzi tried to be nice to Carlyle. Panizzi had made a tour of European libraries, and came back advocating a British Library very much as it is today. 'I want a poor student to have the same means of indulging his learned curiosity,' he wrote, campaigning for increased government support, 'of following his rational pursuits, of consulting the same authorities, of fathoming the most intricate inquiry as the richest man in the kingdom.'

This was fine egalitarian stuff, but Panizzi was not above treating some people as more equal than others if he thought they might be useful to him. Carlyle already had 'clerks' – what would today be called research assistants – working in the copyists' room. Panizzi now allowed him, after all his complaints about the catalogue, to go and find his own books in the shelves rather than wait for them to be brought to his place.

Carlyle's way of showing his gratitude was to attack Panizzi in a footnote to an article he wrote for the *Westminster Review*, making reference to his special treatment. He thanked the 'respectable Sub-Librarian' for allowing him to climb ladders and read 'the outside titles of his books – which was a great help'. Others, he wrote, were less privileged and, baffled by the lack of any proper catalogue, 'after days of weary waiting, dusty rummaging, and sickness of hope deferred, gave up the enterprise as a "game not worth the candle" '. From then on Carlyle could expect no favours. When he uncharacteristically confessed in public that he was perhaps 'a thin-skinned student', Panizzi said he never felt readers' skins, they were all treated equally.

According to legend, Carlyle decided to found the London Library for two reasons. First, by the time he had got from Chelsea to Bloomsbury and the books had been brought to him there was no time to work, and he therefore wanted books he could take home. This is true. Second, when he was working on original papers Panizzi refused to let him have a private room, a favour he had granted to Macaulay. This is less likely. Macaulay was then in the Cabinet, and later, on the death of Thomas Grenville, became a trustee of the museum, but there is no record of him being granted any special privileges before 1840, and he served on the first committee of the London Library.

The legend seems to have grown up after Carlyle's hostile evidence to the Royal Commission in 1849, and from his long-running battle with Panizzi, in which Panizzi was by no means always to blame. It is true that Carlyle always wanted a private room at the museum, and applied unsuccessfully to F. D. Maurice, then on the staff of London University, to get him one in 1838. But the only surviving exchange of letters between Carlyle and Panizzi is to do with a similar request ten years later, long after the London Library had opened. It is worth quoting to show the two men's delight in needling one another.

Carlyle wrote to say that he had stated 'on a public occasion' some time in 1852 that he had not found it possible to get 'any private room or quiet convenient corner for reading and studying in' at the museum.

> There followed, if someone did not mislead me, some contradiction on your part, as if the impossibility had only proceeded from my own want of due inquiry, of due solicitation.

At the present time, I shall be extremely happy if that rumour have been a true one; if I actually can, by any honest industry of mine, procure a quiet place to study in now and then in your establishment. For I am again in want of many helps which are in the Museum, and in the common reading-room, as now experience teaches me, I labour under such disadvantages in using them.

If you could give me a good word of indication on this subject, certainly it would be very welcome, or if I could meet you any day at the Museum, if that were furthersome or necessary. At any rate, if you are obliged to refuse me, I shall know it was with regret. I shall be no worse off than at present, and shall have exhausted the shadow of likelihood there was for me.

Yours very sincerely,

T Carlyle


Panizzi's reply came back by return of post: he did not recollect ever having stated that either Carlyle or anyone else could have a private room to study in at the museum. What he had said was that he was doing all he could to make the Reading Room comfortable for the use of the public. All readers should be – and were, in point of fact – treated alike at the British Museum, and Carlyle must see 'how invidious it would be to make a distinction'.

Panizzi then twisted the knife with a gleeful parody of one of Carlyle's own more absurd extended metaphors.


Our reading-rooms are not of course as quiet and snug as a *private* study: ours is a *public* place. No public conveyance can equal a private carriage: even in a first-class carriage you must occasionally put up with squalling babies and be deprived of the pleasure of smoking your cigar when most inclined to enjoy it; even the luxury of fresh air is sometimes denied a passenger who is obliged to share a carriage with six or seven other travellers.

If, on applying to the Trustees, you find them disposed to make an exception in your favor and they will order special accommodation to be provided for you, I shall obey their directions to the best of my powers, but I do not see how I can of my own accord make any exception in favor of any reader,

however high his literary claims and great my wish to serve him.
I have the honour to be
Your very obed.t faithful servant A. Panizzi

Panizzi knew perfectly well the Trustees were on his side as he had shown them a draft of his letter before sending it.

The hostility continued over the years, and there was one particularly close shave when Carlyle's brother John flattered Panizzi at a dinner party, and a letter from Panizzi was delivered by mistake to Cheyne Row: in any event, Carlyle by 1840 was already furious with both Panizzi and the museum.

From the beginning, the London Library drew its support from two distinct classes of people: from what one eighteenth-century librarian classified as Serious Readers, and from those he described as 'the Gay and Volatile'. Among the first category were John Stuart Mill and George Grote, active as a reforming member of parliament until 1841, and thereafter best known for his *History of Greece*, whose wife, Mrs Grote, was said by unkind friends to have been the origin of the word 'grotesque'. There were dour academics like Professor Key and Professor Malden, as well as deeply serious politicians like Gladstone.

Among the second category were a great many frivolous aristocrats like Lady Ashburton, the 'best-looking ugly woman' Monckton Milnes had ever seen, and for whom Carlyle guarded a brooding passion as his 'radiant goddess', signing himself her 'dark man', and accepting invitations to dinner or to stay at her Hampshire house, The Grange, or her Scottish summer home at Glen Truim. Samuel Rogers went out of his way to upset Jane Carlyle about this, beckoning her over during a party and saying, 'Sit down, my dear. I want to ask you – is your husband as infatuated as ever with Lady Ashburton?'

But the single most influential group in the foundation of the London Library – almost equally divided between earnestness and frivolity – came not from London but from Cambridge. It is possible that even Carlyle was unaware that they were all members of the same discreet club, later officially reconstituted as a secret society. Its existence only came to light in 1863, when it was attacked in *Fraser's Magazine*, and was defended the same year in *Macmillan's* by one self-confessed member, William Dougal Christie.

Not all were members of the first committee, but they formed a dominant caucus, far clearer in their aims than Carlyle himself. They included James Spedding, John Sterling, Monckton Milnes, F. D. Maurice, Douglas Heath, Charles and Arthur Buller, Tennyson, Erasmus Darwin, Arthur Helps, Spring-Rice, Richard Trench and many more. Another member, Arthur Hallam, who inspired Tennyson's *In Memoriam*, died before the library came into existence, but his father Henry worked tirelessly on the founding committee.

The Cambridge Conversazione Society had been started in 1820 by a group of Tory Evangelicals as a debating club. Because of their Low Church sympathies, and because membership was limited to twelve, they became known as 'the Apostles'. Their reputation in the twentieth century, with members like Lytton Strachey, E. M. Forster and, more notoriously, spies like Guy Burgess and Anthony Blunt, would have appalled its original founders, but the generation that admired Carlyle would certainly have recognised some kind of continuity.

They too entertained what would now be called mildly left-wing views, they experienced the same introspective agonies about the purpose and pattern of their lives, they believed in the value of extended confessional analysis of their thoughts and emotions – 'absolute candour was the only duty that the tradition of the Society enforced' – and although only a minority were practising homosexuals like Arthur Buller, their friendships developed in the same hot-house atmosphere of steamy undergraduate passion.

Writing home to his father from Cambridge, Monckton Milnes described his chosen companion, an Irish undergraduate called Stafford O'Brien, as 'one of the dearest creatures I have ever seen'. They were 'inseparable', and his father would, he was sure, approve of their friendship, 'it is so unlike the routine of Cambridge arm-in-arms'.

Their feeling of being an elite did not stem from conventional snobbery; Bury St Edmunds grammar school was as well represented as Eton or Harrow. Arthur Helps, a literary Etonian, actually called the Apostles 'the best protest against worldly success' he ever knew. Their heroes were Shelley, Coleridge and the Romantic Poets, and they unquestionably enjoyed themselves: Milnes and Tennyson remembered rolling on the ground helpless with laughter when Spedding pretended to be a cloud passing across the face of the sun, and when there was a meeting in

Cambridge of Saint-Simonians, devoted to revolutionary progress
on all fronts, free love and the 'speedy development of the free
woman', Arthur Buller had to be restrained from putting on a dress
and 'offering himself a candidate for the Motherhood'.

But the Saint-Simonians, with their promise of a new, mechan-
ically adjusted world, touched a raw nerve with the Apostles.
'Primogeniture,' Richard Trench, later Bishop of Truro, wrote to
another Apostle, William Bodham Donne, 'heredity, all that rested
on a spiritual relation will no longer be recognised, must be swept
away before the new industrial principle.'

The 'spiritual relation' was what they were looking for, and they
had been taught to look for it by their acknowledged spiritual
leader, F. D. Maurice. 'The effect Maurice has produced on the
minds of many at Cambridge', Arthur Hallam told his old Eton
contemporary Gladstone, 'by the single creation of the Society of
Apostles (for the spirit, not the form, was created by him) is far
greater than I dare calculate. It will be felt, both directly and
indirectly, in the age that is upon us.' It would certainly be felt in
the founding of the London Library.

F. D. Maurice was almost certainly responsible for telling Carlyle
about the old London Library. It seems odd that there is not more
reference to it in Carlyle's correspondence, but however thrilled he
may have been to hear of an institution so exactly on the lines
of what he wanted, it is understandable that he should not have
talked or written too much about reviving a library that had gone
bankrupt twice or three times in fifty years, particularly when he
was asking people to invest £10 in it. He could have heard about it
from any number of people: from Coleridge, 'a man', he decided,
'of great and useless genius'; from Lady Stanley of Alderley,
matriarch of the clan that produced Bertrand Russell; or from
Goethe's friend Henry Crabb Robinson, who remembered sitting
by the fire with Coleridge at the old London Library and talking
about his book-borrowing habits. But Maurice is the most probable link.

In December 1838, when Carlyle was having trouble finding
books for his work on Cromwell, Maurice was teaching at London
University and promised to try and use his influence at the British
Museum to get Carlyle his private room. If he did it was without
success, but he kept his other promise, which was to get him books
from Cambridge. Safe in his own little library at home in Cheyne
Row, Carlyle wrote to his brother John to report the arrival of 'a

large Portmanteau of Books from Cambridge University Library: Here they actually stand: sent me by persons whom I never saw; a most handsome and encouraging phenomenon.' They included Rushworth's *Collections* and Clarendon's *History of the Rebellion*, and had been sent off, he wrote, at the request of a friend of Maurice's, Douglas Heath – 'a promising young barrister, a Cambridge man, and a zealous reader of mine'.

In his letter of thanks, Carlyle wrote, 'Neither is the scheme of the "London Library" dead; nay it seems rather to be in a lively way.' This is Carlyle's first mention of the scheme, and it seems unlikely he would have talked about the 'London Library' in quotation marks if Maurice had not mentioned it by name. Maurice's father, too, was a Unitarian minister, trained at the Nonconformist Hoxton Academy and at Hackney, where he was taught by Dr Andrew Kippis.

F. D. Maurice was the incarnation of the troubled spirit of mid-nineteenth century Christianity in England. His father was concerned with the well-being of gypsies and chimneysweeps, putting into daily practice the beliefs of Voltaire who, like his ancient Eldoradan sage in *Candide*, 'worshipped one god, not three as they do in Europe'. His mother, hurled to and fro by the hysterical conversions to the Church of England of her eight daughters, embraced Calvinism and became convinced that not being numbered among the Elect she was damned for all eternity. As the only surviving son, Maurice had grown up with nine members of the opposite sex in varying stages of religious hysteria.

What really captivated the Apostles was Maurice's desperate struggle to retain his sanity by rigorous self-analysis and insistence on absolute honesty as he questioned every aspect of his own beliefs, finally coming to the conclusion that he was a Christian who could not believe in Hell. John Sterling's admiration for him was perhaps the most extreme – 'I am little more than a patch of sand to receive and retain the impression of his footstep' – and Jane Carlyle may have been right in finding Sterling 'wanting in backbone'.

But it was his influence that made them such a powerful lobby, bound to one another by the rule of secrecy and by their habit of mutual confession. These bonds were strengthened at regular dinners in London when those who had, in their rather affected language, 'taken wings' and become 'Angels', met and questioned Apostles still at Cambridge.

Carlyle had first become entangled with the Apostles when he was tutor to Arthur Buller and his brother Charles nearly fifteen years before; what drew them to him now was not only his respect for 'the spiritual relation' but his seriousness. A young disciple of Maurice's remembered all his life the time he had looked up from *Wilhelm Meister*, 'his eyes burning with the light of inspiration, and with a voice trembling with emotion', had quoted one of Goethe's best-known lines: 'Young men! *Earnestness alone makes life eternity!*' Helps, asked once what made the Apostles choose an undergraduate to be a member of their society, said, 'A man to succeed with us must be a real man, and not a "sham" as Carlyle would say.' Maurice might hate his 'pantheism', and hearing people after the lectures 'ranting and canting after Carlyle in all directions', but Carlyle's mysticism, his talk of the Tree Igdrasil uniting all existence, his recognition of the need for radical reform in society all appealed to Maurice and the Apostles as directly and emotionally as it did to the ladies in their ribboned bonnets.

Maurice was one of the original Christian Socialists, and was later to found the Working Men's College. In teaching at London University, instituted to provide education for those unwilling to embrace the beliefs of the Established Church as required by both Oxford and Cambridge, he was carrying on the work of his father. For him, the new London Library would provide the same service as the old London Library, as an armoury for the Broad Church Militant.

Like the old London Library, it would be used by Dissenting clergy. Every committee for the next hundred years was to have its share of bishops and deans and minor divines, and it would be wrong to imagine them as a lot of Canon Fontwater figures who came in to consult *The Craft of Sermon Illustration*. Maurice remained inside the Church of England not because the Church was a safe haven, but because it seemed to him politically to be an organisation capable of bringing about peaceful change in society. Christian education, he believed, could somehow trickle gently down from society drawing rooms to the slums, and the London Library would be a fountainhead. All this would depend on the spreading of the word: by literary-minded parsons and professors and schoolteachers, journalists and historians, authors of popular encyclopedias, but most of all the authors of original work, the crack troops of reform. They would use Carlyle's library, with books they could take home and study in the evenings as they improved themselves before setting out to improve their fellow men. All the Apostles acknowledged the need for reform. Many of them had been at Cambridge when the undergraduates armed against Captain Swing and the Rick-burners: two Apostles later associated with the library, George Venables and Henry Lushington, had written a semi-humorous verse epic about it:

> Deep thinkers left their whys and hows
> And stood prepared to solve with blows
> The riddle of their lives . . .

They had, since then, tried blows when they enlisted for their own version of the Spanish Civil War. Sterling, stirred by the plight of liberal Spanish refugees in London, had persuaded his cousin Robert Boyd to fund and lead an expedition which, they believed, would produce a spontaneous liberal uprising. Trench and John Kemble, son of the actor Charles Kemble and the most self-dramatising of the Apostles, had gone with Boyd to Gibraltar to cross the frontier. Tennyson and Hallam had acted as couriers, bringing French money to the Pyrenees. It was a terrible story of disorganisation and betrayal, and Boyd had eventually died before an incompetent monarchist firing squad on the beach at Malaga.

'I hear the sound of that musketry', Sterling wrote, 'as if the bullets were tearing my own brain.' Now, for a group of reforming intellectuals faced with the real possibility of civil war in their own country, there seemed a chance of solving the riddle not with blows, but once again with words.

It was therefore with a sense of deep political commitment that Spedding and the other Apostles must have watched the audience assembling at the Freemasons' Tavern, two doors away from Spedding's rooms in Lincoln's Inn Fields. It was in a more serious part of the town than Almack's or the Portman Rooms, with fewer beautiful society ladies and more lawyers and members of both Houses of Parliament than Carlyle had drawn before.

Despite its name it also offered a more noble arena for Carlyle's oratory, with soaring pillars, an organ over the doorway and the atmosphere, suitably enough, of a secular cathedral. There, before an altar engraved with Masonic emblems, and beneath a giant marble statue of Panizzi's patron the Duke of Sussex, dressed in the robes of a Knight of the Garter, Carlyle was to give his one and only unpaid public performance.

Lord Eliot rose to open the meeting. He was deputising for the first president of the library, Lord Clarendon. He commended the scheme to the meeting 'and to the reading portion of the Metropolis'. He was supported by Lord Monteagle, formerly Spring-Rice and another Apostle, promising 'the moral and intellectual improvement and the family happiness of a great number of individuals'.

He was followed by young Lord Lyttelton, who condemned the circulating libraries for 'tending to give literature an ephemeral character'. Then, to loud cheers, he introduced Carlyle.

Carlyle began on safe humorous ground by saying he had no intention of criticising the British Museum. 'But, supposing it to be managed with the most perfect skill and success, even according to the ideal of such an Institution, still I will assert that this other library of ours is requisite also!' The London Library would provide books for those who were prevented by their business from going to the British Museum during the day. 'But granting that they could all go there, I would ask any literary man, any reader of Books, any man intimately acquainted with the reading of Books, whether he can read them to any purpose in the British Museum?' This was greeted with another cheer, and from then on he drew cheers and applause whenever he paused to draw breath.

'A Book is a kind of thing that requires a man to be self-collected. He must be alone with it!' More cheers. 'A good Book is the purest essence of a human soul. How can a man take it in a crowd, with bustle of all sorts going on around him? The good of a Book is not the facts that can be got out of it, but the kind of resonance that it awakens in our own minds!' This brought the house down. 'A Book may strike out of us a thousand things, may make us know a thousand things, which it does not know itself! For this purpose I decidedly say that no man can read a Book well with the bustle of three or four hundred people about him! Even forgetting the mere facts which a Book contains, a man can do more with it in his own apartment, in the solitude of one night, than in a week in such a place as the British Museum!'

Having assured them he was not going to criticise the Museum, he now promised them he would not attack the circulating libraries. To make a collection of great books, to get together the cream of the knowledge that existed in the world, you had to be a kind of martyr. 'You could not expect a purveyor of Circulating Libraries to be that!' Such a man did not ask, 'Are you wanting to read a wise Book?' but 'Have you got sixpence in your pocket to pay for the reading of *any* Book? Consequently he must have an eye to the prurient appetite of the great million, and furnish them with any kind of garbage they will have. The result is melancholy – making bad worse – for every bad Book begets an appetite for reading a worse one.'

'Thus we come to the age of pinchbeck in literature, and to falsehoods of all kinds!' His audience was listening to Carlyle the Prophet condemning the Sham, proclaiming the One True Library.

'So, leaving all other institutions, the British Museum and the Circulating Libraries, to stand, I say that a decidedly good Library of good Books is a crying want in this great London. How can I be called upon to demonstrate a thing that is as clear as the sun?' By now the cheering was almost continuous. 'London has more men of intellect waiting to be developed than any place in the world ever had assembled. Yet there is no place on the civilised earth so ill-supplied with materials for reading for those who are not rich.' Then he turned aside from generalisations to delve down for one of his dazzling and mysterious nuggets of fact, gathered from his wilder reading. 'I have read an account of a Public Library in Iceland, which the King of Denmark founded there. There is not a peasant in Iceland that cannot bring home Books to his hut, better than men can in London!' It was an outrage that must be brought to an end.

'The founding of a Library is one of the greatest things we can do with regard to results. It is one of the quietest of things; but, there is nothing that I know of at bottom more important. Everyone able to read a good Book becomes a wiser man. He becomes a centre of light and order, of just insight into things around him.'

It was a bold stroke: join the new library and they would take their place in the glorious line with Odin, Luther and Napoleon. The Hero as Member of the London Library.

'A collection of good Books contains all the nobleness and wisdom of the world before us. Every heroic and victorious soul has left his stamp upon it. A collection of Books is the best of all Universities; for the University only teaches us how to read the Book: you must go to the Book itself for what it is. I call it a church also – which every devout soul may enter – a church but with no quarrelling, no church-rates . . .'

Here Carlyle's voice was drowned by laughter and cheering, and he sat down. Charles Buller spoke, then Monckton Milnes, and Christie brought the meeting to an end, reminding them that they still needed many more subscribers, and with the unspoken memory of the first London Library in mind, its books dusty and stacked in some abandoned storeroom, hoping that anyone who had come – not to scoff, for that was impossible – but simply to hear and look on, would remain to pay.

# The Politics of Babylon

*It is hard indeed to be a serious student of anything without the London Library. In founding it Carlyle served humanity at least as well as by writing* The French Revolution *or* Sartor Resartus.

*The Spectator*, 1952

For all his power as a popular prophet and the political skills of a group of brilliant Cambridge graduates who knew and understood English society far better than he did, Carlyle faced a terrible task. It was one thing to dream of a library, it was another to persuade others to pay for it, find the premises, the books and the librarian.

Worse still, it had to be in London, 'the Brick Babylon'. Both he and Jane had decided to live there, but in his changeable moods it was a place that he could hate as much as he hated London society, and every afternoon in summer, weather permitting, he escaped. At two o'clock his horse Citoyenne was brought to his front door, and he would ride out into the fields beyond Clapham or the hills of Hampstead.

> In ten minutes' swift trotting I am fairly away from the Monster and its bricks; all lies behind me like an enormous world-filling *pluister*, infinite potter's furnace – sea of smoke, with steeples, domes, gilt crosses, high black architecture swimming in it: really beautiful to look at from some knoll-top, while the sun shines on it. I ply away, some half-dozen miles out; the Monster is there quite buried; – its smoke rising like a great dusky-coloured mountain, melting into the infinite clear sky; all is green, musical, bright; one feels that this is God's world this, and not an infinite Cockneydom of *stoor* and din, after all!

Meeting people, planning and organising in that infinite Cockneydom was never easy: even in those days he allowed twenty minutes by cab from Cheyne Row to Pall Mall, and when it was possible he persuaded them to come out to Chelsea. 'Dear Mr. Forster, Can you appear here on horseback, precisely at two o'clock on Saturday, equipt for a canter of two hours? Tomorrow I am, conditionally, engaged to go with Milnes and stir up Pusey into a proper Book-madness!' Pusey, brother of the theologian excommunicated from the Church of England three years later for 'heresy' over his tract on the Thirty-Nine Articles, was an MP and was to pay for the printing of the library's prospectus.

In the evening 'some rational visitor' occasionally dropped in at Cheyne Row for a bowl of porridge or a cup of tea, but more often Carlyle, complaining bitterly before and after, had to go out to dinner, usually in Mayfair and often on foot. Much of his drumming up of support for the library must have been done over the dinner table, when the cloth was taken off and the men drank their brandy.

The campaign had really begun in the winter of 1838, but it did not become a full-time preoccupation until after Christmas, and there is a record of a dinner he went to in February 1839 with Samuel Rogers and Rogers' elderly sister. Rogers himself was then seventy-seven, his best-known collection of verse, *Pleasures of Memory*, having appeared in 1792.

That evening, Carlyle found him less disagreeable than usual, 'his old eyes so full of melancholy, the old grey eyebrows so serenely sad and thoughtful'. Rogers made a spirited defence of the 'poor little Queen, and her fooleries and piques and pettings in this little wedding of hers'. Spedding was there, and so was Monckton Milnes. Carlyle does not mention their having discussed the library, but a letter from Spedding to Milnes later in the week makes it clear that Rogers had promised to help with the campaign, and that he himself had agreed to draft the first prospectus.

This set out the proposal in very simple terms. A reasonable collection of general rather than specialist books could be put together for £2,000. If half this amount could be guaranteed annually, it would be possible to rent premises, pay staff and still have £500 a year left over to buy more books. If shares were sold at £10 each, and the annual subscription set at £5, the library could be started with only 200 members. If fewer than 200 subscribers came forward, their money would be returned.

Milnes was not convinced, and Spedding did his best to answer his reservations, which he said he had heard expressed by many people on the scheme being first explained to them. There might be no big response, but however few subscribers the library started with, it would still be worth while; if more people wanted to join 'it might be immensified to any extent'.

Club libraries, he agreed, existed, but their books could not be taken home, 'and though there may be few literary men who do not belong to some Club or other, there are many literary men who have wives and families quite capable of reading books if they could get them. Consider how many houses there are in London inhabited by rational beings who can read and write, yet into which no book can find its way unless it be either bought, or borrowed from a friend, or circulated from a new public library.'

Milnes seems to have argued in favour of the more serious circulating libraries, but Spedding dismissed them as giving away anything valuable they might have in their stock as 'fallen out of demand': that, he reminded Milnes, was how their friend Alford got his copy of Henry Hallam's *Constitutional History*.

Milnes' final and highly acute reservation, that the kind of people who joined the new London Library 'would never conform to the regulations with regard to time, etc.', Spedding answered very confidently. If they did not conform 'you turn them out, and consider their money as your own'.

Spedding, more than any of the other Apostles, was Carlyle's reliable right-hand man in the early months, a calm centre of competence. He once called the Apostles 'as select a company as ever smoked under the shade of a horse chestnut', and Tennyson remembered him at Cambridge as 'the Pope among us young men, the wisest man I know'. He showed quite astonishing fortitude in a tragedy like the death of his brother, and he was hard-working, single-minded and loyal.

Many years later, when Spedding's edition of Bacon finally appeared, Carlyle called it the 'the hugest and faithfullest bit of literary navvy work I have met with in this generation. There is a grim strength in Spedding, quietly, very quietly invincible, which I did not know before this book.' But Carlyle recognised his debt well enough: when the scheme was going badly it became 'Spedding's Library', and when Spedding briefly found the work too much for him Carlyle was distracted.

Milnes was less reliable, but more entertaining. Carlyle had no very high regard for his poetry, thought he talked a lot of nonsense, but was still very fond of him. 'A most bland-smiling, affectionate, high-bred, Italianised little man, who has long olive-blonde hair, a dimple, next to no chin, and flings his arm around your neck when he addresses you in polite society . . .'

Milnes' feelings for Carlyle were equally mixed. He was a profoundly frivolous man, probably bisexual, and referred to Fryston Hall, his country house in Yorkshire, as 'aphrodisiopolis' on account of the fine collection of pornography he kept in his library there. He enjoyed the horror of his browsing guests when they found, laid between the pages of one book, a piece of human skin taken from the body of a condemned murderer. It was Milnes who introduced the work of the Marquis de Sade to the young Swinburne, who laughed until he wept, and he was never happier than when he was taking part in charades dressed as Mrs Gamp.

If he clung to Carlyle, as he did throughout the launching of the London Library, he clung to him as the embodiment of all the gravity and seriousness he could never muster himself. It was, after all, Milnes who said that Carlyle's writings made on him the impression of the sound of a single hatchet in the aboriginal forests of North America, and he would sit for hours at Cheyne Row drinking in the wisdom, some of which he would write down in a notebook when he got home. 'The immense advantage of our times over twenty years ago', he noted Carlyle saying, 'is in point of seriousness. No Castlereagh would do now – the world is something to us it was not to him.'

As for Michael Astor a century later, the London Library may well have been Monckton Milnes' salvation. The young Florence Nightingale turned down his proposal of marriage – he reflected afterwards that if she had married him he would have deprived the century of one of its greatest saints – successive prime ministers saw only his frivolous side, and refused him public office. But he was to run Christie a very close second for length of service and devotion to the library. In 1951 Mr Cox could remember him coming in seventy years before, stooping but still bright-eyed.

Christie's motives, when he allowed himself to be brought in by Spedding, were more suspect: he was twenty-four, another lawyer, with ambitions to join the Diplomatic Service; Spedding was working at 11 Downing Street, already an influential figure at the Colonial Office. Christie's career was to be marred by bad temper: he was later sacked as ambassador to Brazil, and became known to the staff in his old age at a member of the library committee as 'Old Crusty'. But if he joined out of self-interest he paid for it in hard work, and Carlyle was not exaggerating when he wrote to Christie shortly before the library opened, 'the burden has been almost altogether yours'.

Christie could always be summoned to Cheyne Row: Henry Hart

Milman was fifty, and could not. But Carlyle went about a great
deal on foot, and was always ready to talk about the library, if
necessary, in the street. Milman raised his hat to him, and was
unwise enough to ask how his library scheme was going, and to say
that 'it would depend on how he managed it'. Carlyle, like Christ
gathering the disciples, said, 'Come you and help us!' and Milman
was hooked.

But Carlyle's favourite means of rallying support was by post.
The early Victorians used letters as their descendants use the telephone, scribbling invitations at breakfast that brought guests to
lunch the same day, and Carlyle's London Library notes have all
the urgency of irascible Scots commands barked into the mouthpiece from behind a littered desk.

Some, like his letter to Emerson at the beginning of 1839, were
merely for information: 'We have no library here from which to
borrow books, and we are striving to get one. Think of that!' Those
to his team in London demanded action. 'Let us see one another
face to face', he wrote to Milnes the same week, 'and discover
whether the half-dead embers will not kindle into red when brought
together. I long to see the matter either in decided motion or else
dead and ended.'

Spedding, too, was writing to Milnes, trying to get him to enlist
as a sponsor Lord Northampton, an idle old literary peer Milnes
had met in Italy. Two years before Milnes had offered to edit a
collection of poetry called *The Tribute* for the benefit of an elderly
poet: Milnes had done all the work, Northampton had taken
offence even at being asked to look over the proofs, but Spedding
insisted he was worth canvassing. If they sent out a prospectus
without some established names to endorse it, people would write
the whole library scheme off as 'a job, a booksellers' speculation or
a fudge'.

Rogers turned up trumps, and gave a breakfast party to discuss
the library, taking twelve prospectuses and promising to distribute
them. Carlyle was elated. It was a 'mighty project'. 'I have *preached*
upon it till people take it up. Spedding has promulgated a
Prospectus; Rogers approves, Hallam and a list of official Lords
are expected. And now the Newspaper engine is set a-blowing:
slight thunder from *The Times*, a fierce blast (from me) in the
*Examiner*.'

This, finally, was the best means of all of dominating infinite
Cockneydom, what he called 'the great bellows of the newspaper

Press': the image in his mind was mystical-mechanical, a kind of celestial-Olympian steam engine that could control the intellectual or political climate.

'The experiment', *The Times* felt, 'seems at least to be worth trying, and we have little doubt that it will succeed.'

For the space in the *Examiner* Carlyle had to thank John Forster, the paper's theatre critic. Carlyle had written to him, enclosing Spedding's prospectus, and Forster replied by return of post, sending him a present of 'four beautiful volumes' he needed for his work on Cromwell. Carlyle was apparently delighted. 'I rejoice heartily that you take up this Library Scheme with such prompt zeal. Your help in the *Examiner* will be of *first-rate* value.' He enclosed his piece – 'a crude thing I jotted down two or three weeks ago: if you could in any way pare it into shape, altering, adding, subtracting . . .' – and hoped he would find it worth including in the paper. Crude or not, it was characteristically robust.

He criticised the British Museum, and particularly Panizzi – an exercise he called 'tweaking the nose of the Italian Harlequin', and dismissed the circulating libraries as 'circulating heaps of ephemeral rubbish'. What was needed was a serious lending library. 'Since no government will remedy this want, the public is called upon to unite, and do it. We augur well for the present enterprise,' Forster concluded, 'and shall be happy to report the progress and success of it.'

Despite Forster's immediate willingness to help, Carlyle was mildly snobbish about him: 'Tomorrow night I shall be at home, and very glad to see you,' he wrote to Christie. 'Forster also would do no harm; at any rate, perhaps you could *see* him beforehand, and get out of him what news he had.'

Another Apostle he depended on to talk to and argue about the library was Maurice's admirer, John Sterling. Like Maurice he was a clergyman, and both had edited the *Athenaeum*. That paper too provided a good attack on the shortcomings of the British Museum. At £10 it thought the shares were a little too expensive, but encouraged 'interested persons' to write to James Spedding at Lincoln's Inn Fields.

Some money came in, but by the end of a month the campaign began to waver, and the idea in Carlyle's mind shrank into inverted commas. 'I want to see you about our poor "Library",' he wrote to Forster, 'which I am afraid is like to stick forever on the stocks, unless you give it a shove and launch it. Once fairly floating in the water, I should have good hopes of it; but there it sticks for the present, motionless, or moving at the rate of an inch a week.'

The 1839 lecture season intervened, with Carlyle being asked out every night. 'I dined with Wordsworth at the Marshalls': the same wholesome pacific not altogether watery old man.' The library he seemed bored with. 'Spedding's Library sleeps or is dead.'

His academic friend Craik had suggested he try borrowing books from the London Institution, and he was still being sent parcels from Cambridge. Milnes asked him to breakfast and produced another Cambridge man, the young Lord Lyttelton, who was to be a loyal friend of the library, 'But the breakfast party, usually such a fine work of wit, amounted to nothing. I have gained a sore-head by it, and got home.'

In June he stopped in Mayfair on the way back from another enjoyably infuriating day at the British Museum, to have tea with Lady Stanley of Alderley at her house in Dover Street. Gladstone was there, and became another recruit.

Then, as the gentry left London for the summer, the scheme again went strangely quiet. Spedding returned to his family estate near Keswick, promising to produce a 'Library Program'. The Carlyles set out for Scotland via Liverpool, 'till the hot weather be over'.

Monckton Milnes went to Scotland too, for the Eglinton Tournament, known locally as 'the Torment'. He and his fellow-Apostle Monteith – 'I am very happy today. I have resisted a very irresistible adultery – thank God – I only fear I shall reward myself now by yielding' – debated on which of fifteen or so country houses they should visit during the summer, including a family fallen on relatively hard times who would also figure briefly in the history of the London Library, the Carmichaels at Castlecraig.

The Carlyles returned to London in September, travelling for the first time by train, hurtled along 'through the confused darkness . . . by the huge Steam mystery', to complete his 'Article on the Working People'. This at least reassured the reforming Apostles.

*Chartism* was a fierce and at times Swiftian piece of Annandale gollying that rambled and ranted through History, Geography, Theology and even Science and Miscellaneous. Carlyle acknowledged the terrifying reality of a vast and justifiably angry working class capable of launching an English revolution on a complacent and effete ruling class. At one point, he imagined being interrupted by a heckler: 'Descend from speculation and the safe pulpit, down into the rough market-place,' he shouts, 'and say what can be done!' Carlyle's answer was to recommend that the suffering millions should either be encouraged to emigrate, or – and this was what the Apostles wanted to hear – be educated.

*Chartism* may have reassured Maurice and the more mystical Apostles who thought of the library as a means of inducing peaceful change, but its composition took up time Carlyle could have spent bullying Spedding, who in January 1840 managed, only briefly as it turned out, to resign from the enterprise, saying he had too much work.

Carlyle reacted with Germanic despair, followed by a burst of Spanish bravado. '*Gerade zur unrechten Zeit* [Just at the wrong moment] Spedding has formally given in,' he told his brother, and passed Spedding's letter on to Forster as 'a melancholy emblem of the state our poor scheme lies in at present – till you and your party cry heartily *manos a l'obra!*' He himself began to drive all hands to work like a maniac.

Forster, whom Spedding had recommended as his succesor, produced a new prospectus, and Christie found himself working harder and harder, with Carlyle driving him to write as many as twenty-one letters a day on top of his own work. 'Pray persist, and slacken not. A few such shoulders to the wheel and the very wheel of Destiny must move!'

Every day, too, letters left Cheyne Row, lashing on the labourers, the Carlylean bird's-claw semi-colons cutting into the paper.

> Could not you go, and blow upon Milnes again? The live-coal there is but of a *dull* red as yet. John Mill never emerges in my horizon of late; I believe him heartily well disposed to the enterprise, and he could be set in motion. Agitators are wanted. Agitate! Agitate! Agitate!
>
> I have written to Milman; no answer; indeed not yet time for one. I have set Arthur Buller upon Cole if he do not play me false, and forget. Lord Northampton were my favourite too, I think; but any Lord will do: it is a mere ensign. 'British flag flying at the royal masthead; – all depends upon the gunners! – Fire away!'

In March he got one of his bad colds. 'I cannot sleep,' he told Milnes; 'I have to dine out tonight; I am fast becoming the wretchedest of men. Have you any pity? Not you. Yours ever truly (unpitied), T. Carlyle.'

In April, up to his eyes in preparations for his lectures on 'Heroes and Hero-Worship', he was officially elected 'Secretary, but they do not expect me to act at all'. An advertisement appeared in *The Times* extending the time limit for subscribers to register till the end of May.

'*Stir* the waters,' Carlyle wrote to Christie; '*stir* them, leave no rest till they are all in a white froth – and the Sea-goddess of a Library born, and floated safe to land thereby.'

But the library could not be organised by post, or even in the newspapers; certainly not on horseback, at chance meetings over dinner, or on crowded pavements. In July 1840 Christie finally rented a first-floor office, at 450a West Strand, now the Trafalgar Square end of Coutts' Bank building opposite Charing Cross Station, then still Hungerford Market. It had its own bell, and LONDON LIBRARY COMMITTEE ROOM painted on the door.

The names of the first committee were printed in a circular sent to all subscribers on 10 April 1840. It included Christie, Craik, Charles Dickens (brought in by Forster), Arthur Helps, Professors Key and Malden, the joint headmasters of University College School, Milman, Monckton Milnes, Pusey and Spedding. The only surprise was the name of Carlyle's fellow-'Secretary'. It was Edward Marlborough Fitzgerald, an Irish chancer who had left Cambridge in 1826 after some unrecorded unpleasantness. He had talked his way into the library scheme with a great deal of blarney, and was subsequently never there when he was needed.

As 'Heroes and Hero-Worship' began in Portman Square, the campaign again started to fall apart: at the first committee meeting in May only Carlyle and Craik turned up. Pusey had paid for two thousand more prospectuses, Fitzgerald had promised to distribute them, and had disappeared. 'The beautifullest promises', Carlyle wrote to Forster, 'will avail nothing at all; Pusey's hard guineas will be as light as fairy-money, and all to no purpose, unless they *be* actually distributed, those two thousand Prospectuses – stuck, in real physical fact, into the fists of two thousand individuals of the human species!'

The day after his Odin lecture, Carlyle was still fretting about the lost prospectuses.

I suspect only a small fraction of Fitzg's Circulars are yet fairly off. *We must begin advertising*; we must begin working the great bellows-machinery of the Newspaper Press. To it!

I say to Forster and you; To it, like lions! If I can possibly I will attend you on Saturday; but, alas, in these present weeks I am like a matron in labour, and really do require to be dealt with accordingly. 'As well as can be expected, thank you!'

Four days after his last lecture, Carlyle was after Milnes 'concerning our great Library Scheme; — which you, treasonably, deserted last Saturday' — Milnes' father had been rolled on by his pony while riding in the Malvern Hills — 'but must in no wise desert on Wednesday (tomorrow) at the same place and hour.' Spedding, always recognised by his contemporaries as a saint, was working as hard as ever, and persuaded Lord Clarendon, former British ambassador in Paris, to become the library's first president.

The committee had originally been limited, like that of the old London Library, to twelve. As they laboured through the summer of 1840, meeting usually once a week, it was increased to twenty-four. Lyttelton took the chair, and with the unspoken threat of the old library's dissolution no doubt present in many of their minds, all their attention was on running a concern that would stay solvent. The entrance fee would be increased by stages when the membership reached a thousand, two thousand, and three thousand. They still had only a hundred or so names, but subscriptions were now coming in fast.

The full committee meetings must have crackled with extraordinary energy. The pictures on the stairs today show old men, with Carlyle in a grey beard, looking as he said himself 'like a half-witted old peasant'. Milman, admittedly, was middle-aged, but the rest were all in their late twenties and early thirties.

Carlyle dominated, with his big bare chin, bellowing his joyful enthusiasm for some new recruit or groaning in dyspeptic despair; Forster, deferring to his Prophet, opening doors with a theatrical flourish, but equally ready to roar or thump the table. Spedding, prematurely bald and with a long straight nose, thoughtful and authoritative; Milnes bouncing everywhere, arm round their shoulders, kneeling on chairs in conversation, throwing his head back and shouting with laughter when Carlyle, according to a story Emerson heard over lunch at the Athenaeum, threatened to sacrifice him 'like Iphigenia'.

Listening to them, interrupting, making suggestions, were Dickens, still only twenty-nine, with his mobile, expressive face; Maurice with his fine head and dark compelling eyes, graver and more intense, somewhere between Gregory Peck and Abraham Lincoln; Sterling in his round glasses and clerical stock, the earnest disciple.

There must have been tensions. Gladstone, with receding dark curly hair, already a highly regarded member of Parliament but still without Cabinet office, cannot have been wholly at ease. He admired the Apostles, and had even tried unsuccessfully to found a similar society at Oxford. But Maurice's sister was his sister's paid companion, and Maurice's tormented wrestling with orthodox theology must have distressed him terribly. As a man, too, who believed that life should be lived 'as if before the open grave', he cannot have felt entirely comfortable sitting beside Monckton Milnes, who believed that life should be seen 'through a purple haze of wine'.

Gladstone and Milman represented more conventional Christian *gravitas*, but even Milman shared with Carlyle a fascination for unburying the obscurer roots of Western Culture, and kept an open mind about what he found. His *History of the Jews*, published in 1830, presenting a vivid account of recognisably Middle Eastern life, had outraged his fellow clergy. It also won him the affection of the Jewish community, who had presented him with a piece of commemorative plate. His latest work, which had appeared in 1840, *A History of Christianity under the Empire*, had been snubbed by the ecclesiastical establishment, but applauded by Maurice.

What united many of them, was, surprisingly, a love of the theatre. Milman had had a great hit as a young man with a play he had written called *The Italian Wife*, and had since written lengthy verse epics about the Saxons in Gloucester, the fall of Jerusalem, martyrdom in Antioch, Belshazzar and Anne Boleyn. Helps, too, had composed sub-Shakespearian history plays, rich in insect imagery and featuring characters with names like Michael Podge. He was then writing speeches for Prince Albert and was later to edit the Queen's Highland jaunts, *Mountain, Loch and Glen*.

Readers must have perused his dramatic work closely for intimate glimpses of his royal friends, and they were there to find. In his *Henry II*, for example, he charmingly presents the young Victoria as being no different from the wife of a humble baronet.

Why yes, it must be owned an angry woman,
Whose rage moreover has a cause like this

Is most angelic: the humour's much the same
In queens, as well as in obscure knights' ladies . . .

Helps, however, found himself sitting at the same table as
Carlyle, Dickens and Milnes, all of whose feelings about the royal
family were a good deal less conventional: after Victoria and
Albert's wedding, Carlyle said that 'those two dumpling faces in all
the shop windows make one sick in the street'. Milnes and Dickens
also showed unseemly glee in collecting jokes about the royal
honeymoon and the more comic street ballads sung in the streets at
the time.

Milnes' were judged too obscene to be preserved, but those
Dickens sent him with his acceptance of an invitation to breakfast
might not have pleased Helps had he heard them sung under his
window at Windsor:

> So let 'em say whate'er they may
> Or do whate'er they can
> Prince Hallbert he will always be
> My own dear Fancy Man!

Nevertheless it was Helps who was to persuade the earnest
Hallbert to become the London Library's first royal patron. Carlyle
was impressed. 'How delightful is the news of His Serene Highness
the Incarnate Solecism Prince Albert and our Library!' he wrote to
Milnes. 'You may also remember me to Mrs Incarnate Solecism if
there be any opportunity.'

Forster had been busy with the great bellows-machinery, providing another puff in the *Examiner*, and there had been another long
piece in *The Times*, which struck the deferential tone that was to
characterise newspaper coverage of the London Library ever after.
'Many persons of high station in society' had already declared
themselves anxious to promote it. Now the Prince Consort had
joined them.

One reader who signed himself 'Orbilius' was not impressed,
saying the whole thing was a fraud, a lot of gulls being preyed on by
cormorants, but with the newspaper coverage and 'Heroes and
Hero-Worship' having been such a triumph, they reached their
target of two hundred subscribers. It seemed manifest, Carlyle told
Milnes, that the thing was extensively taking root. 'If we could *heat*
it by one good burst of sun-splendour, or artificial furnace *flash-*

splendour, it would germinate straightway and fill all Cockneydom with its boughs and leaves!' The London Library had become the Tree Igdrasil, the life force.

The only backstage anxiety at the time of the Freemasons' Tavern meeting was that Fitzgerald had now entirely disappeared, last seen drinking at the Carlton Club. Carlyle, not for the first time reaching for a classical reference, likened him to the gods on Mount Ida watching the Trojan War. 'Is not his invisibility there, in the Carlton Ida these two weeks wellnigh inexcusable? Let him descend, with thunder in his right hand, in the Devil's name!' He did not, and the prospectuses were never recovered.

In August the short lease on the Committee Room in the Strand ran out, and Christie had to look for an alternative. He found another first-floor office at 57 Pall Mall, on the north side facing St James's Palace. When they re-assembled after the summer, during which business had been conducted by a small sub-committee including Carlyle, Christie, and Forster, the library was due to open in less than six months. They still had no premises – 'About the getting of our *House* does Venables know anything on that?'; they had no books and they had no proper librarian. All these things were now a matter of extreme urgency.

A circular was sent out to the subscribers, asking them to suggest books, and experts were invited to make up lists for each of the specialist departments. It was Gladstone, for his conspicuous piety, who was put in charge of compiling the library's first collection of theology, and Jane Carlyle's friend Mazzini also made some suggestions. 'Here is a kind of Italian list furnished by a very gifted native of that country', Carlyle wrote, 'not entirely unacquainted with ours. It will require great *sifting*.'

George Grote, the historian and philosophical-radical member of parliament, was asked to draw up a list of history books, and John Stuart Mill, who had proved far from reliable during the past months, was commissioned to draw up a list of works on political economy.

Mill initially hoped to follow the practice accepted by the earlier London Library of paying for his membership with books, which he hoped would be 'commuted' into his annual subscription. 'I would rather not give any opinion at present on the selection of French Memoirs and Histories as many of the books I propose to make over as commutation for my subscription are of that class.' Carlyle, possibly advised as to the state of affairs that kind of deal had produced before, refused. '"Commutation"', he wrote to Christie, 'cannot, of course, be spoken about again; there is nothing more to be said of that.'

Mill took it on the chin. 'I will according to your suggestion pay the entrance money.' On the 'other topic' of his choosing books he was excessively modest. He was sure they had no difficulties on French or German works 'having the aid of Carlyle'. 'I could perhaps undertake Political Economy, or Logic, but the former McCulloch would do much better and either of them I should not do so well as they could be done by many others; however I would do my best on any subject you might propose with which I am completely acquainted.'

Three weeks later he sent a list of books on Political Economy 'which, with the exception of one American book, includes none but English and French'. He was trying to raise a list of German, Italian and American works from a better-qualified friend. 'I have tried to make a similar list for Logic but have given it up in despair . . .'

The question of the librarianship was more stormy. While the books were being bought or collected from friends and piled on the floor of the Committee Room at 57 Pall Mall, a temporary librarian had been appointed called Brittan, who would have liked the job. Instead he had to watch as other candidates were considered.

Each was asked to send in printed testimonials, and an assortment of elderly men, most of them with experience as publishers or booksellers, began to appear at the office. There was a Scot called Simpson who had never been to London and, given the cost of living in the capital, Carlyle reckoned would be better off with his present salary in Edinburgh. There was a Doctor of Letters called Fisher, 'highly recommended for learning, grammatical and bibliographical, for method, diligence, fidelity, etc. – and as to Business, *not yet tried*' who Carlyle was told 'could be got for £100'.

As they appeared in turn, Carlyle's enthusiasm waned and his irritation increased. 'I have just seen Fisher; a solid Irishman, not without sense; totally without experience, without habit of self direction in any kind (I fear), who does not look as if he could go many yards without driving!'

Suddenly, in the middle of all this, democracy caught up with Carlyle and he found himself doing jury service, 'caged in that accursed Dog kennel of a Common-Pleas Court in Westminster'. He did not take it well. 'I will be mutilated, incarcerated, shot and almost crucified rather than go back on such an errand. Macaulay, who saw me in my despair on Saturday I fancied might have told you how it stood with me.' Maurice told him he should get out of it by claiming he was a Dissenting preacher.

Lyttelton, meanwhile, had suggested a librarian called Washbourne, whom Carlyle found 'a serviceable, goodtempered, active, useful-looking man, no great Bibliographer, but he would buy Books &c. very well.'

Then there was John George Cochrane, a Glaswegian bookseller and publisher who had as a young man run a firm in Fleet Street called White, Cochrane and Co. He had gone bankrupt after publishing expensive and elaborately illustrated botanical books, and this had prompted him to write a pamphlet, *The Case stated between the Public Libraries and the Booksellers*, in which he explained the burden for small publishers of having to provide copies of such books for libraries. He set out, with great clarity and wit, the whole early history of copyright law.

Under the existing law all publishers were obliged to send free copies of their work, however specialised and in however many volumes, to eleven separate public libraries, including Oxford and Cambridge, which he maintained could well afford them and made quite enough profit from publishing university books. It amounted, he said, to a tax on publishing. His pamphlet was influential in changing the Copyright Act in 1835, when the list of libraries was reduced to five.

Since then he had managed a German bookshop in Soho Square, and edited their magazine, the *Foreign Quarterly Review*. When that firm too went bankrupt he published the magazine at his own expense as *Cochrane's Foreign Quarterly Review*. It lasted for only two issues. He applied unsuccessfully for the librarianship of the Advocates' Library in Edinburgh, and briefly edited *The Caledonian Mercury* before being asked to catalogue Sir Walter Scott's library at Abbotsford. When he applied to Carlyle's committee he was fifty-nine, and editing a local paper in Hertfordshire.

He was followed by Haas and Baynes, 'the latter of them a shrewd kind of man', and a down-to-earth and very competent Londoner called Hayes. But by now Carlyle was getting confused. Hayes, he wrote to Christie, was at least 'not destitute of wordly experience'. 'It is true that he failed *twice* as a Book-seller in London; or only once!' Christie thought, correctly, that he meant Cochrane, and Carlyle consulted his notes. 'It seems *Washbourne* is the book-seller that failed. Whether Cochrane ever did such a feat is as yet entirely hypothetical for me.'

He was, he confessed, getting heartily sick of the whole business. They had to remember that they were not offering 'laurel crowns and the Bank of England, but hard work and one hundred and fifty pounds a year; Perfection is a thing we must not look for.' As the opening of the library drew closer, Carlyle decided that Cochrane was the best choice, perhaps because he was a fellow-Scot and had challenged the Copyright Act that Panizzi was so fond of invoking to increase his stock of books at the museum. But he wished in the same breath that he was 'out of this thing altogether', and that the library might 'float off without him'.

Christie preferred Hayes. A compromise suggestion was that Christie should stay on as official 'Secretary' or librarian, and that all the work should be done by a clerk till they saw the kind of man they needed. Carlyle was furious. 'It is like sending out a military expedition for conquest of foreign countries under a *serjeant*, with strict provision that *when* he has made conquests, we will send a General.'

But Carlyle wasn't sure he wanted a general: generals had a way of seizing power, and his most revealing note used a different metaphor altogether.

> My notion of the Librarian's function does not imply that he shall be king over us; nay, that he shall ever quit the address and manner of a *servant* to the Library; but he will be a *wise* servant, watchful and diligent, discerning what is what, incessantly endeavouring, *rough-hewing* all things for us; and, under the guise of a wise servant, *ruling* actually while he serves. He should be like a nobleman's steward.

But while Carlyle was doing his best to control things from Cheyne Row, Christie was conducting the interviews, and when he recalled Cochrane, a man twice his age, for a second interview, he clearly allowed his feelings to show. 'I hope you have not frightened away poor Cochrane,' Carlyle wrote shortly after Christmas. 'He seemed in tolerable spirits on Saturday night, and I have heard no whispers of him since.'

Christie predicted that Cochrane would be 'inert'. Carlyle disagreed. He would have preferred a younger man, he confessed, and he detected, he said, 'a shade of obstinacy in him'. But he was not in favour of 'guidableness' in a librarian, any more than he would be in a horse. 'The *guidablest* of all quadrupeds is a starved cadger's garron' – this being Carlyle's auld sporran-hung word for a broken-down horse, a considerably less flattering image of the future librarian of the London Library than that of a nobleman's steward – 'reduced to skin and bone; no kicking or plunging in him; but, alas, withal there is no *go* in him.' Cochrane, he thought, had *go*.

The full committee met in February to interview both Hayes and Cochrane, and took a vote. Cochrane, reporting to one of his sponsors in Edinburgh, observed that 'a knot of Cambridge men' were clearly in favour of Hayes. But on this occasion the Apostles were outnumbered, and Carlyle's candidate was elected.

Cochrane assured them that he would be ready to begin work in March, and that he would 'be in the office on the seventeenth at ten in the morning'. The news did not please the acting secretary, Brittan. When he was asked to stay on until the middle of May he looked, according to Carlyle, 'very pettish'. Faced with what seemed an unguidable quadruped, Carlyle 'had to fling the reins on his neck' and tell him he was free to go.

But the great weight was beginning to lift off Carlyle's own shoulders. He wrote to Christie, who 'had the whole threads of the business in his hand', asking him to meet Cochrane, and to 'give him *hold*, in some way, of the work he has to do. The rest will gradually arrange itself, were a beginning once made.'

He looked forward confidently to the time – 'I suppose in the presence of some General meeting' – when he could lay down the joint secretaryship, and thought Christie would too. 'It is what I want, and long for, no less than you. We shall be then non-Secretaries! The London Library will have the breath of life in it; and may grow as it can.'

# Hobbling after the Macaronis

*It struck me that there might be humble situations such as book collecting etc. which my father would be competent to fill – connected with the new London Library – and that the Bishop of Chichester might know if such be the case or not.*

Samuel Palmer, 1843

The fashionable crowd that surged up the stairs of 49 Pall Mall on the morning of 3 May 1841 included a great many clergymen, a few ladies, and the tight knot of literary figures who had founded the library, led by their prophet, Carlyle. His was one of the first signatures on the page of withdrawal slips, and after all his trumpeting about serious books, he took out *Indiana*, a romantic novel by George Sand.

There was, from the beginning, something irresistibly frivolous about the institution. The first London Library in 1785 had been founded near St Paul's Churchyard, at the serious, bookish end of town, and as it became more fashionable had moved to Jermyn Street. The new London Library opened on the north side of Pall Mall, above a bustling pavement and a row of expensive shops selling clocks, guns, china, glass, candles and lace to the aristocracy. One of them, Elliott's, provided silk underclothes to the young Queen Victoria.

The two rooms the committee had taken were on the first floor of an eighteenth-century house with three high windows looking on to Pall Mall, flanked by decorative pillars and with a wrought-iron balcony. The central round-topped sash had a hooped awning over it in summer, and the windows on either side striped sun-blinds.

For the tenants at street level, Charles and Henry Senior, Foreign Booksellers, the coming of the library and its members was a real windfall, as it was for Mr Wherstone, who sold pictures on the top floor. Given Thackeray's claim to drink five hundred bottles of wine a year, there may also have been some rejoicing at Bell, Rannie and Co., Wine Merchants, who shared the rest of the ground floor with a bootmaker called John Martin.

Opposite, on the south side of Pall Mall, were a few remaining old brick houses, accommodating at pavement level a harp-maker, the Society for the Propagation of the Gospel, and an Army recruiting office, their blackened chimneypots standing out against the high white stucco walls of the new clubs.

There was the Athenaeum with its famous frieze on the corner of Waterloo Place; the Travellers', designed by Barry; and next to it, by the same architect, the Reform, inspired by the Farnese Palace in Rome, where plasterers and painters were still at work for the club's official opening that same year. Towards Marlborough House was the Carlton, designed by Smirke in the Grecian style and accommodating no fewer than thirty-eight members of both Houses of Parliament; beyond it a few more old houses and, also by Smirke, the solid outline of the Oxford and Cambridge Club. All of them had been built within the last ten years.

It was a sight that must have reassured the more serious-minded members of the library: after a century and a half of *Punch* jokes about quaint old buffers silently expiring under copies of *The Times*, it is hard to realise that the clubs were once thought of as voluntary associations of virile and active men devoted to some praiseworthy ideal. In their new palaces they were beginning to favour cooking and comfort, but most of them had been founded without premises in the 1820s with wholly laudable intentions: even the Athenaeum Club had met first in the rooms of the Royal Society at Somerset House to encourage the arts and sciences.

Pall Mall could also be justified on grounds of seriousness by the number of Parliamentarians, some a good deal more serious than Monckton Milnes, who kept first-floor flats and even houses there. Nearby were two other serious bookshops, Wright's and Olivier's, the Royal Society of Painters in Water-Colours and the rooms of the British Institution.

Members of the London Library could think of themselves therefore as part of an exhilarating new tradition, balanced between levity and gravity, Mayfair and Westminster. Like the members of the new clubs they were in fashion, united in the pursuit of a noble goal.

Quite who chose Pall Mall in the first place is not clear. It could have been Milnes, who lived at Number 26, or Venables, who had promised Carlyle he would find 'a house'. But it could also have been Sir Edward Bunbury, responsible for choosing the first books for Travel and Voyages, and a member of the Travellers' Club. Before their new building was finished, the Travellers' had met in those same two rooms. Like many after him, Bunbury was none too clear about the constitution of the new library, and was under the impression, according to Jane Carlyle, that he was on the committee. He was not, but had none the less joined Gladstone and Milman in inspecting the rooms in February 1841.

It would be intriguing to discover whether Gladstone knew the history of 49 Pall Mall. When he first clumped about the uncarpeted floors on a winter's afternoon, listening to the clink of bottles downstairs in the wine merchant's and the tapping of hammers in the cobbler's shop, he must have realised that the old house, built in the middle of the eighteenth century, had some kind of a past. The building still retained something of its old elegance from the time when it had been a notorious eighteenth-century gambling den.

It had been opened in 1759 as an 'alehouse' by William Almack, at one time also proprietor of the assembly rooms in which Carlyle delivered his first lectures. He had been valet to the Duke of Hamilton, and 'Almack's' was the club from which both Brooks's and Boodle's ultimately descended. From the start it was frequented by the same race of grandees that a hundred years later was to patronise the library. 'Poor Sir Harry Ballendene is dead,' Horace Walpole wrote to tell the Hon. Henry Seymour Conway in 1761. 'He made a great dinner at Almack's, drank very hard, caught a violent fever, and died in a few days.'

In 1762 *The Gentleman's Magazine* announced that a new club would meet at 49 Pall Mall. This was to be the Macaroni Club, and again there was an uncanny resemblance between its members and some of the younger readers later associated with the library. It was, according to Walpole, 'composed of all the travelled young men who wear long curls and spying-glasses'. They were, someone else said, 'the younger and gayer part of our nobility and gentry', anxious to set themselves up as 'standards of taste and polite learning, the fine arts, and the genteel sciences', but who also 'gave in to the luxuries of eating and extravagancies of dress'.

Within twelve months, according to Walpole, they had 'quite absorbed Arthur's' – an earlier incarnation of White's – 'for you know old fools will hobble after young ones'.

A third 'society' met on the same premises, called the Ladies' Club or Coterie. Ladies could play loo after supper, or meet in the morning 'either to play cards, chat, or do whatever else they please'. Men were allowed to join, but there was a rule that no gentleman could blackball another gentleman, and no lady blackball another lady. It was tremendously exclusive, numbered five dukes among its members, and after moving premises several times eventually went bankrupt in 1777.

Almack's continued to use at least part of the house, and Walpole reported that 'the young men of the age lose five, ten, fifteen thousand pounds an evening there: it is worthy of the decline of our Empire or Commonwealth.' Gibbon, whose complaints about the amount of money he had had to spend on buying books to write his *Decline and Fall* were quoted at the head of Christie's prospectus for the library, did not agree. He described it as 'a place where I have spent many agreeable hours . . . the only place which still unites the flower of the English youth. The style of living, though somewhat expensive, is exceedingly pleasant, and notwithstanding the rage of play I have found more entertaining and even rational society here than in any other Club to which I belong.'

Brooks, the manager of Almack's, made a fortune out of lending money to members late at night, and in 1778 was able to buy the club's present premises in St James's, 'there being no reason', as one member put it, 'for preferring a bad old house to a good new one'. The bad old house became first a hotel, and was subsequently divided up into offices. Then, with the coming of the new serious clubs, it got a fresh lease of life. There was a Large Room at the front, overlooking Pall Mall, and a second room at the back, used by the librarian and the committee.

Either the Travellers' Club or the Royal Botanic Society, who had been there since 1831, had made various modern improvements: gas pipes across the ceiling to a 'handsome massive four-light gas burner', complete with reflectors and chimneys, three washstands with blue china basins and brass taps fed from a tank in the roof by thick exposed lead pipe, and the three iron stoves, 'inlaid with brass and set in stone with black marble jambs'.

The rooms were therefore in relatively good order, and Gladstone, Milman and Bunbury only asked for the decorative pillars at the front of the building to be repaired and painted. If the library succeeded, members expected to move, as the clubs had, to somewhere grander. They therefore recommended that the rooms should be taken on a seven-year lease, choosing to rent rather than buy the huge iron stoves and the gas lamps. The rent included a coal cellar dry enough for storing books, and, hoping to expand, they took first option on Wherstone's picture gallery on the floor above if it should become vacant. They also asked a firm of carpenters,

Stevensons of Theobald's Road, to make shelves for 10,000 books. When the members arrived at the beginning of May, three-quarters of these shelves were still empty.

Cochrane, newly elected librarian, had signed the lease with Clarendon and Pusey, and had taken an equally prominent role in assembling the 2,500 books they now possessed. He had spent a lifetime buying and selling books, and liked to boast that there were few persons who could equal him in his knowledge of foreign literature.

From February onwards the sub-committee responsible for buying the books had met every week. It included Carlyle, Craik, Forster and Christie, Spedding, and two more Apostles, Venables and Edward Fitzgerald, translator of Omar Khayyám. They went through the suggestions of the experts, and of ordinary subscribers, ordering those books approved by a majority of the sub-committee. In some cases, books were presented: Helps brought in a complete edition of Goethe printed on vellum, given by the Prince Consort, and almost all the members of the first committee gave something.

But there were still a great many titles in the suggested lists that Cochrane had to buy. In some cases he went to auction houses to bid for entire libraries, like that of the late William Hill which he had noticed within days of beginning work was coming up at Evans's. In other cases he made a deal with booksellers, and here some of the Apostles' reservations seem to have been justified.

As a twice bankrupt bookseller of fifty-nine, suddenly finding himself the agent of some of the most eminent and respectable men in the country, the temptations must have been considerable. Exactly what happened is not clear, but he appears to have made private arrangements with particular bookshops for their mutual benefit without telling the committee. Two months before the library opened he entered into a 'agreement' with a firm called Whitaker's which was subsequently cancelled by the committee. Christie, who had led the opposition to his appointment, was put in charge of all future deals, and instructed to explain clearly to all publishers and booksellers the terms on which the library was prepared to buy books.

Cochrane was also asked to make an official entry in the minutes that when he next asked the auction houses Evans's and Sotheby's to keep a look-out for books for the library he would make it clear that they would receive no commission.

This does not seem to have shaken his authority, and he enjoyed a greater measure of power over the committee than many of his successors, who have been obliged to exercise it more slyly by editing and manipulating the minutes. It was Cochrane rather than Milman, the first chairman, who wrote to the committee telling them that their numbers would be reduced, now that the library was open and working, to a more manageable size.

But Cochrane's main failing, as Christie had predicted, was indolence: he did not turn out, after all, to have 'go'. Carlyle, answering letters of complaint, did his best to defend him. 'The poor Librarian, for all his defects, rejoices to do for any member whatsoever is really in his power and is a most obliging good-natured man, eminent for patience and cheerfulness.'

'He did much really useful work in a quiet lucid way, in spite of his indolence,' Carlyle admitted to Lyttelton at the end of Cochrane's librarianship, 'and for practical help as a *bibliographer*, he was far the best I ever met within this country. True, he by no means shone as a distributor of books, and could never bring himself to believe that the wish of everybody without restraint to anybody *cannot* by any skill be complied with.' It was 'the wish of everybody without restraint to anybody' that clearly got the poor old Scotsman down: from trying to please the customers in a small German bookshop in Soho Square, he found himself dealing with international statesmen, absent-minded literary figures whose names were household words, the very spoilt and the very rich.

Brittan, the temporary secretary, had gone in February with a £10 bonus for his trouble, and Cochrane was left on his own, with one porter. A week before the library opened he had been allowed to engage one assistant, Upham, who was sacked for incompetence six months later.

Part of the success of the library's launch, as it has been of its survival, was the weight of Big Names: Carlyle, Macaulay, Dickens and Thackeray, then the grander foreign ambassadors like Bunsen and Van de Weyer, and finally everyone who was anyone in politics and society, like Gladstone, Milnes, Clarendon and Lyttelton. To have called them back in all the social excitement of the opening, to have insisted on signatures, or kept them waiting until the books were properly registered, would have demanded greater courage than Upham possessed, and Cochrane himself was almost certainly too busy enjoying the company of the great and famous. From the records of books borrowed in the first few days of May, still preserved in the library, it is clear that the result was chaos.

Special forms had been printed with the words 'Received from the London Library' and a dotted line for a signature. On each of these, as their successors would 150 years later, Cochrane or Upham wrote the member's name and the title of the book – at this early stage without any reference number. The member borrowing the book was then to sign underneath, acknowledging his responsibility to return it. That some of the books came back is clear, as they are still in the library, but how Cochrane or Upham can have traced them from the issue slips is hard to imagine. In some cases the form is cancelled with a smudged stroke of the pen, in others marked with an 'R'; the rest bear no mark at all.

The wide-ranging passions associated ever since with members of the London Library are in evidence from the start. On the first day John Fisher Esquire of Hackney took out Harris's *Wild Sports of Africa*, Wilkinson's *Egyptians*, Sir J. *Romilly's Memoirs, Vol. 1*, Carlyle's *Miscellanies, Vols 1 & 2*, and something heavily scored out to do with China. Fisher does not seem to have collected the books himself, and Jas Dunne signed them out for him. There are a couple of correctly signed entries, including John Sterling's brother Edward taking out *Curiosities of Literature*, Wycherly, Congreve, Vanburgh, and Farquhar. Then as an afterthought he has added Balzac's *Scènes de la Vie Parisienne*, for which he signed, and Walpole's *Letters*, for which he did not.

More earnest borrowings follow by some of the founders, Milman scoring highest points for seriousness and breadth of scholarship. 'Mr Carlyle of Chelsea' himself is represented by a signature very different from any on his letters: it could possibly be his own, written at the end of a long arm with a bad pen while he was talking to someone else over his shoulder, but it looks more like an attempted forgery by Cochrane or Upham.

Carlyle's attitude to the rules, which were ordered to be printed and pasted into the front of all the books a few days later, was always nonconformist. Several of the books he failed to return have since come to light as far afield as America, and his outrage at being asked to return books was extreme: 'Don't trouble me about this book,' he wrote when he was asked to bring back George Eliot's translation of Strauss's *Life of Jesus* which he had borrowed six months before; 'I have never had it, never saw it, nor wished to see it, nor shall wish to see it!'

Jane Carlyle's behaviour was if anything worse, being more frivolous, although her account of it leaves a clear impression of how handy the library soon became as a place of refuge in Pall Mall, even from the rain. One afternoon in January 1843, she was on her way to visit Erasmus Darwin, Charles Darwin's younger brother and yet another Apostle. He was an invalid, and one of the first to appreciate the benefits of being able to have books sent to his home.

At one o'clock, there being every appearance of a clear dry day, I set out in an omnibus to buy tea and coffee at *Fortnum & Mason's*, meaning thereafter to pay a *charitable* visit to poor Darwin, who was (and is) confined to the house with cold, but no sooner had I issued from the omnibus according to programme, than contrary to all human expectation it began to rain on me, so I made for the nearest refuge that offered itself, viz. the London Library. Being in the Library what could I do but choose myself some books? Everything I asked for was as usual 'out' – so *as usual* it ended in bringing away French novels – a book of Sand's which I had not before seen and two of – Paul de Kock! Having still however some sense of decency remaining, I coolly entered my name in the ledger for these books *Erasmus Darwin*! to the wonderment of the book-keeper doubtless, who must have thought me an odd sort of *Erasmus*!

Her complaint about books being 'out' was a standard one, and there were others. Edward Fitzgerald said the 'confounded London Library' was never open when he wanted it, although its official hours were ten to six. A more far-flung member, Mr H. I. Cameron of Dingwall, north of Inverness, wrote in the autumn of 1841 to say that he and five other subscribers found 'the regulations of the Library for the use of books of such a nature that it was physically impossible for them to comply', and asked for their subscriptions back. Pickford's had been employed to deliver books to country members, but they had clearly taken too long getting there.

But for every complaint there were several letters of appreciation: Leigh Hunt was the first of many writers to thank the staff in a preface, and the membership continued to grow, enabling Cochrane to buy more books. Donations also continued to come in, and a library guide published in 1843 specifically mentions more gifts from the Prince Consort, and from Sir Charles Pasley, who provided an entire library.

Pasley was the first of many military men of a literary bent to join the library, a brilliant engineer who had served under Wellington in Spain. He was, according to a later librarian, 'a short, stiff, grey-headed man who speaks with a slight Scotch accent and with decision. He reads much, going back with pleasure to the Greek and Latin studies of his youth. To amuse his waking hours at night he reads a volume of Fielding or Smollett.' He also had a short temper and was to persecute the staff for the next twenty years.

By the time 49 Pall Mall had been open eighteen months such new acquisitions had filled the empty shelves in the Large Room, and the carpenters were back making new bookcases on the landing: it was clear the time would come when the library would have to expand.

In 1843 Wherstone went, and they were able to make a Reading Room upstairs. It was well stocked with newspapers and periodicals, though Jane Carlyle still complained, when she called in at the end of April 1844 to look at the *Revue Independante* – 'just the only French Review they do *not* have'. For this room they bought a clock and inkwells. They also had a set of mahogany steps made for the Large Room.

Cochrane, meanwhile, had produced a first catalogue in 1842, dismissed by one critic as 'no better than a bookseller's list', which already contained 13,000 volumes. Nearly a thousand more were added during the following month. During that first year, 14,834 books had been lent out, and Cochrane had rationalised the issue system, with alphabetical lists of members and titles drawn up at the end of every day.

To help him with this Cochrane had taken on a young man of twenty, a fellow-Scot called Macpherson, and shortly after Upham was sacked, two more assistants, Dryden and Jones. Dryden was soon dismissed for embezzling £45, though the committee took a typically cautious line in not prosecuting for fear of incurring additional legal costs. John Edward Jones, on the other hand, is one of the most intriguing and mysterious figures in the whole history of the library, and a worthy representative of the many clerks and assistants who have warmed the hearts of members by their love of books and eagerness to help, but who have appeared in print in dedication after dedication simply as 'the staff of the London Library'.

Soon after joining Jones applied for an increase in his wages, and Cochrane told him that 'from expressions which had passed at the Committee from several members, he felt obliged to tell him that he was afraid, not only that his application would be unsuccessful, but that the probability was that his services would be dispensed with.' A member called Williamson had shouted at Jones for failing to keep a book he had asked for, he had defended himself, and Williamson had written to the Committee to complain. Jones characteristically went behind Cochrane's back to engage the support of Arthur Helps, author of *The Claims of Labour* in which he had written at length about the interdependence of employers and those who worked for them, and Jones was let off with a caution. But the episode was typical of his long career at the library.

He joined the library in August 1844, and Mr Cox, interviewed in 1952, said he had 'vivid memories of Mr. Jones', but the interviewer did not press him, and his vivid memories died with him. Jones was tall, energetic and moody, and obviously competent: he not only became Cochrane's assistant, but expected to succeed him. He was also the one member of the staff to charm Jane Carlyle, perhaps because of his ability to take intense dislikes, perhaps because of his sudden flashes of disgruntled gloom.

In 1845, the library moved to St James's Square. It was, socially, a retreat into a more parsimonious world, the austere heartland of entrenched aristocratic privilege. The neighbours were not breeches-makers and milliners. Except for one establishment listed as 'Balls' Lodging House', St James's Square was largely occupied by bishops and peers of the realm.

When Robert Adam had been asked to rebuild Beauchamp House, the library's new home in the north-west corner of the square, in 1772 for Sir William Mayne, he had conceived it on very elegant lines. The façade was to be in plain stone, with a frieze of classical reliefs. In his plans the front door opened into a hall, on the right of which, on the site of the present leather bench, hatstand and Suggestions Book, was a circular, stone-flagged front parlour with niches for statues. The main area of the Issue Hall was an 'eating room', reached from the front parlour through a semi-hexagonal antechamber. Beyond it, at the back, a study, lined with bookcases.

The stairs occupied the same position as they do today, but curving round an almost-square space through a ninety-degree turn: on the left, halfway up, below the level of the present

Gentlemen's Lavatory, was a service stair and a water closet, and at
the top, facing north, a door into an anteroom, with the drawing
room on the right occupying almost the same area as the present
Reading Room. On the left was a gentleman's dressing room with a
'powdering closet', and another stair to a bedroom above. Adam
also planned a possible extension to the north, where the Art Room
is today, with a large bedroom and dressing room on the ground
floor.

His designs were never built, and what Cochrane, Jones and
Stevenson the carpenter found when they first looked at it was 'the
worst house in the Square'. It had the narrowest frontage, and
while other buildings had been faced in stone, it still had its old and
flaking brick façade. It had been built in the middle of the seventeenth century, and had stood empty for a year, with rotten win-
dowframes and shutters, broken locks and missing keys, cracked
and discoloured ceilings, and floors which in some places had given
way altogether.

Beauchamp House was named after the ancestor of a twentieth-
century member of the library, Lady Mary Heber-Percy, formerly
Lady Mary Lygon. William Lygon, Lord Beauchamp, bought it in
1799. It was already an old house and had been gradually extended, over two centuries, with stables in what is now Duke Street,
and what was called a 'backhouse', a kind of garden room, a
'bathing place' somewhere under what is now Topography, stone
walks in the garden, and a lead cistern dated 1700. By the middle of
the eighteenth century it had become so ruinous that its owner 'fled
out of it for fear it should fall on his head'.

When Lord Beauchamp died in 1816 his widow Catherine stayed
on, allowing the house to become more and more derelict. She died
in 1844 and it was eventually bought by the library's old neighbours, Foster and Sons the auctioneers, who offered it to the
committee. With no capital to buy it, they agreed to rent
Beauchamp House on a twenty-one-year lease. Foster undertook to
make the necessary repairs to the floors and windows, the ceilings
were 'washed and stopped' and either 'whitened' or 'distempered'.
All the woodwork inside and out was repainted.

It was summer, and not many of the committee were in town, but
a little party of the more serious figures including Craik, Professor
Wilson and Dr Twiss came round to see if any of Lady
Beauchamp's old furniture was worth having. They 'saw nothing
desirable to purchase excepting the hall lamp, a writing table, and

one of the carpets, which Mr Cochrane was desired to look after and purchase if at a reasonable price.'

On the same visit they decided that the entrance hall would need a small inner lobby, and Mr Abraham the surveyor put in an estimate to make 'a pair of folding doors at the entrance of two and a half inch deal, painted grain wainscot, and varnished, glazed with best British plate glass' for £21. They also that afternoon 'determined that the front room facing the Square should be made the Reading Room as preferable on all accounts for that purpose.' Looking forward to the winter, they asked Cochrane to find out how much it would cost to put in a new grate for a fire in the new Reading Room.

Work began in September. In addition to Foster's repair work, the library spent nearly £800 – a third of its annual income from subscriptions – on making new shelves and on buying furniture. There were inevitably delays: Foster's men got behind, and this slowed down the carpenters, but circulars were finally sent out to all members asking, with only limited success, for books to be returned for the move in November.

After two more postponements, Jones, the two other clerks, two extra porters and the 'car man' began transporting nearly 20,000 books on 11 November. Four days later the move was completed, and the library reopened in December 1845. Cochrane was delighted with what he called the library's 'new and permanent domicile' and the committee voted that John Edward Jones and the two other clerks should share a £5 bonus.

In all other libraries naked flames were forbidden because of the fire risk, but as this was a private library for practical use rather than an irreplaceable collection, the committee authorised the use of camphene lamps, burning a mixture of oil and turpentine. For the first time, on winter afternoons, the windows of the London Library glowed with light, and the clanging of the handbell at closing time was heard in St James's Square.

# Gladstone's
# Neapolitan Duck

*The London Library is not typically English; it is typically civilised.*

E. M. Forster, *Times Literary Supplement*, 1941

'Dear Mr L.', Gladstone wrote in his clear round hand on a piece of writing paper no more than three inches square, 'I hear that Mr. C. is somewhat better. All we can do is to prepare for the contingency should it arise.'

A week later on 4 May 1852, he wrote again. 'Dear Mr. Lacaita. I have just received an intimation that Mr. Cochrane died this morning. The Committee of the Library are to meet on Saturday. The time has therefore come for you to make up your mind. Will you breakfast here on the 13th?'

Cochrane had soldiered on at St James's Square with John Edward Jones, a favourite of both Thomas and Jane Carlyle, who believed himself to be Cochrane's natural successor.

Now, extraordinary as it may seem, Gladstone was about to launch an almost unknown Italian who had been in the country less than four months as his candidate for librarian of the London Library. What made the plot so disreputable was that it was a direct reward for political services. For Carlyle it was to become the affair of 'Gladstone's Neapolitan Duck'.

Having moved from three rooms and a coal cellar into a large town house, the library had far too much space. They therefore approached the Statistical Society, who had rented a very limited amount of shelf space at 49 Pall Mall, and offered them a room at St James's Square.

The Statistical Society, like the library and the new clubs, was part of the wave of earnest endeavour, and three of its leading lights, Henry Hallam, Lord Lansdowne and Spring-Rice, were members of the library. Founded in 1834 to try to throw a statistical net over the mysterious shifts in economics, politics, public health and public morals, they were responsible for the census of

1839–41, and were so successful in inculcating an anti-Carlylean view of life as a monitored scientific process that by the end of the century almost every newspaper carried a breakdown of births and deaths in the capital, showing how many had died from cholera, influenza or measles.

Originally they had met in rooms at the top of a flight of sixty-nine steps in St Mark's Place. Though for the most part young, eager and progressive, they had found the stairs too much for them, and in 1842 they had rented very commodious ground-floor premises in Regent Street. This cost them £200 a year, and although it included the services of a hall porter, a housekeeper, and the cost of making coffee at their meetings, they decided that it was too expensive. St James's Square, being cheaper, made better statistical sense, and they moved in.

The committee also rented out one room to the Philological Society, many of whose members were also subscribers to the library. They met once a week to discuss Middle High German sound-shifts and the role of the fricative, and were ultimately responsible, forty years later, for the *Oxford English Dictionary*, produced by James Murray in his Canterbury Cap, labouring away in a corrugated iron shed in his garden in north Oxford.

These neighbours were to lend the library an additional sense of purpose and progressive endeavour for the next thirty years. They also got the library into trouble with the local council. Mr Buzzard, clerk of the parish of St James's, Westminster, took them to court for rates, claiming that the Learned Societies Act of 1843 only allowed exemption if the library was run exclusively for the pursuit of learning. By taking rents from the two societies they were in business as landlords.

It was Cochrane's finest hour: he was to be called by the Royal Commission on the British Museum some years later, but this was the only occasion on which he appeared in public on behalf of the library. He went into the box, spoke not about the rates but about the many distinguished and eminent men who formed the library's committee, about the Prince Consort and Lord Clarendon, and the magistrate instantly dismissed the case. Buzzard eventually appealed, and the library had to pay a few pounds to the parish as long as the societies stayed. But a century later Buzzard's ghost was to return and haunt them with a vengeance.

Jane Carlyle continued to be critical. In September 1847 she walked up to the library, and found it 'too bad for anything'. 'The officials mortal drunk, or worse – overtaken with incurable idiocy! Not a book one could touch without getting oneself filthy. I expressed my horror of the scene, and was answered: "Are you aware, ma'am, of the death of Mrs. Cochrane?"' She was not, and nor was Carlyle, taking as he did less and less interest in the affairs of the library. Jane remained heartless. 'I brought away the last four numbers of *Vanity Fair*' – then being published in instalments – 'and read one of them in bed, during the night. Very good indeed, beats Dickens out of the world.'

After her death, Carlyle found the passage in her diary, and wrote, 'Poor old Cochrane! The only real bibliographer in Great Britain!' It seems possible, after a frustrating life as a bankrupt bookseller and journalist, that Cochrane had indeed taken to the bottle. It would account for the charges of 'indolence', and would explain why Carlyle almost always referred to him after his appointment as 'poor Cochrane'. But when poor Cochrane died in office in 1852 the membership had risen from five hundred to a thousand, the stock of books to 60,000.

Unlike Gladstone, the man Disraeli accused of not having one redeeming vice, Carlyle was moved by the news of Cochrane's final illness, and mourned his death. Gladstone's unchristian interest was motivated by guilt towards another man. When Lacaita arrived in England in January, Gladstone wrote to him from Hawarden, 'You being in England takes a weight off my heart and my conscience in some measure.' There were few people Gladstone had dropped more completely in the soup.

Giacomo Lacaita was a grave and bearded Italian with liquid brown eyes and dark wavy hair that shone with Macassar oil. He was in some ways a tragic figure: an exile whose wife was to die in childbirth, and whose son was thereafter brought up by in-laws who despised him. But he was also hugely comic. A charmer and a howling snob, he was briefly and incompetently librarian at Chatsworth and was finally to be knighted and elected to the Athenaeum, according to his own account, with more signatures of support than any other candidate in the history of the club. The knighthood was for accompanying Gladstone, in the role of linguist and reciter of Italian poetry after dinner, on his famous diplomatic trip to Crete.

It was on this occasion that Gladstone, as Europe's greatest orator, insisted on speaking in Greek, and was congratulated afterwards by a Greek admirer who told him how wonderful it had been, regretting only that he had not been able to understand it as he did not speak English.

Lacaita was born in the heel of Italy near Taranto, the son of a provincial chemist, and he had met Gladstone in Naples in the winter of 1850. As the protegé of an elderly American chargé d'affaires, Enos T. Throop, he had tried unsuccessfully to earn his living as a barrister, and had eventually become the darling of the English colony as legal advisor to the legation.

Gladstone had come to Naples for a holiday, advised that his three-year-old daughter Mary's eye infection would benefit from the climate, and met him at dinner with the Carmichaels, who had come south for Sir Thomas Carmichael's gout. They despised the Italians, and longed only to return to the Scottish hills, which they compared to inverted teacups. Lacaita had been unwise enough to fall under the spell of their dumpy eldest daughter, Maria. She was, according to her family, 'not handsome' and never stopped talking. Lacaita had only proposed, according to their son, 'after many heartburnings'. They were now secretly engaged.

Gladstone was immediately charmed by Lacaita's ability to quote at length from Dante and Ariosto, and a passionate holiday friendship developed, with long walks by moonlight 'between the orange blossom and the whispering darkness of the surf'. Gladstone noted in his diary that he liked Mr Lacaita more and more, and Lacaita clearly got the measure of Gladstone at an early stage, telling him how he had learned from Enos T. Throop 'the duty of speaking the truth on every occasion'.

A great deal of Gladstone's diary at the time is devoted to which was the cheaper of two milkmen, one of whom threatened to kill the other for his custom, and Lacaita seems to have helped him to find somewhere economical to rent. He also drove their carriage with great dash on excursions in the mountains.

The political climate in Naples was less benign. The Bourbon King of Naples, Ferdinando the Second, known as 'King Bomba' for his belief in the artillery barrage as the most effective method of diplomacy, had little time for civil liberties. Lacaita had always been a cautious liberal, keen to offend no-one, but some of his 'chats' with Gladstone inevitably turned to politics.

In the middle of Gladstone's holiday Lacaita was arrested by Bomba's secret police. All his papers were confiscated, sealed in three sacks, and one letter discovered, according to Lacaita, that was considered damning. Some weeks before, he had organised a picnic for Gladstone's friends the Leslie Melvilles, during which he and the girls had decided, as a game, to take a vote on everything they did. Anna Leslie Melville's thank-you letter contained the phrase, 'Mamma desires me to say that it will give her great pleasure if you will come this evening and complete the final dissolution of the "glorious republic".'

This, Lacaita said, after two 'tiresome' days of reading through all his bills and laundry lists, excited the secret police, and he had great difficulty in proving that he and all his grand English and Scottish friends were not dangerous republicans. A week later Lacaita was let out, according to his own account, with a warning that the Leslie Melville letter had been lodged with the public prosecutor. Like many of Lacaita's stories, there is something fishy about this, as the letter was still among his papers at the time of his death.

Gladstone, in any event, was by now in a state of high righteous indignation, and when he met him next at dinner he wrote in his diary, 'Mr. Lacaita is out. *One* of about 150 arrested here within the last few weeks.' He was determined to make capital out of it at home, and was anxious to collect a strong case against Bomba. Through Lacaita and Brown, the correspondent of the *Morning Post*, he arranged to visit Baron Poerio, in whose chambers Lacaita had first studied. He had been in prison for nearly a year for his republican views, and was being kept in leg and wrist irons that were never unlocked, shackled to another man in a low-roofed underground cell.

Gladstone returned to London, joined the shadow Cabinet for the first time, having been offered everything except the post of shadow foreign secretary, which was already promised to Palmerston. Writing to Lacaita in April 1851, he promised him that 'on *every* ground, as well as on account of the effect that any hostile proceeding might have on you, I have sought in the first instance to go to work quietly . . .' His idea of 'going to work quietly' was to publish two pamphlets addressed to the Foreign Secretary, the *Letters to Lord Aberdeen*, calling down the terrifying wrath of British public opinion on King Bomba and his ministers.

There is no direct evidence that Lacaita was in cahoots with Bomba's secret police, but his account of the events that followed is not entirely convincing. He told Gladstone that he was suspected, if not of having written the *Letters to Lord Aberdeen* himself, at least of having been Gladstone's main source. But far from being arrested, he was advised, and in no great hurry, to go to England with Bomba's blessing and an official passport, to raise money for a new railroad. When his son was going through his papers he was surprised to find that the country house at Leucaspide in southern Italy where Lacaita died had been paid for by a railway company, and it is safe to say that in coming to England Lacaita was not playing an entirely unambiguous role.

As far as Gladstone was concerned, however, he was a political refugee, and his responsibility. Lacaita was certainly short of money, and his domestic prospects were not bright. Lady Carmichael, known to her family as 'Lady', had finally been told the news. 'She said', Maria wrote to tell him, 'she hoped you would not be able to come to England, that she could see no ray of comfort and no chance of happiness for me, that she did not think she could receive you here, that by birth and connections she thought you were not my equal, that she thought poverty most dreadful.'

None the less his passport came through in December, and he sailed for Genoa on the steamship *Vesuvio*, bound for London where he arrived in early January 1852. His travelling-companion was Panizzi. Lacaita went straight to Gladstone's house in Carlton Gardens, and Gladstone, who was out of town, wrote to him to arrange a meeting. Lacaita did not let him off the hook. 'I was delighted to see again and *without any alarm* your handwriting. Don't write any more about Naples.' Then, the charming holiday friend again, he went on: 'You see I have brought some Neapolitan fine weather with me.' They met in Oxford and, with Cochrane's health failing, Gladstone proposed the librarianship.

Lacaita liked the idea, but was understandably dubious about his qualifications. Back in London in February, however, he began to like the idea very much. He was asked to dinner with Lord Minto, where he delighted Lord Lansdowne, a member of the London Library committee, who took him on to another party at the Palmerstons. There he was particularly well received, having worked for Palmerston's younger brother, William Temple, at the British Legation in Naples. Before long he was going out to dinner four or five times a week, and had soon charmed several other members of the committee, including the Prussian Ambassador Bunsen, Lyttelton, Hallam, Bunbury and Monckton Milnes.

Gladstone had already begun canvassing, and had written individually to several members of the committee. Lyttelton, a loyal supporter of Gladstone, wrote to Carlyle. If it was intended to test Carlyle's possible reaction to the scheme, the response from Chelsea must have brought great comfort to the Lacaita faction.

> My name, I understand, is still on the Committee; but I have taken almost no share in any kind of Library business since those old days when you used to attend. Of course, if we lose poor Cochrane, it will behove us all to use all possible care to get a fit successor. If I have any thing to do with it (which seems doubtful) I can only engage to endeavour with all my industry to get the fittest attainable.

His first reaction to the idea of Lacaita becoming librarian was particularly comatose and unsuspecting. 'Mr Gladstone's friend appears to be an interesting man; and his qualifications, if he present evidence of them will deserve to be well investigated.'

Lacaita had by now been to Castlecraig for what he described in his diary as 'Scenes', and after a great deal of weeping and hysteria 'Lady' had agreed to them being married, providing, as he was a Catholic, that they were married twice. The liquid-eyed Lacaita acquiesced without a murmur, and arrangements were made for the Catholic marriage to be celebrated in a rented house in Edinburgh, followed by a Presbyterian service in the Tron Church. Then Cochrane died, and Gladstone ordered him to cancel everything. Keen that her future son-in-law should have a job, 'Lady' agreed to a postponement.

On 8 May Gladstone spent the afternoon at a sale at Christie's and then went to St James's Square at four o'clock for the committee meeting at which they were officially told of Cochrane's death. Gladstone had already made it generally known that he favoured Lacaita as Cochrane's successor, but agreed that there must be an opportunity for other candidates to come forward. He listened in silence as Milman declared the post of librarian vacant and announced that two advertisements were to be placed in *The Times*, and one in the *Athenaeum*, offering a salary of £200 a year with unfurnished apartments. Applications were to reach the library by 22 May.

That evening Gladstone summoned Lacaita to Carlton Gardens. Lacaita was once again in a panic: Panizzi had written to him in Italian, assuring him he had 'powerful friends', but he was still not convinced. He had, it was true, some knowledge of Italian poetry and as a hobby sometimes bought second-hand books with fine bindings, but that was the extent of his qualifications.

Gladstone reminded him that he was thirty-nine, would soon be married, and had no other means of earning a living. In the end the prospect of dinner every night with the aristocracy seems to have convinced him he should stand, and with Gladstone's political weight behind him he must have thought he had a reasonable chance of success. He had reckoned without Carlyle. Looking back forty years later, Gladstone remembered what followed as 'a lovers' quarrel', but at the time it seemed a very ugly fight, with both sides risking public humiliation if they were defeated.

Carlyle remained for a while wry and dismissive. 'From Gladstone's own account to me, I figured him as some ingenious bookish young advocate, who probably had helped Gladstone in his Pamphlets underhand – a useful service, but not done to the London Library particularly.' He did not like Gladstone, considering him to be an opportunist – 'He has no convictions, but he is a long-headed fellow' – and at their first confrontation he hardened his line. 'The proposal is quite inadmissable, the post ought to be given to an Englishman.' The battle lines were drawn.

Carlyle withdrew to Cheyne Row with influenza, foreseeing 'a reprehensible and ominous affair'. As at the time of the foundation, he reached for his pen, and began to fire off letters. 'I am struck down to the earth with Influenza, incapable of stirring out for near a week past, and forbidden even to speak above five words in the half-hour, under penalties.'

His first tactic was to delay the election. There were, he knew, a great many applicants for the job and that number was growing; Gladstone's proposal had produced even more argument among the committee as to whether they wanted a working librarian or a gentleman librarian, and among the members there was a growing ground swell of hostility to Lacaita.

Over two hundred applications had come in already, and in the middle of May he persuaded Jane to go to St James's Square, to communicate his notions to Forster:

> . . . namely, that Jones should be interim manager; that first of all a thorough examination and illumination of the Library's *condition*, from the very heart to the surface of it, should be had; – whereby we might know what *kind* of

Librarian might now be the best for us; – and that not till after that should any Election, or movement towards an election, be made by any one of us.

He also told her to 'signify to Jones in some kind way' that their asking him to be interim manager did not mean he would automatically succeed Cochrane, 'tho' his deserts were known and would be attended to'.

Jane Carlyle then made history by becoming the first woman to attend a committee meeting, and the last for another thirty years, but in the 'bustle' afterwards, she missed Jones and failed to pass on Carlyle's warning. Jones therefore left the library believing, as the shortlist was prepared from the sheaves of applications, that he was the Founder's favourite.

But Jane did succeed in convincing Forster: he agreed to resist Lacaita, and, in any forthcoming struggle, was prepared to swear his allegiance to Carlyle 'on the Koran'. He did not believe, however, that they had the remotest chance of winning. Gladstone, Forster wrote to tell Carlyle, was 'stirring Heaven and Earth' to bring about the election of 'his Neapolitan'. The committee – Milman, Lyttelton, Milnes, Hallam, etc. – represented 'a clear majority of malleable material, some of it as soft as butter under the hammer' of a powerful politician. They were 'perfectly certain', Forster thought, to do whatever Gladstone suggested.

Jane was 'quite of Forster's way of thinking', and so initially was Carlyle. But he was determined at least to put up a good fight. 'Gladstone', he wrote to his brother, 'will probably succeed: but he shall not do it without one man at least insisting on having Reason and common Honesty, as well as Gladstone and Charity at other men's expense, satisfied in the matter; and protesting to a plainly audible extent against the *latter* amiable couple walking over the belly of the former.'

By the time Forster's gloomy letter arrived, written after his conversation with Jane at the committee meeting, Carlyle became more pugnacious. 'This project of Gladstone's must be resisted *à l'outrance!*'

Despite Forster's 'evil prognostics', there were what Carlyle called 'possibilities'. 'And if there were not, such must be *made*, and prosecuted with energy and without delay.' Resistance was growing among the members. Lacaita wrote to Gladstone in alarm.

Immediately after the committee meeting on 22 May, he had been told by Captain Galton, who was a member of the library, that he had been sent a petition protesting against Lacaita's appointment.

'It seems that the petition has been drawn up by an *employé* in the Board of Trade. I think Mr Cole, or some such name, who is a great friend of some of the principal candidates.' This was Sir Henry Cole, a founding father of the V&A, who had joined the library in 1841. 'It seems also that they are trying to have the appointment referred to a general meeting of all the subscribers, which I am told will be next week. Should you wish to see me, any message from you will find me at the Athenaeum from one to two o'clock today.'

Gladstone got his letter after lunch, and did not reply till the next day. He was not over-optimistic. Lacaita's being a foreigner who had only just arrived in England 'might be against him', there were a great many candidates, and it would be no disparagement to him if he were passed over. 'But you have nothing to fear from such a circular as that which you describe, and of which I regret to hear simply on account of the parties who may have got it up.'

The threatened extraordinary annual general meeting did not materialise, but the committee met a week later. Carlyle and Helps were formally re-elected to the committee, and the meeting to elect the new librarian was set for 12 June. Carlyle continued to pound his old friends with a barrage of metaphors, most of them domestic rather than heroic. Having raised the spectre of Gladstone and Charity walking over the belly of Reason and Common Honesty, he set about demolishing Charity first. Charity, as he explained in a letter to Forster, in this case meant helping Lacaita, who badly needed a job.

> The Committee (of which every one of *us* is a constituent atom) has no more right to do this thing, than your Henry would have, if you sent him out for a cut of salmon, to buy it, with your money, of some meritorious Fishmonger (Neapolitan or other) who had a cut *extremely in need of being sold*. With what face would Henry present malodorous salmon to you: and brag of his 'charity' done at your expense! This seems to me the exact position we occupy, whether we recognise it or not; and we, each of us, shall intrinsically deserve horsewhipping if we play false to it, and don't bring home simply the *best salmon* we can find!

Poor Arthur Helps, caught between his obsequious editorial activities at Windsor and the composition of a fragile letter on slavery inspired by reading *Uncle Tom's Cabin*, published that year, was summoned to London.

'The London Library is in danger!' Carlyle began. It could not be used for the convenience of this 'miniature Panizzi'. All the other 'native candidates' were 'superior in real fitness to the young Neapolitan Advocate just arrived on our shores, whom Gladstone has decided to lead in over the belly of both Rhyme and Reason, and make a king over us! To myself all this is a thing evidently contrary to not the London Library alone, and to its clear interests and rights, but to the common honesty of every one of us to whom said interests and rights have been tacitly but most validly delegated for management and supervision.'

Helps was to come to London at least a week before the crucial meeting of the committee, and plot. 'Unless actually held, as I myself am, you are actually bound to this somewhat as your groom would be if he saw one of your horses about to be stolen by a cadger, and could prevent it by a little running.'

'I have', Carlyle went on, 'no candidate of my own; on the whole, no wish in the matter except that what is honest be done by the Committee. Sure enough, Gladstone might saddle Kossuth' – the Hungarian exile recently arrived in the country who was astonishing the crowds with his grasp of English oratory – 'or King Bomba on the L. Library, or put the L. Library altogether in his pipe and smoke it to white ashes, without entirely ruining one's prospects in this immense Universe!', but Helps was to come if he could.

It was, for the twenty other members of the committee who arrived at St James's Square on 12 June, a potentially comic confrontation: Gladstone, the fervent moral giant, accused by the grumpy Scots prophet, now fully recovered from his influenza, of using the librarianship of the London Library as a political bauble.

The shortlist consisted of eleven candidates, including Lacaita, Jones and a little-known country squire from Norfolk, James Bodham Donne. In favour of Lacaita was a thick folder of testimonials from peers who had met him in Naples, members of parliament who had met him at dinner since his arrival in England, and, guaranteed to inflame Carlyle, a warm recommendation from Panizzi.

'Gladstone, with Bunsen and Lyttleton and Lansdowne to back, made due appearance', Carlyle wrote to his brother afterwards, 'and had all along been very diligent and eager for his Neapolitan Signor of Merit.' Jones' name was soon forgotten in what became a straight fight between Gladstone and Carlyle, one backing Lacaita, the other Bodham Donne. Gladstone, it seems, spoke first.

Milnes once said that Gladstone's idea of impartiality was to be furiously in earnest on both sides of the question: on this occasion he was furiously in earnest only on the side of Lacaita. As he stood there on that hot summer afternoon in the Reading Room, looking round him from under those heavy brows, his noble head still quite well covered with black hair, he must inevitably have impressed his listeners simply by his presence. He was one of the most charismatic politicians of the day: he was also, Milnes' jokes apart, an orator of genius. When Gladstone spoke, according to Curzon, there was a feeling as though the air was fanned by invisible wings.

'Speeches were spoken,' Carlyle recalls, 'manoeuvering went on.' Carlyle, when he spoke, likened Gladstone to Apollo, descending in all his glory to address them. Carlyle described himself, as he had described Cromwell in 'The Hero as King', as the wild man Orson, lost son of an emperor but reared by a bear in the woods, 'Old Orson with his Club'. Gladstone said afterwards it was the most artful speech he had ever heard.

There was 'real politeness, candour and delicate management', and Carlyle eventually called on the chairman, Lord Devon, to take a vote as 'they were not convincing one another'. Written votes were collected, and Lord Devon counted them 'amid considerable stillness'. Then he announced the result: 'For Donne 18, for Lacaita (the Signor of Merit) 4'; after which, as Carlyle concludes, 'We departed most of us with mutual congratulation.'

Found among Lacaita's papers after his death was the letter Gladstone wrote him immediately after the vote.

London Library Committee Room
June 12th 1852

My dear Mr. Lacaita,
Mr. Donne is elected. *You were the only other person for whom there were any votes* out of the one hundred and seventy-three candidates: in point of fact, his only competitor; which is the fullest admission from everybody that your gifts, qualifications and character were faultless. Had your repu-

tation in this country not been made before, I confidently assure you that this day would have made it.

I remain,
Most sincerely yours,
W.E. Gladstone

Lacaita got married, and wrote to Gladstone from his honeymoon in the Lake District on blue paper stolen from the Athenaeum. What neither he nor Carlyle probably knew was that Bodham Donne was an Apostle.

# The Coming of Pegasus

*Books are the first luxury abandoned; for if a man puts down his carriage, or leaves off champagne at his dinners, all the world discovers his poverty; but unobserved he can borrow a publication he wishes to look at from a circulating library . . ."*

John Murray III

In the 1850s the library was faced with commercial competition that nearly drove it out of business. The committee blamed the Crimean War and the upheavals caused by the Indian Mutiny, but the real threat came from a national lending library that had its own horse-drawn delivery vans, its own carefully packed book-crates and even tin-lined cases to send orders overseas, like the covers of its books all bearing the symbol of Pegasus, the Flying Horse.

The London Library would find it hard to compete: it was still being run by a committee of gentlemen amateurs, and Thackeray for two successive years took over the accounts. John Edward Jones in particular had a good deal to be gloomy about: he had not only been passed over but he was now assistant librarian to a man with almost as little experience of libraries as Lacaita. William Bodham Donne was forty-five, and like his rival Lacaita had never had a proper job.

Donne was also one of the most affected men of his generation, with a passion for the theatre that by far exceeded any interest he had in the library. Worse, and particularly distressing in a librarian with the opportunity of meeting so many writers, he was a belle-trist. He thought of himself as a reincarnation of Madame de Sevigné, and liked to drop a Shakespearian reference or phrase in French into practically every sentence. 'My wit like Iago's acts like bird-lime, it plucks out brains and all (*voici mon apologue*).'

Although he professed to find writing a strain – 'As I grow old I become more fastidious in my composition. I never had, nor ever shall have, the "pen of a ready writer" ' – he kept up a self-consciously literary correspondence with Fanny Kemble, sister of

82

his lifelong friend John Kemble, now Examiner of Plays, for whom he occasionally deputised.

In infancy, so he said, he had been recommended to Charles Lamb as a child of great promise, though they never actually met. He was delicate, and was educated at home until his father's death when he was twelve. He was then sent to the King Edward VI School at Bury St Edmunds, where he was a contemporary of three future Apostles, Spedding, Edward Fitzgerald and John Kemble. At Cambridge he distinguished himself as a scholar, but refused to take a degree, following the example of F. D. Maurice in challenging the old Act of Conformity that required all graduates to be members of the Church of England.

Since then he had married, had five children, and lived quietly in the country, producing an anthology on travel called *Old Roads and New Roads* and editing a book about magic and witchcraft, both of which were published in the year he took over from Cochrane, in 1852. They suggest a range of interests very typical of the London Library reader. He also wrote occasional critical articles about his friends' work and had continued to attend the Apostles' annual dinner in London, at which he frequently took the chair.

His fellow Apostles must have sensed mid-life stirrings of discontent: earlier in the same year he had been asked whether he would become editor of *The Edinburgh Review*, and had turned it down on the grounds that 'his habits were too retired to keep him in the current of public opinion'. He now stirred himself sufficiently to accept nomination for the librarianship at St James's Square and even came to London for the election, though he affected only bored curiosity as to the outcome. He stayed in Charlotte Street, where he took his daughters to see a conjuror and visited two elderly actresses who lived near by.

Carlyle accepted him as 'a friend of Spedding, Milnes and etc., a scholar of distinction, "Man of Business", (they say), a small Norfolk Squire who – even the Justices of the Peace love him – appears to be, if *testimony* can be credited, little short of an "Admirable Crichton", fit to be the envy of surrounding Libraries.' Carlyle was wrong again. An 'Admirable Crichton', fifty years before Barrie's play was written, implied admirability rather than butlering. Crichton was a sixteenth-century scholar and swordsman, and Sir Thomas Urquhart had called him 'admirable'. Bodham Donne, for all his popularity with the committee, who were delighted to have a fellow gent in charge, was far from admirable as a librarian. 'Testimony', according to Hagberg Wright, a professional administrator of libraries who later cast an eye over the accounts under Donne's management, 'was perhaps too kind in calling him "A Man of Business" '.

The most striking thing about Bodham Donne was his grandeur. His wife had died ten years before, the children were brought up by his mother, and when he was appointed he moved into poor Cochrane's old flat at the top of the library. He called it disparagingly 'this precipice', but lived there in some style, entertaining a good deal and having food sent in from a French caterers in the Opera Arcade. He was looked after by an old housekeeper, Mary Trollope.

Members of the library found her wonderfully amusing and old-fashioned for her habit of clumping about St James's Square in pattens, wooden platform-clogs used by milkmaids for walking through the mud, which had not been seen in London since the turn of the century. She adored her employer and thought him far grander than anyone else in London. On one occasion, Lord Derby's butler asked her if she'd like to go round and see the table laid for a Cabinet dinner. The table was covered in fine linen, crystal and gold plate, but Mrs Trollope was not impressed. She looked at it, pursed her lips and said, 'That's nothing to what we have at Mr Donne's.' According to the clergyman who attended her on her deathbed, 'It was of no use talking to her of the glories of the Saints: *she* will only talk of the glory of the Donnes.'

Handing out books in a lending library, however distinguished the clientele, was therefore a bit of a come-down. He did his best to cling to his retiring habits, and spent his days writing in the Librarian's Room on the ground floor at the back. When Jane Carlyle called in the month of August, two months after he took over, 'to get Madame de Staël's *Mémoires* for Count Reichenbach', she was told that the librarian was in his room, and wrote in her journal: 'He never comes out of that end room seemingly.'

Her informant was Jones, who in July had received an award from the committee of £30 'for extraordinary services' and had had his salary increased from £104 to £117 a year. Donne allowed him to take over the part of the job that, once the initial excitement had worn off, he least liked doing, which was meeting the subscribers. 'He is', Donne told Christie, 'the only person who knows the pulse of the members and who can measure the degree of pleasing or offending them.'

But Jones was still in a sulk, and told Jane that he was going off for three days 'for a little pleasuring'. He had also decided to leave the library. 'The tall young man', she noted, 'was on the eve of his departure' and had 'found on trial of six years that the place didn't suit him.' He was going to take a job in a silk manufactory at Derby, 'a very good opening indeed'.

Jones never went to Derby, but laboured on under a man who was to give the library less than six years' trial before discovering that it did not suit him at all. Soon after moving in, Donne wrote:

I believe people think I have a light place. I wish they could try it a week. I don't think you have, and I don't see how you should have, any notion of the amount of correspondence attached to the Librarianship; there are ordinary letters to answer; extraordinary and unreasonable grumbles to soothe or to scold, and literary questions or hints to respond to daily, besides the accounts – and then there is the (to be) classified catalogue to prepare in slips and arrange under heads.

He did not even begin this for another three years, and never finished it, but the idea weighed on his mind.

I never attempt to do any work but library work from eleven to six p.m. Seven hours of work of any kind, even if routine work, takes the freshness out of one, and I am seldom good for much again until eight.

If, after a life of literary leisure in the country, he was unaccustomed to work, he made matters worse by allowing his passion for the theatre to draw him into working for the Lord Chamberlain's office, licensing plays, and when his old friend Kemble went to Germany he asked Donne to take over as Deputy Examiner.

Then comes the Lord Chamberlain generally four times in the week, and no small amount of correspondence and book-keeping in the course of the year, over and above the reading and making out the licenses.

He was writing to Richard Trench, who had asked him, eighteen months or so after his appointment as librarian, to give a course of lectures at King's College, London. Donne refused, saying he was afraid that 'the scheme would not be palatable to the Committee or the subscribers generally'.

This was probably true. Cochrane had left the library in a mess, and the first thing Donne did when he took over was to send a printed letter to all members asking for overdue books to be returned or re-entered. He also sent off letters to those who had not paid their subscriptions. But whereas 'excellent old Cochrane', as Carlyle now began to call him, had managed to charm the members with his bookseller's chatter, Donne put their backs up. He was popular enough with his old friends on the committee, but complaints from the members about his running of the library poured in, and in 1853 he was asked to appear before a special sub-committee to deal with them.

The complaints fell into three categories: the first was Jane Carlyle's old refrain, that standard works always seemed to be 'out'. Donne said there was nothing he could do about that: members paid no attention when they were asked to return books. He had sent out the circulars, he had threatened fines, but all to no effect. There was a good deal of head-shaking by the committee, and some irritation when it was discovered that one of the chief complainers was William Ewart, MP for Dumfries and the main driving force behind the Public Libraries Act. As a London member he was allowed to have ten books out at a time, and he at that particular moment had twenty-four.

The second source of irritation was that Cochrane and his staff failed to keep any proper records, so that it was impossible to know whether books had been returned or not. Here Bodham Donne resorted to the traditional defence that it was all very well to draw attention to things when they went wrong, but that a lot of the time they went right.

The third and most damaging complaint, for which Bodham Donne could not be held responsible, was that books, particularly the latest books, could be obtained a great deal faster and more cheaply from Mudie's.

To understand the threat of Mudie's, the library with the Flying Horse on its books, it is necessary to remember the power of the so-called circulating libraries. They had a bad reputation. According to their critics, like Carlyle, they circulated rubbish, and rubbish that was likely to corrupt. In a famous scene in *The Rivals*, Sir Anthony Absolute uses an image that may have been at the back of

Carlyle's mind when he fused the Tree Igdrasil with the London Library 'filling all Cockneydom with its boughs and leaves'. 'A Circulating Library in a town', says Sir Anthony, 'is an evergreen tree of diabolical knowledge. It blossoms throughout the year. And depend on it, Mrs Malaprop, that those who are so fond of handling the leaves, will long for the fruit at last!'

But it was the success of the circulating libraries in the eighteenth century that had made possible the growth of the more earnest subscription libraries, founded like the first London Library with reading rooms and serious collections, and the two had always been to some extent in competition. One late eighteenth-century proprietor of a big subscription library divided his readers into the Sedate, the Historian, the Theatrical Amateur, and the Gay and Volatile, and members of the latter category were always liable to stray away to handle the leaves of the evergreen tree of diabolical knowledge.

The founders of the London Library had made a point of not buying novels when they were first published, and the reason was as much to do with money as with morals. The new three-volume novels were astonishingly expensive by mid-nineteenth-century standards, costing a guinea and sometimes more. The library bought later editions, which were cheaper, but that was of no comfort to those writing to complain to the committee, who wanted to have the latest triple-decker hot from the press, and could get it from Mudie's.

Charles Edward Mudie, a Scotsman like Carlyle, had opened his Select Library a year after the London Library, and was already wiping out his competitors. His father had run a lending library in Chelsea forty years earlier, with a subscription of a guinea a year, and young Mudie charged the same. This was half what the London Library charged, and there was no £5 entrance fee. He was also savagely undercutting those of his rivals who circulated the expensive three-volume novels, and who were charging five or six guineas a year.

He imposed strict regulations. New novels could only be borrowed for a week, and no book longer than a month. Anyone who kept a book out longer had to pay the full purchase price, there was no committee to appeal to, and Mudie had not been at Cambridge with anybody who could put in a word.

Mudie's Select Library rapidly became a national institution. 'As children must have Punch and Judy, so I can't do without my

Mudie.' Unlike some of his rivals he did not specialise entirely in trash: he stocked Emerson and Carlyle, and undergraduates from the new University of London borrowed his books. So did F. D. Maurice.

In time Mudie established an elegant Reading Room in New Oxford Street and books were delivered all over the country by Mudie's vans, and eventually all over the world in his tin-lined cases. In them, so legend has it, Mudie's books survived even shipwreck. They were bound in bright yellow, and became standard furniture in every Victorian home.

The publishers Smith Elder tried to break the three-volume pattern by issuing one-volume novels at six shillings each in a series called 'The Library of Romance', but under pressure from Mudie, who said they were 'inconveniently long', they were then issued in two volumes, and would probably have appeared in three if the series had not been abandoned.

Mudie has been credited with making the three-volume novel possible, and for maintaining its popularity for almost fifty years. When the company went public in 1864, Mudie himself retained half the stock: the other half was bought by John Murray and various other publishers. He had set the pattern for circulating libraries for a century to come. Boot's Booklovers' Library, Harrods and W. H. Smith, with whom Mudie's finally amalgamated in 1894, all followed in his successful wake.

Mudie's London premises remained open under their own name until 1937. Wyndham Lewis went there in the twenties and described it as 'a superbly Forsyte institution, solid as roast beef'. 'It is about the only place in London where you can still find muttonchop whiskers, lorgnettes, tall hats from late-Victorian blocks, feathered and flowered toques, and that atmosphere of unhurried fastidiousness, leisure which has quite gone.' Harrods bought what remained of their book stock and the old Reading Room in New Oxford Street was destroyed by a German bomb.

Looking back at the end of the century, the chairman of the committee, Edmund Gosse, wrote that it had been 'peculiarly the age of the triumph of fiction'. Henry James, whose father had been put up as a founder member by Carlyle himself, talked about 'the prolonged prose fable' as 'a flood that threatened the whole field of letters with submersion'. It was a flood that very nearly submerged the London Library. The Serious Readers and Historians who had embarked ten years before, pledged to provide books for the elite who would educate the masses, found themselves shouldered out of the way by readers, Jane Carlyle among them, who wanted the latest three-volume novel. Bodham Donne quoted Christie's original prospectus, and even had a special notice printed in bold black type which was displayed throughout the library. It was not their policy to buy new novels, and members would save themselves time by not asking for them. There was very little money; what there was should not be spent on what he called 'supplies for the *vulgar*'.

Discreetly, however, the committee took out a subscription to Mudie's. Whether the London Library issued them in their Pegasus binding is difficult to tell. It was a desperate bid to keep the Gay and Volatile membership, but it seems to have worked, and the subscription was maintained for many years.

But Bodham Donne was convinced that he had saved the library by a more subtle scheme, allowing people to join the library annually, without the £5 entrance fee but paying £3 instead of £2. 'I know', he told Christie, 'that in a lucky hour, by introducing a new rate of subscription – the three pound annual – I saved the Library from inanition.'

In terms of preserving the serious character of the library it backfired. It attracted the wrong kind of people, and increased the demand for light literature. 'For the most part', wrote Bodham Donne, 'the "three-pounders" were engaged in business or professional studies, and used the books for relaxation.'

Donne himself managed to fit in a good deal of relaxation. In the first eighteen months, living in his bachelor luxury and looked after by Mrs Trollope in the rooms above the library, he had old friends to stay, like Edward Fitzgerald. Writing to Donne's mother from the librarian's flat, Fitzgerald conveys a mood of gentle lethargy rather at variance with Donne's account of his exhausting hours of work. At other times, Bodham Donne, again with his old Cambridge friends, idled agreeably about in London:

Having breakfasted with Crabbe, I accompanied Spedding in the evening to Captain Sterling's, brother of my old friend John. In his garden at Knightsbridge, apart from the dwelling house, he has built himself a huge room of cast iron, and mounted on rollers so that it may not become a fixture, and belong to the owner of the ground. This building is called 'The White Cottage' yet anything less like a cottage you cannot well imagine. It is more like a barrack room. But it is admirably warmed and lighted, and some fine old paintings on the walls. Here on Sunday evenings occasionally the gallant captain receives his friends, and permits his friends to introduce their reputable acquaintance – *comme moi* – so Jem took me.

Edward Sterling was a founder member of the library and a regular borrower of books, and it is odd that Donne had never met him, but he was no doubt in his room, composing letters scattered with Latin tags and *bons mots*.

He took tea with Fanny Kemble or watched as she was drawn by Samuel Lawrence, who had already, as the librarian put it, 'made a copy of my cranium and phiz in Crayons'. In the winter of 1854 he spent evenings with her at her house in Savile Row. She had given him Charles Kemble's watch – 'a very good one' – and they were going through a tin box filled with the old actor's red pocket-books from 1790 to 1817. Apart from records of his stage performances they contained 'the most interesting anecdotes about the people he associated with' and the two of them sat for hours reading them aloud to each other. They would have made better speed, he said, 'were it not that almost every page suggests something or other and sets us talking. So we advance as slowly as the Dominie in arranging Col. Mannering's Library.'

His tone of amused contempt for the work of the librarian would have irritated members of the London Library no end. From a photograph taken at the time, with his high forehead, large silk bow and a self-consciously witty twist to his mouth, it is easy enough to imagine him floating through the Issue Hall, his mind full of some show he had seen the night before or some amusing thought that had occurred to him that he wanted to tell Spedding or Fanny Kemble, entirely ignoring Jones and the other toilers in the storehouse of knowledge.

With a librarian who was such a flamboyant admirer of the stage and theatre folk it was ironic that the most terrifying threat to the library during his time there should have come from a theatrical project.

The house next door, now occupied by the Clerical, Medical and General Insurance Company, had belonged for almost a hundred years to the Anson family, and was standing empty when the library moved in. Shortly after that it was let to the Army and Navy Club on a short lease, which ended in 1850, and became a picture gallery. Then, in November 1853 a piece appeared in the *Art Journal* under the headline A NEW THEATRE IN LONDON.

> Strange as it may seem, there is to be a new theatre in London: a company (consisting principally of French gentlemen) has been formed for the purpose of introducing dramatic performance in a somewhat new form in England. They are to consist of concerts and ballets, and are to be conducted, we understand, on a large and liberal scale, to be sustained by the best singers and dancers of the continent; the leader, Monsieur Berlioz.
>
> The house to be converted into a theatre is that mansion in St. James's Square, formerly the Army and Navy Club, and more recently a public picture gallery. The theatre is to be arranged to contain two thousand persons, and there will also be elegant and spacious rooms for promenades etc. The project is to rival all similar establishments of the world in the elegance and beauty, and pure taste of the whole of the decorations.

The *Art Journal* predicted that it would be a great success, if only because 'everything connected with it will be of a singularly graceful and refined character.'

When the London Library Committee met a few days later there was near hysteria. The house next door was going to be turned into 'a Theatre, Casino, or other place of common resort and entertainment'. The librarian was told to investigate the story, and 'to watch all proceedings tending to confirmation of the same, with a view to the effectual prevention of such or any similar design'. The plan fell through, and in 1855 the house was let to the Junior United Services' Club.

Tennyson called in to see Donne at the library, 'looking very grave with his beard and moustaches', to tell him he had bought his house on the Isle of Wight. 'He affirms it to be, both for its privacy and its prospect, a very Paradise. He has made me promise to visit him, which I certainly will do one of these days.' He was working 'in good earnest' on his *Morte d'Arthur*. Bodham Donne wrote disloyally that he hoped it was not like *Maud*, 'for that grates on my ear and passes all my understanding'.

The Brownings were living in Devonshire Place. 'Mrs Browning has been delivered of *Aurora Leigh*, i.e. of many hundreds of verses, which I have not read and do not intend to read, not out of disrespect, but simply because I do not understand either her writings or her husband's, and – a sign of age I suppose – require poetry to be some years old before I can relish it.'

Spedding was still in town, 'correcting his slices of Bacon and disseminating such fallacies about things as would shock you to be told.' Like many of his successors, Bodham Donne quite enjoyed entertaining eminent members in the Librarian's Room, even if they wrote for *Punch*. 'Tom Taylor comes to see me today; he is engaged on something that requires all our books in any language relating to Flanders and the Flemings, though whether it be a play, a poem, or a tale is not indicated.'

Charles Reade, who was delving in the library for his fictionalised story of the love affair of Erasmus' parents, *The Cloister and the Hearth*, was more irritating. 'He sits watching one, when he calls, with head on one side like a magpie, and derives seemingly much amusement from the contemplation.' Donne's theatricality and laboured French witticisms must have made the old man laugh a lot, but the joke escaped Donne. 'He may think of turning me into the *père respectable* of a romance.'

He was occasionally amused by letters he got at the library, like one from a clergyman asking urgently for *La Dame aux Camélias* in time to write his sermon, but in general it was tedious.

The summer of 1856 was unusually hot, and when London emptied in July Donne stayed at St James's Square, trying to start work on his catalogue. 'I sit here sometimes for days on end without seeing a soul, but a man who has on his hands the compilation of a volume as big as a Church Bible, viz. a classified Catalogue of near 80,000 volumes, does not need any interlopers.'

Fanny Kemble, in America, was amazed at the number of books and asked if she'd read it correctly. 'Yes,' Donne answered, 'the London Library *does* contain 80,000 books, and I am the luckless wight whose duty it is to sort and give an account of those same . . .'

At other times he was more philosophical – 'It is not a bad position. I am useful in it to many persons, and utterly without ambition' – but that same year he made his first attempt to escape, applying for the job of registrar at London University. He was very difficult about it – 'canvassing in any shape being utterly distasteful and detestable to me' – and was not accepted.

The work he enjoyed most was licensing plays. He seems to have

accepted that there was not a great deal he could do: he had banned
*La Dame aux Camélias* in 1852, and when *La Traviata* opened in
1856 he merely noted that 'she has at last escaped from her four
years' bondage, and is now performing at the opera, in the full
bloom of her original horrors.'

The theatre managers loved him. He happily accepted the crates
of wine they sent him, was always punctual, and as stage-struck
putty in their hands must have been just the man they wanted in the
job. When he came to the end of his time as Deputy Examiner they
insisted on coming to the library to present him with a silver
inkstand. Kemble died in 1857 and Bodham Donne was asked to
become Examiner. He immediately resigned from the library.

Lacaita was still available. His wife had died, his son Charles was
being brought up by 'Lady', and he was loafing rather aimlessly
from country house to country house. His mother-in-law suggested
he should make some money. 'Go into society,' she told him, 'call
upon your great acquaintances. English people like to patronize,
and there is no saying when influence may get you something.'

Lacaita did not need any encouragement to go into society, and
was now seeing practically all the London Library Committee
regularly at dinner. He had still not forgiven Carlyle, whom he met
shortly after Donne's resignation at Milnes' rooms in Pall Mall.
'Carlyle was holding forth about the late Sydney Smith, and maintained that Smith had no wit, no talent, no amusing or intelligent
conversation of any sort! I own the more I see of Carlyle the greater
is my dislike to him.'

But it was Bodham Donne who finally scotched the scheme,
advising Lacaita as one gentleman to another not to touch the
library with a bargepole. Donne said he did not know Lacaita, 'but
had been taught greatly to admire him by those who did'.

There can be no doubt of *his* fitness, or of the agreeable
relations between the Secretary and the Committee; that is the
*couleur de rose* side of the matter: there are, however, less
pleasant circumstances between some of the members and the
Secretary, which may make a gentleman pause before accepting an office in all other respects agreeable.

The chances, or rather the certainties of these disagreeables
should I think be candidly put before any friend who might be
desirous to propose himself: a stranger would, of course, as I
did, take his chance and rough it.

I do not know that I am particularly thin-skinned, and certainly, though not of the best temper in the world, have sufficient command of the temper I have, as well as sufficient interest in the welfare of the Library, not to quarrel directly with some of its subscribers. But even had it, on other grounds, been for my interest to retain the Secretaryship longer, I doubt whether I could much longer have put up with the almost daily provocations to *explode*, which the unreasonableness of many, the unpunctuality of many, and the utter want of common civility in some, tend to excite.

All will be well that ends well; and I shall take care to keep the peace (as I have kept it hitherto) during the remainder of my term. But as Bob Acres felt his courage oozing out of the palms of his hands, I feel my temper oozing out of the tip of my tongue and my pen very frequently. Therefore I think it most prudent to resign betimes, though other causes occur to this conclusion.

I should be sorry that an accomplished and refined gentleman, like Mr Lacaita, should take the post under the delusion that he will have in it either much leisure for his own pursuits or much peace of mind in his public duties.
Believe me, my dear Sir,
Very sincerely yours,
Wm. B. Donne

Bodham Donne went on to become a favourite of the Queen, organising plays at Windsor, though he continued to take a keen interest in the library and stayed on the committee for many years.

Lacaita almost immediately fell on his feet. He became 'Secretary' to Lord Lansdowne, a man so old that he had a copy of Boswell's *Life of Johnson* given him by the author. Lansdowne, he wrote, explained to him that 'he had a person who wrote for him ordinary letters and bills, but gave me clearly to understand that his chief object was to enable me to be in Town and attend to my literary pursuits.'

Once again, John Edward Jones, loyal, hard-working and a friend of the members, seemed destined to succeed.

# Death in the Periodicals

*The so-called instinct of Self-preservation is a fiction. The*
*only impulse at work there is the shrinking from Pain; and*
*this in the matured experience leads to the intelligent act of*
*self-preservation.*

George Henry Lewes, *Problems of Life and Mind Vol. 1*

Just before five o'clock on a Wednesday afternoon in May 1875, a
young man called Bryan Courthope Hunt walked up the steps of
the London Library. He was twenty-three, with high cheek-bones,
rather full lips and looked not unlike the young Mick Jagger.
Downstairs, at the Issue Desk, he returned a fairly heavy book,
bound in cloth boards and red leather, and still on the open shelves
of the library, the first volume of George Henry Lewes's *Problems
of Life and Mind.*

He asked for the second volume, and Charles Scarse, the clerk on
duty, told him it was out. When he was asked later how Hunt had
taken this he said he had been rather busy at the time and had only
glanced up, but he thought Bryan Hunt was 'rather indifferent
whether the book was in or out'.

Hunt then went up the white marble stairs into the Reading
Room. He said good afternoon to Jones, who was working at his
desk, and went on up to the Magazine Room, which was on the
second floor at the back, and a place, according to Jones, where
very few of the members went.

Jones had known him for some years, as the son of Thornton
Hunt, first editor of the *Daily Telegraph,* who had died two years
before, and the grandson of Leigh Hunt. Jones knew that he was
not a member, but as both his father and grandfather had been
familiar figures at the library he would probably have been allowed
to go on using it. What neither Jones nor anyone else knew was that
Bryan Courthope Hunt had in his pocket a loaded pistol.

Robert Harrison, appointed instead of Jones to succeed Bodham
Donne, was, according to his own account, the son of 'a gentleman
in easy circumstances who was induced to enter into a partnership
that proved disastrous'; according to others, of a bankrupt brewer

from Lancashire. Harrison and his eleven brothers and sisters had been brought up by their mother, the daughter of a hat-maker from Stockport, who somehow succeeded in supporting them by flower painting, something she continued to do until she was eighty-eight.

He had in earlier life worked in a bookshop in High Holborn, and then gone as tutor to an aristocratic family in Russia. When he got home he was appointed to run the Leeds Library, which according to his letter of recommendation he had found 'in much confusion', and had left after introducing 'very satisfactory arrangements'.

This must have sounded encouraging to the committee in St James's Square: Bodham Donne had been made an Honorary Life Member when he left, but under his management the library's annual income had fallen from £3,000 a year to less than £2,000, and membership from nearly a thousand to just over eight hundred.

The committee itself had lost a lot of its energy: Christie had become a member of parliament and then British Ambassador in Brazil, Spedding was entirely absorbed in his academic work, Carlyle never came, and Milman had more than enough to do as Dean of St Paul's. On several occasions committee meetings were cancelled because nobody turned up.

Despite the subscription to Mudie's, competition from the circulating libraries was still fierce: Hookam's of Bond Street claimed to have a larger collection of important works than any other library in the kingdom except the British Museum. One even set up in 1865 under the name of the London Library Company.

Desperate measures were considered. One was to jettison the old idea of buying only established works and to open a special department of the library for new books and novels. This was not adopted, but Harrison extended the arrangement with Mudie's to borrow up to a hundred books at a time. Another more despairing proposal, proof that the London Library was still far from being the sacred institution it has since become, was to amalgamate with a firm calling itself the English and Foreign Library Company. This too was turned down.

Someone else suggested making the library more useful to those who had to work during the day. In 1866 the library had gone to the expense of installing gas lamps and for three months in the spring of 1868 the library was kept open from six to eight in the evening. The president, Lord Clarendon, wanted to extend this till ten at night, 'not during the summer months, when people were generally out of town, but in the autumn quarter'. Between six and eight o'clock, he told the annual general meeting, when men had eaten and were full, they were not much disposed to study; but when the process of digestion was over, many persons – particularly those who were busily employed during the day – found rest and the best sort of recreation in a couple of hours' reading before bedtime.

Some people objected that this would make the library too much like a club, 'which was not desirable'. Clarendon did not agree. Why should it be more like a club of an evening than in the morning when members congregated in its rooms for the purpose of reading? 'A library must necessarily always be deficient in the attributes and attractions of a club, which comprise wines, dinners, cards, billiards, newspapers, etc.; above all, the idle gossip, which in a library could never be found.' This produced 'loud laughter'.

Thanks to Harrison, some of the idle gossip is preserved in a ledger bound in green parchment, alphabetically indexed and labelled Carriage Arrears. At the top of every page, written with a broad nib, are the names of individual members, and underneath are the amounts owed for having books delivered to their homes in 1848 and 1849. What makes the book so remarkable is that it belonged to John Edward Jones, who checked and signed every column, and that Harrison used it to make notes for his memoirs. As if in answer to Jones' protest he has written on the flyleaf:

> I have taken this book for my own scrawling, because it is no longer of use for anything else. It was set aside before I came to the Library, and as on taking office the arrears for carriage were for certain reasons abandoned, I am at liberty to throw away these old accounts. R.H. 1859

It bears witness to years of tension and silent conflict.

Jones, passed over again, had another pay rise and was again thanked by the committee. But as Bodham Donne told Christie many years later, 'Jones and the present Secretary did not agree from the very first. It is very grievous when there is not unity between the manager of an institution and his principal clerk, but', he said, no doubt with a hint of *après lui le deluge*, 'there never has been such unity at the London Library since I quitted there as Manager.'

Harrison was thirty-seven, only a few years older than Jones. He was to remain in the job for another thirty-six years. As early as 1864 Harrison complained to the committee that Jones 'had refused to follow his directions', and was told not very helpfully 'to make the order peremptory'. The relationship between the two men can only be imagined: Harrison greeting distinguished members, watched by Jones; Harrison taking them into the Librarian's Room that Jones might have occupied, and closing the door; Jones tidying the Issue Desk after the library had closed, hearing Harrison going upstairs to the librarian's apartment that might have been his, and having instead to put on his hat and go out into the dusk of St James's Square.

Harrison, in his notebook, never mentions Jones by name and rarely goes in for introspection: there is, it is true, a poignant page where he wonders whether he might have influenced world events by dropping a word in favour of the North during the American Civil War to a man then helping to frame British policy. Could a jocular remark he made to a secretary at the Russian Embassy somehow have affected the outcome of the Franco-Prussian War? But these thoughts really only confirm his respect, as a good nobleman's steward, for the members.

There is also a touching account of the members showing their gratitude. He and his son Bo were on holiday in Salisbury in Easter 1869, and in the cathedral they met Auberon Herbert, a member of the library. He asked them to Wilton on a day when the house was not open to visitors. On the way they saw Gladstone, then prime minister, walking on the road, and discovered he was staying at the house. They were asked to lunch, and afterwards they shook hands with Gladstone: 'I told Bo to remember that a prime minister had shaken hands with him.'

It was a big lunch party, and Harrison was not sitting at the same table, but he thought Gladstone, who was then just sixty, looked very well. 'When the ladies were trying to persuade him to take a glass of wine he resisted gently, saying "At my age I must not do such things!" '

But more members of the library were about to arrive. 'Luncheon was over and I had risen to take leave when in came Lady Ashburton' – the best-looking ugly woman Monckton Milnes had ever seen, Carlyle's favourite hostess and the first woman to become a life member in 1841. 'Her party included Lord Houghton [Monckton Milnes] and Mr. Brookfield [husband of Thackeray's mistress], who shook hands with me and must have been mightily astonished at seeing me there!'

He hears the occasional funny story, like the time Tennyson, who claimed to be intensely shy and to dislike being recognised in public, went with an equally shy fellow-poet, Allingham, to see Dr Lynn the conjuror at the Egyptian Hall in Piccadilly. Lynn did not know what Tennyson looked like but chose him as his stooge, and to Tennyson's acute embarrassment pulled an egg out of his ear and another out of his beard.

But most of what Harrison noted down was the kind of inconsequential talk he would have exchanged with members while he helped them to find books, and the notebook is the nearest we shall probably ever get to the real history of the London Library: what Carlyle would have seen as the budding and branching of the Tree Igdrasil, the growth and spread of ideas in the library, occurring through chance meetings between readers, books opened by chance releasing long-dormant thoughts, Alexander Herzen gossiping to Harrison in the Librarian's Room, Harrison ordering his works, Isaiah Berlin coming across them on the open shelves a century later and going on to edit *My Life and Thoughts*. Such encounters occur at the London Library a hundred times a day: conversations rarely written down, often forgotten, which if they could be recorded would reveal an astonishing spreading web of mental activity with the library at its centre.

Harrison's notes are scrappy and scribbled at random but they are the most powerful surviving transmitter of impressions of what it was really like to breathe the hot, dusty air inside the London Library in the 1860s and 1870s. It also contains an eyewitness account of what happened to Bryan Courthope Hunt.

In 1865 John Edward Jones' old friend Jane Carlyle was still dropping in to St James's Square. Harrison made a great fuss of her, and Jones must have felt particularly bitter when he saw the door of the Librarian's Room close behind them and heard Jane Carlyle's laughter. But a lot of her charm and sprightly Scots phraseology survives in Harrison's account, scribbled down immediately after she left.

Mrs Carlyle complains of her husband having gained nothing from his recent trip into Scotland than a morbid sensibility to the noise of railway whistles. He did not notice them while engaged on his various works, but now that his occupation is gone he hears the noises and cannot sleep for them. She thinks something better than stuffing the ears with cotton wool might be invented to exclude sound.

Going on to speak of deaf people and their trumpets she said that Harriet Martineau used one and at their house one day Carlyle was talking to her while suffering from a cold in the head which made the water run from his nose. Mrs C. amused herself by watching the trickling stream and by speculating on the effect of a drop getting into the trumpet. If it reached the tympanum of the listener the effect, she thought, would be something like the crack of doom. At least the attitude of these three persons would make a picture that posterity would like to see.

Perhaps the most moving note of a conversation with Carlyle is after Jane's death, when he told Harrison that it was 'the same as if he had lost his skin, she was everything to his comfort'.

He loved Carlyle's jokes about how boring it was listening to Macaulay, who he 'characterised happily enough when he repeated the first line of the song "Flow on thou shining river!"' Carlyle was really in no position to talk, and Harrison was told of an occasion when the two of them had been arguing about Cromwell at dinner and Macaulay had called Carlyle a 'windbag'. Carlyle must have resented this all the more for being a term he had invented himself.

But he preferred Macaulay as a comic figure. One member told Harrison he had been standing next to him at a funeral at the Abbey when the mourners had had to wait for an hour in the Jerusalem Chamber, and that 'he kept up a stream of talk with Mr. Benj. D'Israeli and Mr. Van de Weyer for three quarters of an hour without intermission. This however was nothing to a breakfast at some Queen's Counsel's house when (the lady says) he talked from eleven o'clock till two without a single "flash of silence" as Sydney Smith called it.'

Bodham Donne, who still came in a good deal to dazzle Harrison with his aphorisms and to bring gossip from Windsor, told him that the Queen once asked Macaulay something about a famous Indian emerald. 'The essayist not only gave the required information but bored the Queen to death by about forty minutes' talk on all the emeralds that ever existed in the world.' Macaulay had also upset the royal family by using Windsor Castle notepaper, when he was staying there, to write a letter to *Blackwood's Magazine*.

Jones was no doubt carrying heavy piles of books up and down stairs while Harrison listened to such tales; Harrison would probably have argued that part of his own job was keeping the members happy.

Harrison writes in conclusion to his stories about Macaulay:

The only time I have seen the great man was about a fortnight before his death. He was not pleasant, either in look or manner, about the middle size, rather under, of ungainly thickness in the body, with a leaden complexion and grizzled hair. His manner was abrupt, and to some remark I made about a Dutch journal recently put in the Library he scarcely gave any answer, and in an ungracious manner turned himself off.

His disease, poor man, must have affected his temper very much. His heart was probably more like a sponge than anything else.

Harrison was always fascinated by medical details, and in December 1863 he records the death of Thackeray, found dead in his bed from an 'effusion on the brain'. He remembered Thackeray telling him that he had always suffered from bilious attacks:

. . . a stoppage of the biliary duct he called it, when talking to me in the Library one day, by which he was always prostrated. He had an attack at Bradford about seven years ago on the very night he was expected at Leeds to deliver one of his lectures on the Four Georges. We were talking of that incident when he told me of the disorder, which however he always thought he could master by means of calomel.

He told Mrs Coulson (the surgeon's wife) when dining at their house in the Regent's Park some months ago that he drank not less than five hundred bottles of wine a year, for when at home he drank one bottle to dinner, and when out which he often was he drank more.

He was I believe a great frequenter of the Garrick Club where he invariably (as my informant saith) finished the evening, wherever he might previously have been, with gin and water.

There was a steady stream of visitors from abroad who were allowed to use the library on a temporary subscription. Alexander Herzen was then editor of the exile magazine *The Bell* and a keen collector of any damaging gossip about the regime in Russia. Although Harrison spoke some Russian, and built up the library's collection of Russian literature, they talked in French, and he told Harrison a story about Kleinmichel, Minister of Means of Communication under Nicholas the First, a buffoon risen from the ranks. He appears in Herzen's *My Life and Thoughts* as a byword for stupidity, and on this occasion didn't understand about the time in eastern Russia being different from that in Moscow.

The historian Motley came in on his way to be American Minister in Vienna, and 'the Hon.ble Charles Sumner, Senator for Massachusetts'. Sumner was a passionate campaigner against slavery, and had recently been beaten with a heavy stick in the Senate by the nephew of Senator Butler of South Carolina for insulting his uncle. He visited the library in October 1859, and Harrison described him as 'a fine tall man with much talk'. This was largely about the beauty of old England and Westminster Abbey being like a poem. After 'much talk' Harrison has added a spectral exclamation mark.

Longfellow, 'the American poet', called in at the end of 1859, and impressed Harrison with his vivid use of metaphor. 'He illustrated the condition of a narrow-minded man by means of that wooden instrument which is used to expand the fingers of tight gloves – "He wants the glove sticker putting into his mind." '

Harrison, surprisingly, had no need of the glove sticker, and his attitude probably reflects fairly accurately the broad-mindedness of the London Library as a whole. He was a regular churchgoer, and was mildly shocked when a preacher he complained about was credited with a joke about Harriet Martineau's 'dogmatism': 'Dogmatism is very bad, but bitchmatism is intolerable!' He made the note 'Strong and wholesome doctrine, but not delicate!' But he was delighted when Buckle, who had come under fire from the clerical establishment for his *History of Civilisation*, told him how friends, afraid he would be blackballed from the Athenaeum, had threatened the Bishop of Winchester that if it happened they would blackball every bishop, dean, rector and curate who stood for election for the next ten years.

The clergy still made up a large proportion of the intellectual establishment, and many of those he saw at the library were

parsons, not all of them overemployed. One repeated the rhyme – 'I
have lost my portmanteau!' 'I pity your grief!' 'My sermons were in
it.' 'I pity the thief!' – and told him proudly that he had translated it
into Greek, Latin, French, German, Italian, Swedish and Chinese.

But the mood was changing: the days of John Stuart Mill's
friendship with Carlyle were long since over, and in retrospect the
burning of the manuscript of *The French Revolution* by his maid
had taken on a symbolic significance: Carlyle's old romantic,
mystical-spiritual message that had so appealed to Maurice and his
followers was now increasingly dismissed as rubbish by Mill's
disciples.

The creed in fashion was Positivism, a term first used by Henri de
Saint-Simon, whose followers had shocked the Apostles at
Cambridge by rejecting the 'spiritual relation': after him had come
Auguste Comte and John Stuart Mill himself, insisting that science
was the only valid knowledge, and dismissing metaphysics and
religious ideas as so much mumbo-jumbo. Many Positivists, like
Frederic Harrison, did their best to turn it into a new religion, with
positivist hymns, collected and edited by his wife, and a positivist
calendar featuring heroes very unlike Carlyle's, not dreamers but
doers, worthy human beings to be venerated for their contribution
to Progress. Like Herbert Spencer, another of its leading exponents,
Frederic Harrison was now on the committee of the library, this
was the new orthodoxy, and Robert Harrison the librarian
accepted it as such.

Another member of the committee, George Henry Lewes, who
was to play a major role in the events that brought Bryan
Courthope Hunt to the library, and who devoted himself to popularising such ideas, was a progressive both in his writing and
his way of life. He rejected Carlyle's idea of the Hero in favour
of something a great deal more scientific and democratic – 'The
great thinker is the secretary of his age. If his quick-glancing mind
outrun the swiftest of his contemporaries, he will not be listened
to' – and he was living in high-minded adultery with Mary Ann
Evans, George Eliot, whose *Adam Bede* had been published in
1859. But Harrison treated him with as much deference as anyone
else.

He includes an account of Lewes getting his own back on Bulwer
Lytton, who had come into the Librarian's Room without acknowl-
edging him, by drawing his attention to a factual error in Lytton's *A
Strange Story*, then appearing in serial form. 'The great man (MP

and Rt. Hon)', Harrison wrote, 'bore the snub before me without wincing.'

Lewes had a mobile, ape-like face – the Carlyles called him 'Monkey Lewes' – and he was the kind of man for whom the London Library had been invented. As a former medical student who had abandoned his studies because he couldn't bear to see people in pain, he had published psychological and scientific papers, including a public challenge to Dickens questioning the plausibility of Old Krook's spontaneous combustion, and under the pseudonym of Slingsby Lawrence he had translated several French farces. In some of them, being the son of an actor and grandson of the popular comedian Charles Lee Lewes, he had himself played a leading role.

He was also known as the author of a life of Goethe and as a populariser of the German philosophers, but he was best known as the lover of Mary Ann Evans, and his affair with so stupendously ugly a woman was a great joke of the period. While he studied the nervous system of the lower animals for his book *Seaside Studies in Ilfracombe, Tenby, the Scilly Islands and Jersey*, she had compared her own appearance adversely to any sea-slug he might find at the bottom of a rockpool.

Although Harrison does not mention the gossip, the sequence of entries in his notes makes it clear that it existed. One paragraph refers to Lewes coming in and talking to Richard Congreve, the Positivist, about Buckle's *History of Civilisation*; the next is an account of a conversation with John Chapman about George Eliot.

Chapman had actually introduced Lewes to Mary Ann Evans, and he talked to Harrison about the shape of her head. He said she 'possessed one of the most massive intellects of our time'. Combe the phrenologist had once told him that he had never seen a woman's head indicative of so much power, and, he concluded, 'very few mens' heads'.

Despite her regular borrowing from the library, and her habit of leaving books in the country when she was in London and vice versa, Harrison does not seem to have known her well. Chapman told him she was 'an agreeable conversationalist, full of knowledge – but her external graces are small and few, coiffure and toilette generally being of the negligent sort.'

Lewes had only recently moved in with her; his connection with Bryan Hunt went back over twenty years, to a time when he and Bryan's father Thornton Hunt had worked together on a radical newspaper called *The Leader*. Lewes's young wife, Agnes, had fallen in love with Thornton, and there is a charming pencil sketch by Thackeray of the three of them at the time: Agnes Lewes at the piano, with a long pretty neck and her hair tied in bunches, her husband standing behind her, beating time, and watching them with a smile and his thumbs in his waistcoat Thornton Hunt.

Agnes Lewes had three brown-skinned children by Thornton, and Lewes, true to his progressive principles, condoned it. Thornton also continued to have children by his own wife, one of them Bryan Courthope Hunt.

As a child, Thornton had played with Shelley, who twisted his greasy forelock into a horn to frighten him. Both Shelley and Leigh Hunt had dreamed of liberated communes, and Thornton when he grew up actually established one in Hammersmith, calling it the Phalantsery. It was a joke based on the word *phalantsère*, used by Fourier in his scheme for an ideal society to mean a group of buildings occupied by a 'socialistic community' of eighteen hundred persons. The household in Hammersmith consisted of Thornton's family, in-laws and maiden aunts, Agnes and George Lewes, and all their children.

Lewes's friendship with Thornton was now over, and the moral chickens had come home to roost. Lewes had been unwise enough to mention money, a subject none of the Hunt family could bear, and Thornton had challenged him to a duel. Bryan Courthope Hunt had spent his adolescence with his family in Euston, vaguely aware of unacknowledged step-brothers and -sisters in Kensington sporadically supported by his father, who worked most evenings until very late at the *Daily Telegraph*.

In many of his letters written from the newspaper office in Peterborough Court, Thornton Hunt talked about the importance of personal influence, and he had done his best to get jobs for all his children: he had written to Gladstone, A. H. Layard and even Walter Pater, trying to find a job for Bryan's brother Walter, who was now manager of an engineering works in Notting Hill. But Thornton Hunt had died when Bryan was twenty, and had not been able to do much to help him.

His uncle said Bryan was not like anyone he had ever known, that his intellectual condition was extraordinary, and that he had half expected him to go mad. He suffered as a child from heart disease, and had recently been trying unsuccessfully to find work. When he had been given a medical examination he was found unfit, and according to his brother Walter this had preyed on his mind. He had shut himself in his room to write, had begun to drink or take drugs, and shortly before his visit to the library he had been destroying papers.

The book he was reading at the time was George Lewes's *Problems of Life and Mind*, a series of papers about psychology and the determined nature of emotional response. Harrison remembered him as being fond of reading, and 'acute in matters of that kind'.

Ten minutes or so after Jones saw him go into the Magazine Room there was the sound of a shot. Scarse downstairs at the Issue Desk heard it, so did Jones, and so did Samuel Butler, author of *Erewhon*, who was also in the Reading Room. He was looking through books about Canada, where he was to go a few weeks later. Harrison did not hear it, as he was in his office on the ground floor at the back of the building talking to Carlyle, now seventy and affecting the grey side whiskers and irascible-melancholic manner of his later years, waiting impatiently for the second volume of Motley's *The Rise of the Dutch Republic*.

Both Scarse and Jones said afterwards that they had paid no attention when they heard the report. This seems extraordinary, but photographs of the rooms as they were then show a building that was never intended to be used as a library, like a private house in Moscow after the revolution: ornamental fireplaces packed round with books, books stacked on the mantlepiece, shelves hooding once-elegant doorways, more bookshelves up the walls to within centimetres of the delicately moulded ceilings. Any sound would have been muffled, and could have been confused with the din of workshops and horse-drawn traffic in Duke Street.

Bryan Hunt had not killed himself. His first shot had cracked his skull, but he was still conscious. The pistol he had used, a Derringer, required the barrel to be unscrewed and reversed before he could fire again. This he somehow managed to do. Those who heard the second shot said it came between three and five minutes after the first.

This time Scarse went upstairs to investigate, and found Hunt, still alive, lying in a pool of blood with the pistol in his right hand and one cartridge case beside his head. He immediately ran downstairs and called Harrison, who went with him to the Magazine Room.

'When called to the dying man,' Harrison wrote in his notebook with his characteristic interest in medical matters, 'I found brains and blood oozing from his forehead and that there was no hope of saving his life. He was in strong convulsions. I sent off for a policeman and ran myself to Dr. Tegart, whose assistant came in five minutes, and in a quarter of an hour the unhappy suicide was removed to Charing Cross Hospital where he died two hours later (at seven o'clock).'

When he ran into the Librarian's Room to get his hat on the way to fetch the doctor he told Carlyle what had happened. 'He showed', according to Harrison, 'no symptom of emotion.' Carlyle, impatient for his book, then went up to the Reading Room and asked Jones to fetch it for him, adding as an afterthought, 'Another of Thornton Hunt's bastards gone.'

Jones then had to go into the Magazine Room to get a ladder to fetch *The Rise of the Dutch Republic*, so shocked by what Carlyle had said that he even told Harrison when he got back with the doctor. 'This, if true,' Harrison wrote in his book, unwilling to believe anything he heard from Jones, 'is simply revolting, considering the intimacy that had existed between him and Leigh Hunt the older. I asked Mr Samuel Butler, who heard him, if those were the words used, and he replied "Something to that effect." '

Even then, Harrison could not bring himself to mention Jones by name. 'In order to get the book Mr C. wanted, the assistant had to reach over the dying man's body for the steps. This of course', Harrison adds, cooling down and remembering his affection for the Founder, 'was not known to Mr C.'

At the inquest, Jones described what he saw as he fetched the ladder: a policeman was kneeling over Hunt, taking a spent cartridge case out of the pool of blood by his head, and with some difficulty removing the pistol from his tightly clenched hand. He then pulled back the trigger to remove the second cartridge case. Bryan Hunt was still alive when a medical orderly arrived a quarter of an hour later. The policeman who helped take him to hospital reported that on the way Hunt was sick in the cab.

A week later, George Lewes went to a watercolour exhibition in Pall Mall. Afterwards he called on Dr Mackey at the Reform Club to talk about a house that he and Miss Evans had thought about buying, and decided it wouldn't suit them. He then crossed Pall Mall into St James's Square, where he heard the news. The note in his diary is fairly terse. 'At London Library heard of Bryan Hunt having shot himself after bringing back Vol 1 of *Problems &*.'

True to form as a member of the staff of the London Library, Scarse told him that Hunt had asked for Volume Two before he shot himself, and true to form as a literary member, that was the only additional fact that G. H. Lewes recorded in his diary.

# Old Men
# and New Women

*This is the London Library, Madam, not a ladies' powder room!*

T. S. Eliot, at an Annual General Meeting
of the London Library

In 1881 Carlyle died, grumpily satisfied with the library he had called into existence: 'To me it yields on the whole,' he told a friend, 'though by no means what I wish, yet some average approximation what I hoped.' On the death of Clarendon, he had reluctantly accepted the position of president of the library on condition that he was never asked to preside.

The same year James Spedding was run down by a hansom cab and, saintly to the end, spent the few days before he died insisting that the cab-driver was innocent, and that he had stepped out from behind a cart without looking where he was going.

Of the other founders, four were still active: Monckton Milnes, plump now and bald but still spry, succeeded Carlyle as president; Gladstone, who had become a national monument; Christie, grown very bad-tempered; and Tennyson, whose only reaction when he was asked in the Reading Room whether he would take over in turn from Milnes as president was to enquire whether it meant him paying more money.

The new members of the committee, most of them men in middle age, did not hold them in any special esteem. Herbert Spencer, who had started his working life on the footplate of a railway engine and saw progress as an inevitable evolutionary process, had been suggesting long before Carlyle's death that those members of the committee who did not attend should be replaced by people who would. When the old guard resisted, he suggested a vote.

Forster, whose tailor's bills during his last years include a recurrent item 'to putting larger seat into Mr. Forster's trousers', made what the librarian described as 'a funny display of temper', accusing Spencer of not being a gentleman, and saying that such things were never put to the vote. He then walked out. Spencer did not

109

press it, Carlyle continued to be automatically re-elected until his death, and continued to stay away.

But the most passionate Positivist on the committee was Frederic Harrison: for him, as for the Apostles thirty years earlier, the library was not simply lending books; it was lending weapons with which to fight the good fight. Frederic Harrison was an early campaigner for the formation of a Labour Party, and in his essay *The Choice of Books*, he asked the kind of question that most members of the library, by dipping and browsing, hope they can avoid ever having to answer: since nobody could ever read more than a small proportion of the books already on the shelves, let alone the barrage of new books being pumped out of the presses every day of the week in fifty different countries, what should responsible people read?

Frederic Harrison's answer is that most new books belong in the dustbin, and he provides a reading list based on Auguste Comte's own fairly conventional selection of established classics suitable for busy Positivists building the new rational world.

But the very fact that there were men on the committee who were asking such questions indicates a new mood, and there was a recognition that they had inherited a very vague and amateurish organisation. They were also egged on by energetic younger men like Leslie Stephen and his friend the lawyer Frederick Pollock. Frances Partridge remembers Pollock 'coming into one of Henry James's tea-parties at Rye in golfing bags, with his hands held up in front of him like a dog who had been taught to beg', and was told he was 'frightfully intelligent'. Both he and Stephen were early members of the Alpine Club, who went for long vigorous walks at the weekends, their 'Sunday Tramps'.

They faced two very serious problems: the first was that the library was only renting its premises, and secondly that it was, through bequests of books and a steady accumulation of new stock from second-hand sales and bookshops, rapidly running out of space. If they were not thrown into the street by Foster, the auctioneer who owned the freehold, they would soon be forced out by the sheer weight of books.

Earlier efforts to buy the freehold had foundered on the realisation that although it now had 90,000 books, a salaried librarian and a staff of seven including Mr Slaughter the porter, the library still did not really exist as a permanent institution. 'It is neither in the position of a corporate body nor yet, it is believed, an ordinary partnership,' and its condition therefore was 'very complex and indefinite'. It was decided to make it a joint stock company and, under a dispensation from the Board of Trade allowing non-profit-making societies to drop the 'Ltd', was registered simply as the London Library.

The committee then felt themselves in a stronger position to raise money to buy Beauchamp House, and in 1878 they approached Foster, asking him if he was prepared to sell. He was not. The lease had been renewed in 1866, and still had another eight years to run.

Relations with Foster were more cordial than appears from the minutes. According to Harrison's notebook the auctioneer dropped in regularly for a chat, telling him a story on one occasion about the meanness of Lord Palmerston, who had run up bills of nearly a hundred pounds with the chimneysweep. Eventually the sweep terrified Palmerston's 'powdered footmen', by threatening that he would come round *with all his boys* and wait in the hall until the money was paid. The fact that the story was about what happens to gentlemen who try to take financial advantage of the lower orders suggests that Foster's calls may have had an element of business in them, and he was almost certainly waiting for a better offer.

He succeeded in any case in putting the committee into a panic, and for the first and only time in its history there was serious talk of evacuating St James's Square and re-opening the library in a house in Northumberland Avenue. The alternative, suggested at a general meeting of the members, was to raise a really large amount of money and to buy not only Beauchamp House, but Fortnum and Mason's stables, from which a warm smell of horse manure had permeated Theology throughout the library's existence at St James's Square, together with a house in Duke Street occupied by a plumber called Storr, all of which Foster had let it be known he might be prepared to sell.

It was an ambitious scheme, and many years later Sir Frederick Pollock (known to Virginia Woolf as 'Fred') remembered the conflict in the committee between those who advocated caution and those who believed the risk was worth taking. Gladstone later claimed the credit for pushing the scheme through, but it was the old guard that needed persuading, and it was Spencer who was commissioned to negotiate with Foster.

A circular went out to the members. The committee, they were told, doubted whether 'any Society of this kind has ever acquired so wide a reputation, and such valuable possessions, with so precarious a tenure for its domicile.'

After barely breaking even, the library had been running at a profit of just over £500 for the last two years, and by saving the £500 a year they were paying Foster for St James's Square, with just over £200 rent coming in from Storr and from Fortnum and Mason, Spencer persuaded them they could finance a loan of £20,000. This loan would be raised from members in the form of debenture stock at $4^1/_2$ per cent to be repaid over twenty years, and offered in blocks of £100, £500 and £1,000.

Erasmus Darwin, still clinging on as an elderly invalid, and Gladstone's son John both invested £1,000 each, the remainder was raised in smaller amounts, and the freehold was finally signed.

The second problem was the slowly growing pressure of books. First the Philological Society, then the Statistical Society were forced out of their rooms by the lava flow, and finally the librarian himself was asked to abandon three rooms of his apartment on the top floor to make way for more shelves.

Harrison seemed at first to take the idea rather well. He had been talking for years about moving to the country, and when he told Bodham Donne that he looked forward to being 'forced out by the folios', Bodham Donne had said, 'Ah, you want to *exfoliate!*' For these three rooms, the committee offered him £80 a year as compensation.

Over the years, Robert Harrison's attitude to the committee had changed: having begun his jottings full of awe for the members and their most trivial remarks, he took in later years to using Jones' old ledger for totting up his own royalties. The committee had employed Joseph Gostick to help him with the preparation of a new catalogue, and the librarian from then on devoted himself to working with Gostick on a very lucrative school textbook, *Outlines of German Literature*.

When Harrison wanted to use St James's Square for the first meeting of what was to become the Library Association of the United Kingdom, of which he was the first treasurer, he did so on his own initiative, and only afterwards approached George Lewes, with a great affectation of deference, to ask the committee's permission. When he was asked to give up his rooms, he banked his £80 compensation, and at the end of the year was still using them. Such was the vigilance of the committee, for all their progressive zeal, that no-one seemed to notice.

Except Jones. At last, after a lifetime of bitter resentment, he saw his chance and took it. Harrison had persecuted him for years, telling him he was overpaid, and that they could get someone else to do his job for half the money. Now Jones wrote to every member of the committee.

Sir, I feel it my duty to call your attention to the following item in the Balance Sheet of the London Library, viz. 'Rent of Librarian's apartments, £80.' I impugn the validity of this charge and am ready to attest it before the Committee if allowed to do so.

Bodham Donne and Christie found Harrison's behaviour 'unintelligible'. Harrison was asked to leave the Committee Room, Jones' letter was discussed, and Christie and Herbert Spencer were instructed to look into it. They decided that Jones was entirely in the right, and demanded that the librarian be punished. He should not only give up the rooms he had promised to give up, but should be paid nothing whatever for doing so. They only stopped short of sacking him on the grounds that it would be cruel to his wife and children.

Christie and Bodham Donne both assured Jones that his knowledge of the library and its members more than justified his salary, and that however much they paid they would find it hard to replace him. 'I rejoice', Bodham Donne told Christie, 'in the undivided recognition of Jones's conduct and merits.'

Harrison's rage was terrible. He was now suffering from bad gout, and his hatred of Christie revealed depths of intolerance never hinted at anywhere else in his bland collection of anecdotes. 'I think W. D. Christie', he wrote in Jones' old ledger, his pen cutting deep into the paper, 'must be a half-breed. He never could have mixed with English gentlemen so long and preserved that vile nature if he were of pure Saxon or Norman descent. A negro or South American Indian would surely be found in his pedigree' – one imagines his eyes narrowing – '. . . if it could be traced, which I doubt.'

But there was, ultimately, no justice for Jones. Harrison was determined to outwit Christie and, making use of divisions in the committee, succeeded in getting the support of Lord Stanhope. Whether or not Stanhope shared Forster's dislike of Herbert Spencer, he took advantage of Spencer and Christie missing a

committee meeting to push through what amounted to a full reha-
bilitation of Harrison, with an increased rent allowance of £100 a
year in return for giving up the three disputed rooms; when Christie
and Spencer tried to reverse the decision a fortnight later they were
outvoted.

Losing the rent from the Philological and Statistical Societies
meant that the library was now free of its bill of £70 a year for rates
in St James's Square, and when Harrison finally moved out
altogether they seemed safe from the Inhabited House Tax. The
library was not to be troubled with such things for another eighty
years.

But if the committee, smugly and exclusively masculine since
1841, thought that their troubles were over, they had reckoned
without Dr Pankhurst.

Richard Pankhurst had been a member of the library for some
time, and at the annual general meeting in the spring of 1890 he
appeared in the company of a young Fabian, Ellen Cahill. Those
who looked round before the meeting began must have been mildly
amused to see Pankhurst with a woman who was not his wife. He
was now fifty-five, and despite his small, closely set eyes, his little
pointed red beard, his squeaky voice and plump, scruffy appearance, he had the reputation of still being very attractive to women.

That afternoon Mrs Pankhurst was almost certainly at the shop,
called Emerson and Company, which was intended to raise money
for their political work. It specialised in Japanese screens and
William Morris fabrics, and their first premises had been in
Hampstead Road, where working-class locals were mystified by the
milking stools Mrs Pankhurst sold, painted with her own hand in
pastel colours and covered in bright flowers by her sister Mary. It
had now moved to Regent Street, but was still losing money.

Tennyson, as president of the library, was expected to take the
chair, but he had been ill on the Isle of Wight and didn't fancy
endangering his health by coming to London. His place was taken
by Sir Mountstuart Elphinstone Grant Duff, a Balliol man and
lifelong friend of Lacaita.

The old Italian charmer, now sporting a fuzzy grey beard and an
eyeglass, had retired to Southern Italy, and only left home very
occasionally for lunch in Paris with the Prince of Wales or a
weekend with the Empress Eugénie at 'her new place in
Hampshire'.

He, Grant Duff and younger men like Fred Pollock were mem-

bers of several exclusive dining clubs, and of Lacaita's own
Breakfast Club, which had met at Lacaita's rooms in Duke Street,
where he was looked after during his time in London by an Old
Etonian landlord with a working-class wife. In his diaries Grant
Duff reflects on how well all the early members of the Breakfast
Club have done, Lacaita with his knighthood, and himself as the
recently retired Governor of Madras.

Grant Duff was an unlikely figure, like Spencer one of the first
lecturers at F. D. Maurice's Working Men's College, and at one
time a member of Gladstone's Cabinet. He was, as one contemporary put it, 'a man of almost dainty refinement', and terribly short-
sighted.

He opened the meeting by finding his way through a few reflec-
tions on the history of the library. In a month they would be
celebrating the fiftieth anniversary of Carlyle's speech at the
Freemasons' Tavern, which had been 'attended by several men of
great eminence'.

Privately he did not set much store by the present committee, and
never gave their meetings more than a brief mention in his diary as
somewhere he went before the Literary Society, but on this occasion he managed, by holding his notes very close to his thick
spectacles, to decipher a few anecdotes. He recalled the
Macconochie Trial, at which all the books consulted by both sides
had been borrowed from the London Library. He said that the
records of past annual general meetings 'bore most gratifying evidence of the support our Institution has ever received from men of
high distinction', and contrasted the thin times in the past, when a
drop in the membership had been blamed on the Great Exhibition
or the Crimean War, with the brighter prospects today. He sat
down to moderate applause.

It was then that Ellen Cahill stood up. She proposed that in
future at least one member of the committee should be a woman.
This was seconded by Dr Pankhurst.

Grant Duff peered along the committee table for someone to
answer, and Sydney Gedge rose to speak. He was the son of an
Apostle who had been at Cambridge with Maurice, an MP, and the
lawyer who represented the library. He told them this was a legal
and not a political question. Miss Cahill and Dr Pankhurst did not
seem to be 'alive to the meaning of what they were proposing'. It
would mean rewriting the regulations of the library, which established the right of every member of the library to serve on the

committee. There was nothing to prevent a woman, or six women if they so chose, from being elected, but insisting that the committee *must* include a woman was to tinker with the process of free election. A parson on the committee, Dr Rigg, was more conciliatory: he invited Miss Cahill to join them at their next meeting when the matter could then be discussed at greater length.

This infuriated a member sitting in the body of the meeting: if they were always compelled to have one woman on the committee, why not one agnostic or one Dissenter, or one of any other category of person?

During these speeches Dr Pankhurst and Miss Cahill were observed to put their heads together, and Pankhurst said he wanted to place no limitation on the freedom of election. In view of what Mr Gedge had explained he was prepared to consent to the withdrawal of the amendment, and had advised Miss Cahill 'not to press it'. This was typical of Pankhurst's approach.

He had married Emmeline when he was forty-four and she was twenty, and had promised her in one of his most passionate love letters, 'Dearest Treasure, every struggling cause shall be ours.' The struggling cause that concerned both of them most was what their three young daughters called 'silly old women's suffrage'. At their home in Russell Square they entertained Louise Michel, known at the time of the Paris Commune as 'La Petroleuse', Elizabeth Cady Stanton, who brought out the first feminist version of the Bible, and Antoinette Stirling, the American contralto who was famous for singing 'The Lost Chord' and not wearing corsets.

But Pankhurst had been campaigning for women's rights long before he married Emmeline. He was a Doctor of Laws at London University, and he had always argued his case calmly, quoting in one instance the rights of abbesses and peeresses in the Middle Ages. But he found the struggle at times very frustrating: once, after yet another meeting at Russell Square, he suddenly roused himself from gloomy musing and said, 'Why are women so patient? Why don't you *force us* to give you the vote? *Why don't you scratch our eyes out?*'

He was, for all that, a very gentle revolutionary: his servants believed him to be deeply religious, hearing him read Shelley and Walt Whitman aloud in the bath every morning and assuming that he was saying his prayers. His children, none the less, were booed at school because he refused to allow them to attend Scripture lessons, and he was known, as a Republican, to be 'against the Queen.'

THOMAS CARLYLE,
ÆT. 58.
Best likeness known to me:
T. Carlyle (April 1869).

'Best likeness known to me.' Founder, Thomas Carlyle.

A room in Beauchamp House before the rebuilding in 1898.

Hagberg Wright, librarian from 1892 until his death in 1940.

'Mr Cox at the Issue Desk', a 1952 *Punch* drawing by Mays.

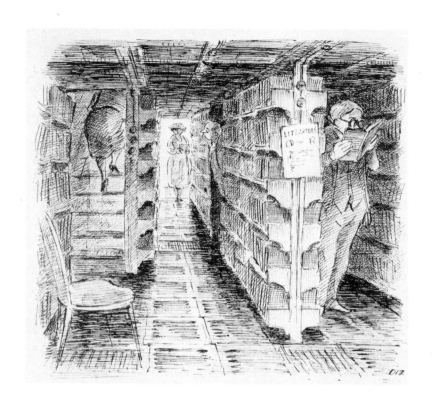

'In the Stacks', by Edward Ardizzone.

The London Library was characteristically tolerant, welcoming Pankhurst as a member among peers and Tory ministers, a man the *Spectator* called 'a French Red', who was in favour of nationalising the land, and who once described the House of Lords as being 'without doubt the most preposterous institution in Europe'.

Opposition to the Pankhurst scheme came from Frederic Harrison too. As a disciple of Comte, who instituted a 'Day of Good Women' in the Positivist Calendar, he still believed that women should serve their husbands. His own wife said it never seemed strange to her that her gardener, who could not read or write, was allowed to vote when she was not. As well as making a collection of Positivist hymns she wrote a book attacking women's suffrage.

The library was by no means a traditional male ghetto. Of the original five hundred members in 1841 as few as fifteen were independent women, members in their own right, and Lady Ashburton was the only woman in that first year to become a life member. But under Cochrane the number of women members rose to over two hundred. During Bodham Donne's librarianship it fell sharply, and by the time he handed over to Harrison there were only thirty-four. One of Harrison's more successful schemes to recruit new members was to allow wives to use the library, officially, unlike Jane Carlyle who took it for granted. Membership began to increase again, and women therefore could and did argue that it was they who had saved the library. A hundred and sixty-four women were now members in their own right.

But for earlier women members, like Harriet Martineau getting Monckton Milnes' *Poetry for the People* sent to Tynemouth in 1844 – 'I wish you cd. see how delectably dirty and broken backed this copy is' – the question of sexual discrimination at the library would not have crossed their minds. It was not mid-nineteenth-century practice for women to serve on committees where they might be called upon to vote.

Ellen Cahill left the meeting defiant, saying that they couldn't hope for anything from the committee, and promising to ironic cheers to propose a woman the following year. She proposed two: one was Miss Shaw-Lefèvre, rebellious daughter of a man she referred to as 'an obsolescent politician'; the other Beatrice Potter, later Beatrice Webb. Herbert Spencer's expression behind the committee table must have been a study, as Beatrice Webb was then staying with him in St John's Wood.

Both Sidney Webb and Beatrice were members of the library. They had met the year before, and were now in the first flush of their long love affair, convinced, like the Pankhursts, that 'together they could move the world'. Sidney now got up to second her. He was, as Beatrice described him:

> . . . a remarkable little man with a huge head on a very tiny body, a breadth of forehead quite sufficient to account for the encyclopaedic character of his knowledge, a Jewish nose, prominent eyes and mouth, black hair, somewhat unkempt, spectacles and a most bourgeois black coat, shiny with wear; regarded as a whole, somewhat between a London card and a German professor. To keep to essentials, his pronunciation is Cockney, his H's are shaky, his attitudes by no means eloquent, with his thumbs fixed permanently in a far from immaculate waistcoat.

He said he thought the committee had failed to keep up with economic questions, and he suggested that Miss Potter might be of great value to them in that respect.

Fred Pollock, from behind the committee table, said (in spite of a year's warning) that the idea of ladies on the committee 'ought not to be sprung upon the members in that way'. It was a great innovation and ought to be discussed by the general body of subscribers. Others agreed, and one old gentleman produced laughter and cheers when he said he had no objection to seeing ladies on the committee, but if this was a political question, 'he must rally to the support of his down-trodden sex'.

After further discussion, and some speeches of support, there was a show of hands: Miss Shaw-Lefèvre was rejected by forty-six votes to twelve, Beatrice Potter-Webb by forty-four to thirteen.

But the members were now getting restive. In 1892 Grant Duff again found himself in the chair at the annual general meeting and, perhaps sensing trouble, dispensed with the traditional chairman's speech. He proposed instead that they should simply adopt the annual report, which covered among other things the replacement of gas by electric light.

Immediately a man jumped up, complaining that the rules of the library had been changed at a meeting of the committee in February to which he had not been invited. Indeed, no-one appeared to have been told about it. The London Library belonged to its members, not to the committee. A woman member, Mrs Heatherley, joined in the attack: the committee was not what it had been. It was a very poor committee indeed. She proposed that the annual report should be rejected, and was seconded by Dr Drysdale, who congratulated Mrs Heatherley, amid loud laughter, on being 'the representative of a sex which he hoped would be of more use in the future than it had been in the past'.

In 1894 Spencer and other progressives decided to jump before they were pushed. At the annual general meeting, the committee put forward its own candidate, Alice Stopford Green. She was proposed by the historian Lecky, Unionist MP for Dublin University, and she was elected.

Born outside Dublin, the daughter of an Anglo-Irish parson, Alice Stopford Green was an attractive woman with melancholy blue eyes, a wry Irish twist to her mouth, and a reputation for good talk. She once defined the aim of conversation as being 'to *shut up* your companion (alias for the time being *opponent*). If he is feeble he deserves it, and if he is strong, it is a duty we owe to society to silence him for once.'

She was more than a match for any man on the committee. She had had a tough upbringing. One of their governesses punished her little brother when he broke a milk jug by using his head to mop the milk up with, and her social conscience had been developed early by her father who encouraged them to write texts on pieces of card and scatter them on the way to church with a view to converting the working-class Papists.

In her late twenties she had married the historian J. R. Green, author of *The Making of England*, then an invalid of forty, and had robustly nursed him through his final illness. Since his death she had written *The Making of Ireland*, history written as she saw it from the point of view of 'the little man at the parish pump'.

As a widow she applied for the post of Mistress of Girton. She had the support of Florence Nightingale, who disapproved of the college for encouraging 'an angry and aggressive agnosticism rather than original research' and for not giving the girls sufficient say in the catering arrangements. But despite Florence Nightingale's belief in Alice Green's 'pluck and wit', she was not elected.

She did however become a force in her own right in London society, entertaining at her house in Kensington Square with her own maid, a butler and a cook. She preferred, in the main, the company of men, and had the reputation for contriving to invite them without their wives.

She also carried on a turbulent love affair with John Frances Taylor, Irish correspondent of the *Manchester Guardian*. Yeats said he was the greatest orator he had ever heard. He had a violent temper, was a passionate Irish nationalist and hated Ulster almost as much as he despised the British Empire. He found English liberals in London 'a canting, puling, whining, lying gang of prigs, pedants and precisions'. Alice never married him, perhaps thinking he would disrupt her dinner parties.

Beatrice Webb was particularly irritated at Alice's election to the committee of the London Library. She was an old friend, admired her 'razor-like intellect', and had been on a walking holiday in the Alps with her. But when Alice visited them that year Beatrice got the impression that she had 'gone off them', keeping up 'an almost irritating criticism of our way of life with our sordid simplicity, lack of culture, and general lower middle-classness.'

> Alice Green seemed to believe that the *distinguished* i.e. those accepted by high society should live apart in an inner circle of luxury, charm and ease. Of course she does not express herself so crudely but presents the aristocratic view of life with as much intellectual glamour and picturesqueness of presentment as she formerly did her democratic creed.

Alice Green annoyed Beatrice Webb most of all by suggesting that it would be more in keeping with her work on trade unions if she gave up all personal luxuries and wore a uniform. 'I refused somewhat brutally, saying I could not afford to be eccentric in small matters and should still buy a new hat before I went investigating.'

Just what a formidable woman Alice Green was can be judged from the memoir of a prominent Quaker who met her some years later when she asked him to lunch with General Smuts. After the soup, lamb chops were brought in, and General Smuts was offered tomatoes. Smuts refused them, saying he did not like tomatoes. Mrs Green flew into a rage, telling him how many hours she had spent trying to find tomatoes, and asking him whether he realised they were out of season. 'At that time I disliked tomatoes, which I believed made me ill, but when it came to my turn to be helped my courage failed me and I ate them, preferring to be ill rather than face Mrs Green's displeasure.' As the cowering members of the London Library Committee must frequently have learned to their cost, mother knew best. 'I was not ill', the writer concludes, 'and have eaten tomatoes ever since.'

Alice Stopford Green stayed on the committee of the library for twenty years. It was Leslie Stephen who was credited with muttering into his beard as she left the Committee Room: 'Never a woman again!'

# Haggy Takes Charge

*A man must shine very brightly to shed any lustre on the London Library.*

Desmond McCarthy

From 1892 to 1940 the London Library was in the hands of a man who possessed all the qualifications Carlyle thought desirable in a librarian. He was the brother of a general, a friend of Tolstoy, prepared to work if necessary eighteen hours a day, and was enough of a gentleman's gentleman – 'every syllable and consonant perfectly pronounced, if you know what I mean', as Patrick Leigh Fermor remembers – to make the members feel secure.

Miss Bolton, whose tiny handwriting is preserved in all the corrections to the old bound catalogues, remembered how well he got on with Mr Cox, the gruff old cockney who presided over the Issue Desk till well after the Second World War. 'They were two of a kind, you see.'

Whether Charles Hagberg Wright would have agreed with that judgement is doubtful. His grandfather on his mother's side was head of the Swedish Royal Mint, and his father was a parson whose family had a small estate in Yorkshire. He affected what was sometimes known as a 'tea-strainer moustache', waxed at the ends in earlier years. His hair was parted high on the crown, and his eyebrows arched quizzically over rather quaint but steady dark eyes. He always wore a stiff white collar and a black velvet jacket with braid at the cuffs.

One committee member, Harry Yates Thompson, benefactor of both the London Library and the British Museum, called him 'Haggy', and frequently had him to stay at his house in the country. According to a surviving Yates Thompson relative he 'treated him like a kind of domestic pet'.

Hagberg was thirty when he was appointed, and a bachelor. At the Royal Academic Institution, Belfast, he and his younger brother were both wholly overshadowed by Almroth Wright, the eldest, later knighted for his services to pathology. The youngest brother became a general; Hagberg became a great librarian.

122

He loved books to the point of mania: friends on holiday with him to Rome remembered him buying a life of St Elizabeth of Portugal and a treatise on silica and kindred minerals, and enjoying them together, one page of each at a time, with a kind of sensual relish. He was an inspired organiser, a man of great vision, and a master of what would later be called marketing and publicity. The London Library as it exists today is largely his creation.

Ten years earlier, in 1882, the young Frederick Cox had joined the library as a messenger boy – 'It was Frederick do this, Frederick do that in those days' – and John Edward Jones had finally retired in 1886. He was given a reasonable pension, thanked by the full committee, and despite his life of martyrdom was remembered by members as 'the amiable sub-librarian'.

Harrison's last year in office was enlivened by a remarkable contest for the presidency on the death of Tennyson. The candidates were the ancient prime minister, William Ewart Gladstone, and Leslie Stephen, middle-aged and largely unknown to the general public.

Stephen was a popular chairman of the committee, and was best known to the members as editor of the *Dictionary of National Biography*. He had been a friend of the publisher George Smith of Smith, Elder and Co., and had edited his *Cornhill Magazine*.

Works of biographical reference had not been popular, several recent efforts had come to grief after the letter A, and Smith went into the enterprise expecting to lose money, meaning to finance it from another of his interests, Apollinaris, the Victorian equivalent of Perrier.

Leslie Stephen began work by placing an advertisement in the *Athenaeum* magazine for 'a new *Biographia Britannica*' – the original had been edited by Dr Kippis, founder of the first London Library – and asking for suggestions. You had to be dead to qualify, articles would be confined to facts and dates, but he hoped to include some 'characteristic anecdotes'.

He wrote the first specimen essay on Addison, and the inevitable horde of baying lunatics appeared from every point of the compass, suggesting the names of fourteen hundred hymn writers in the first few weeks. Even with more interesting figures, he was appalled by what he called 'the insane verbosity of the average contributor'.

'I never knew before', he wrote, 'how many words might be used to express a single fact,' and he sat up in the office till late at night, grimly hacking off the convolvulus tendrils of late Victorian prose.

'I read piles of manuscripts, cutting left and right, and reducing some "copy" to a third of its original mass.'

The plan was to publish quarterly, beginning in January 1885 until the work was completed in June 1900. It is an amazing tribute to the confidence and discipline of the age that the work was finished slightly ahead of schedule.

Furnivall of the Philological Society was a consultant, and so was Edmund Gosse. Stephen's assistant editor was Solomon Lazarus Lee, who took over when Stephen's health began to fail under the strain. He later changed his name to Sidney Lee, and his annotated copy of the *DNB* is still on the shelves of the library.

The London Library became a recruiting office. The librarian himself was enlisted to do a great deal of the donkey work: two As, forty-three Bs, twenty-eight Ds and a few Es, Fs, Hs and Js, for which he insisted on the inclusion of a life of his mother, the flower painter, and his two brothers William Frederick Harrison (1815–80) and George Henry Harrison (1816–46). Mountstuart Grant Duff wrote the life of Henry Austin Bruce, first Baron Aberdare; Sydney Francis Gedge provided the life of his Apostle father, Sydney Gedge (1802–83); and Dr Rigg, the parson on the committee who had been so kind to Miss Cahill, no fewer than 641 entries.

But however greatly his work might be respected, Stephen could never hope to compete with Gladstone for the awe with which he was treated on his occasional visits to the library. Mr Cox remembered his two detectives waiting outside the Reading Room while Gladstone went in to thumb through the magazines. Gladstone also liked to boast, as an 'aboriginal member', about his role in finding their first 'relatively contracted premises' in Pall Mall.

The librarian was overwhelmed with reverence, when the Prime Minister called in to look up a quotation for his *Juventus Mundi*, at how far superior Gladstone's inaccurately remembered line was to the original Horace.

As a notorious public skinflint, too, Gladstone was revered for his practical concern about the economic well-being of the library. Talking to Bodham Donne once he had asked him how much they spent on shelves. Rather surprisingly, Donne knew the answer, which was tenpence a foot. Testing Donne further, he asked him if that included the shelf that ran across the top, which supported no books. Bodham Donne said it did. Gladstone grunted. 'That is a cheaper rate than I can do it for. It costs me a penny a book!'

124

There is still a letter in the archives in which he complains about having to pay the full rate when he used the library so rarely. He suggests that a £1 a year fee should be introduced for people like himself who only wanted to use the Reading Room and never took books off the open shelves. He ends by threatening to resign if his terms are not agreed.

The result of the election for president must have struck him as a rebuff. It was reported in full in the *Hyde Park Gate News* in November 1892.

Mr Leslie Stephen whose immense literary powers are well known is now the President of the London Library. Mrs Ritchie the daughter of Thackeray who came to luncheon the next day expressed her delight by jumping from her chair and clapping her hands in a childish manner but none the less sincerely. The greater part of Mrs Stephen's joy lies in the fact that Mr Gladstone is only vice-president. She is not at all of a 'crowy' nature but we can forgive any woman for triumphing when her husband gets above Mr Gladstone.

The reporter was Leslie Stephen's daughter, later Virginia Woolf, then aged ten.

Harrison's gout finally got too much for him that winter. He resigned, and like Bodham Donne was made an honorary life member. The same year the principal librarian at the British Museum was paid £1,200 a year and the Keeper of Printed Books £750. The librarianship of the London Library was advertised in *The Times* at an annual salary of £400, with no guarantee of a pension. But competition to take the job was surprisingly fierce.

There were 253 applicants, including writers, naval officers, lawyers, schoolmasters, accountants, one town clerk and even the head of a steamship company. In the end the choice was between Macfarlane of the British Museum, George William Wheeler of the Bodleian and the assistant librarian of the National Library of Ireland, Charles Theodore Hagberg Wright.

This time there was no talk about guidable quadrupeds or starved cadgers' garrons: the committee wanted someone who knew about business and had administrative capacity, good health and good character, education and social status, previous experience as a librarian, knowledge of languages, literature and bibliography. They unanimously chose Mr Wright.

Leslie Stephen told H. A. L. Fisher they 'had secured a most wonderful young man for the post of Secretary to the Library: a great linguist, a brilliant organiser, and a man of considerable personal charm.'

Hagberg immediately took on more staff, raised wages in exchange for abolishing overtime – the chief clerk came out of this half a crown a week better off – and reduced to a half-day the one day off a working fortnight the staff had taken under his predecessor.

The subscribers were also made aware of a new broom. Life members who had not used the library for years were struck off, and ordinary members whose subscriptions were in arrears or who had failed to return books were fiercely pursued.

But Hagberg's real rage was reserved for the building. The problem of space was now desperate. German Literature and Philosophy had been moved up to the attics, the parliamentary Blue Books were piled in the cellar, and other books of every colour appeared in heaps in the passages and even on the marble stairs.

There was no proper ventilation, the coke-fired boiler in the basement gave off eye-watering fumes, and years of 'intolerable heat' from the old gas lamps had rotted the bindings of books on the top shelves. These could only be reached in any case by way of long ladders, and several clerics had risked death in pursuit of higher things.

Hagberg's answer was not only to reorganise the tens of thousands of books, but to pull down what he called 'a last-century dwelling house' and build a proper library.

Convincing the committee of the need to demolish Beauchamp House, even at a time when acres of Tudor London were being cleared to build offices, was not easy. Convincing the public was even more difficult, and the *Spectator* launched a campaign to stop him. Hagberg and the committee, they argued very reasonably, should sell the old house and use the money to build somewhere else in London where there would later be room to expand.

Hagberg Wright stuck to his guns. He might not have any compunction about vandalising a seventeenth-century town house, but he knew the market value of tradition. Newspapers, even popular ones, announcing the next annual general meeting of the London Library – not normally worth more than an inch and a half at the bottom of a column – seemed unusually well informed. All of them mentioned the London Library's literary tradition and the great names that had been associated with it. They all paid tribute to the fact that it was one of the five largest libraries in the United Kingdom, and that it was 'the leading lending library of its kind in Europe'.

The way in which the identical phrases recur in every newspaper indicates the hand of a practised public relations expert lobbing column-fillers to the overworked journalists. That hand was clearly Hagberg's.

One sentence in particular occurs in every piece: 'A complete census of the Library was taken at the beginning of the year with a very unexpected result [some versions use the word 'surprise']: it was discovered that the Library contained no fewer than 168,000 volumes.'

This could hardly have been unexpected or a surprise to anyone who had ever bothered to open the library's printed annual report, which carried a clear table showing how many books and how many members the library had going back twenty years. But the 'surprise' became Hagberg's trademark.

Later in 1895, for instance, the *Sketch*, 'through the kindness of Mr. Wright' was afforded 'a peep behind the scenes at St. James's Square'. Hagberg warned the man from the *Sketch* 'that he had some surprises in store', and then bowled over the readers of the popular press with revelations that even in those days can hardly have taken their breath away. Four readers were waiting for the *Acta Sanctorum* – 'none of them clerical people' – and one reader was at present studying the history of duelling. 'In conclusion Mr Wright told me a very amusing open secret. "We can often", he confessed, "predict what a great novelist's next work will be like from the books he has out of the Library." '

Hagberg was establishing a technique that would be used again and again to raise money for the library: he was selling its exclusiveness. Even Mr Pooter, if he could afford the entrance fee and the subscription and persuade someone to recommend him, could find himself chuckling knowingly at the Issue Desk as another great novelist at his shoulder took out ten books on underpants.

The press always seemed to take the bait, and throughout the 1890s the London Library, now frequently referred to as 'the London' as if it were a smart gentlemen's club, began to glisten in the middle-class awareness with a mysterious gleam of social desirability mingled with literary romance.

Hagberg was only developing a technique pioneered by Carlyle himself, in making use of 'the great bellows of the newspaper Press'. With its help, Wright prepared the annual general meeting for his bombshell. Leslie Stephen was at a funeral, Sydney Gedge took the chair, and the members seemed at first disinclined either to pull down their old home or to raise the £17,000 he needed to rebuild it.

Then Hagberg produced a piece of paper, obtained at his request by Leslie Stephen. Francis Knollys, secretary to the Prince of Wales, had mentioned the matter to their patron. For Leslie Stephen himself, the idea of the Prince being their patron was a great joke, and he often told the story about the dinner to celebrate the completion of the *DNB*. Looking down the table at a clerical figure, Canon Ainger, the Prince asked Stephen who he was, and Stephen told him he was an expert on Lamb. Sawing away at the meat on his plate, the Prince repeated the word 'lamb?' in great puzzlement.

Knollys was desired by the Prince of Wales to inform them that as Patron of the London Library he was very glad to hear that a movement was on foot for extending the usefulness of the institution by providing an adequate building for the important collection of books in its possession. The scheme met with the entire approval of his Royal Highness, as he was well aware of the deep interest the Prince Consort had taken in the library, and how invaluable it has proved to be to all those who are in any way connected with history and literature.

From the wording of the letter Francis Knollys could have mentioned it to the Prince as he was spraying perfume into his beard on the way to some amorous encounter: the Prince could well not have answered, walked out and left him in a thinning cloud of cigar smoke, but it did the trick with the subscribers.

Convinced that the scheme was divinely inspired, the members approved Hagberg's plan, and authorised the committee to raise the £17,000, only stipulating that the fund should reach £5,000 before they started building. The rest would be borrowed, as before, by offering members debentures at a fixed percentage.

Hagberg's mastery of the media is evident from another interview he gave after the meeting.

' "Will you tell me, Mr Wright, what the proposed changes at the London Library will mean?" "They will mean", replied the librarian, "a total reconstruction of the present premises and additions on the north side. As it is we are awkwardly cramped. I have history in three different rooms and fiction in more than one place, so that it has become quite impossible to carry on the work properly." '

An architect, Osborne Smith, who had done work for the Bodleian Library and British Museum, had already been engaged. ' "A scheme has been drawn up for very extensive alterations in the building we now occupy, and for bringing in the house you see there through the window." Mr. Wright, from his chair of office, pointed to a building adjoining, lying immediately behind the Windham Club.'

The Windham, now Grindlay's Bank, was the first house on the north side of the square, a residential club used by various peers and members of parliament, and the building Hagberg Wright was pointing at was a workshop behind it used by their tenant, Storr the plumber. They would also build westwards towards Duke Street.

When it was finished, Hagberg said, they would be able to provide room for nearly double the number of books. 'At present we possess 170,000 volumes – that is the utmost limit of the capacity of the present premises; but as we are buying at the rate of 5,000 volumes every year, you will readily understand how necessary it is to provide further accommodation. I calculate that there will be room for 300,000 volumes when the alterations are completed.'

The interviewer calculated that if they went on accumulating books at that rate, 'within fifty years' the library would again need more space. '"There's no doubt it will," said Mr. Wright, rising and producing a ground plan of the entire premises; "but you will see here" – pointing to the plan – "we can build from the back to an extent that will provide accommodation for another 300,000 volumes, although that will be an extension for the next generation to undertake."'

The kind of quiet confidence Hagberg Wright displays in this interview, foreseeing developments that are now actually being undertaken a hundred years later, must have been profoundly reassuring to the committee and the members, and they must have been equally grateful for the way he reminded them of their great literary tradition.

From the evidence of corrected proofs still in the archives, Hagberg actually wrote a major editorial on the library in *The Times*, and what he didn't write he obviously planted.

Somebody has said that the Committee of the London Library would not form a bad nucleus for an English Academy of Letters, including as it does at present Mr Leslie Stephen, Mr Herbert Spencer, Mr Lecky, Mr Huxley, Mr St. George Mivart, Mr Frederic Harrison, Mr Edmund Gosse, Mr W. S. Lilly, and one Lady member, Mrs J. R. Green. The apostolic succession of the Presidents is from Lord Clarendon to Carlyle and etc.

This sequence of great men, more than once referred to in all innocence as an 'apostolic' succession, was to figure large in the fund-raising campaign that followed.

There was a brief counter-attack by the conservationists, but Hagberg fobbed them off with the promise that photographs would be taken of all the main rooms before demolition began, and pressed on with the fund-raising. *The Times* reported that only 376 members had so far contributed to the Building Fund. This left 1,903 who had not. 'It has to be pointed out that if each member contributed £2 10s 0d the necessary sum would soon be obtained and leave a margin to the good.'

*The Times* was not the only paper to be taken over as house magazine of the library. Later in the year the *Birmingham Post* printed a list of 'distinguished names' who had already promised 'to subscribe a portion of the £5,000 required to carry out the very necessary reconstruction of the well-known premises in St. James's Square'.

A month later Hagberg tightened the screws by sending round to the newspapers the exact amount each contributor had given. 'Mr. James Crossley Eno [the Liver Salt King] has given £500 and Mr H. Yates Thompson and Mr W. Lindley £100 each. Among other subscribers are Mr. Gladstone, the Archbishop of Canterbury, the Earl of Rosebery, Admiral of the Fleet Lord Hay' and so on. Some papers included the news that Lord Rosebery had given exactly a tenth of what the Liver Salt King was able to afford, and others actually asked at the end of the story that 'contributions should be forwarded to the Librarian, Mr C. T. Hagberg Wright, at 12, St James-square S.W.'

But after nearly a year, Hagberg was still £1,500 short of the money he needed to start. He persuaded the committee to go ahead anyway, Cubitt's submitted an estimate of £16,000, and the work began.

The plan was to build the new 'stacks' at the back of the house first. The idea of 'book stacks' came from America, and had already been used by Osborne Smith in his extensions to the Bodleian and the British Museum. Books were stored back to back in double-sided shelves, seven feet high for easy access without ladders, and set on iron-grilled floors that allowed the light to filter down from an opaque glass roof. The building was steel-framed, which was to save it from total destruction when a bomb hit it in 1944.

The stacks were promised for the beginning of July. July came and went, as did August: they were finally ready at the end of September. Hagberg Wright then gave proof of his generalship: the old brick-fronted library was closed, and he and his staff trans-ferred nearly 200,000 books into the new steel-framed store at the back. This was then sealed against brick-dust, and Cubitt's began demolishing the old house, leaving the basement kitchens, a few rooms in the attic, and some of the load-bearing walls intact.

The library re-opened by way of a passage from Duke Street, not used again for another eighty years, when WPC Fletcher was shot in St James's Square during the siege of the Libyan Embassy. The whole move was completed in exactly three weeks.

Hagberg immediately started on his other task of recataloguing all the books in a little house in Duke Street, leaving Leslie Stephen, no longer a young man and very deaf, to supervise the building work, reliving his old mountaineering days as he clambered up the wooden scaffolding in St James's Square to inspect the new stone façade.

It was this façade that most impressed the journalists on 5 December 1898, when the new building opened. One also picked out as a 'crowning glory' the stand for bicycles close to the front door.

On the ground floor they found a spacious hall, fitted all round with shelves on which the newest books were displayed; above them were more book-lined galleries, reached by wrought-iron spiral stairs. The ceiling, 'in the Adam style', was supported by square and fluted pillars, resting on pedestals in oak panelling, and surmounted by ornamental capitals. On their right were 'ample counters' and desks for the issue and return of books. The colour scheme was a creamy white with gold edges. On the left they saw a wide staircase with a handsome teak balustrade, leading up to the new Reading Room on the first floor.

All this, Hagberg told them, had been built at no cost to the taxpayer, and the committee was hailed as 'a standing contradiction of the accepted theory that literary taste and financial capacity do not run in harness'. According to the *Manchester Guardian*, it was 'a striking example of the spirit of self-help which enables Englishmen of all classes to obtain by friendly combination the advantages which in other countries have to be sought from the State'.

There was a new-found respect for what the *Moniteur International* called '*cette belle institution*'. The *Daily Telegraph* said the library 'had surely attained to the zenith of a useful and progressive career', and the *Manchester Guardian* compared it to the great poet who awoke one morning and found he was famous.

Typically, Hagberg had invited the press in two days earlier for a few 'surprises' before the official opening, and *The Times* devoted two columns to a preview of the new building. The new Reading Room was 'magnificent': it was, as a sop to the conservationists, as far as possible an exact reproduction of what had been there before but with high windows for better light, 'arranged and decorated in the manner of the last century'. Osborne Smith had also incorporated two marble fireplaces that had been in the old house.

The opening ceremony began at three o'clock and lasted for two hours. The committee and their guests were on one side of the room, roped off from the elegant crowd. The man from the *Chronicle* caught the atmosphere best. 'It was', he said, 'a unique gathering – mostly of grave, serious folk, little inclined to laughter or enthusiasm – keen-eyed, critical, and contemplative workers in the literary fold. Books, one might say, on looking at such an assemblage, are a wearying trade – with a tendency to produce baldness.'

Leslie Stephen spoke first. 'A tall, thin man, with a long beard and melancholy eye – at a distance he might play Don Quixote with applause. But there is a whimsical contrast in his oratory, for while he seems ever about to dissolve in tears his lips drop pleasant witticisms.'

He hailed the London Library as 'one of the chief glories of her Majesty's reign', then, more characteristically, talked about its position at the corner of St James's Square – 'a square full of peers and bishops and bankers and everything the soul of man reveres'. He said they had not rebuilt out of any unhallowed lust for bricks and mortar; it had been a matter of build or burst.

The next speaker was Viscount – formerly Sir Garnet – Wolseley, the man who had arrived in Calcutta as the guns were firing a last salute on the death of Wellington and who had become his natural successor. He had written that any young officer seeking to distinguish himself should set out to get himself killed, and he had certainly done his best. Badly wounded in the thigh leading his first attack in India, he had lost an eye in the Crimea, and led assaults on French Separatists in Canada, rebels in China, King Koffee in Ashanti, and the Mahdi in the Sudan. As commander-in-chief, he had rationalised and modernised the Army. His name had become a byword – 'All Sir Garnet' was the slang phrase for 'All in order' – and George Grossmith impersonated him when he played the modern major-general in *The Pirates of Penzance*.

He told a story about the time when Thackeray was writing *The Virginians*, and came in to consult the librarian about General Wolfe. He had been shown various books about Wolfe's campaigns, and then said, 'No, I don't want that. I want to know what kind of breeches he wore, and whether he took snuff or not!' Then Wolseley became more confessional. 'In my' – the gruff clearing of the throat before the next word is not conveyed in the text – 'humble way, I too like books – I like the feel of them, I like their backs!'

The man from the *Chronicle* was rather moved: 'As he warmed to his subject, the true man came out in him, peeping through a stiff and somewhat conventional little speech.'

Lecky then popped up, 'bursting forth into an unbroken, singsong monologue on the futility of mechanism in education', and told a traditional library tale about Carlyle marking passages he found particularly stupid with a pair of donkey's ears.

The greasy gleam of bald heads, the flicker of hard eyes, and the pre-deodorant stuffiness in the crowded room on that early December afternoon can only be imagined.

There were then speeches from the Bishop of London, 'one condemned from no fault of his own to be respectable'; from the Permanent Secretary of the Board of Trade comparing Blue Books to Blue Stockings: 'both are accused of dullness by the ignorant, and are referred to slightingly on very imperfect acquaintance!'; and from Monckton Milnes' son, who declared he didn't think there was any institution dearer to his father's heart than the London Library. He praised Hagberg's 'lack of mawkish diffidence' in wringing money out of the members, and handed over to Frederic Harrison, who introduced Hagberg as 'our Mr Panizzi'.

Topping the bill, the thirty-five-year-old Hagberg acknowledged a storm of applause, and told three jokes.

One member asked for something on the raising of Lazarus: to be impartial, I sent him the Bible and a book on Christian myths. Someone else wanted a book about a Royal Princess who worked as a cook in London, and made nice curries. There was also a question put to me, perhaps the Bishop of London could help me on this, 'Who was the Coptic saint who made a mummy talk in the third century?'

The tired company, according to the *Chronicle*, laughed their first good laugh over these stories, and then broke up to wander over the buildings and feast their eyes on the new sumptuous abode. They discovered electric lamps, placed a few feet apart, that 'could be turned on at pleasure, each by its own tap'. If there was any fault to be found it was a fault inevitable where space was of such value, that the books on the lower shelves of each story could 'hardly be examined without some back-breaking'.

Afterwards Leslie Stephen, Hagberg and the committee members had dinner at the Criterion in Piccadilly Circus. It was cooked by Spiers and Pond, Refreshment Caterers, with light music played on one of the Erard's pianos 'exclusively used' in the restaurant's private rooms. As he worked his way through the *Hors d'Oeuvres, Croûte au Pot, Crème Jackson, Turbot Bouilli Sauce Hollandaise, Faisan Rôti, Baba au Rhum, Coupe Jacques, Patisserie et Fruits,* Hagberg must have wiped his waxed moustache and considered that he had every reason to congratulate himself.

Next morning he was able to tell the *Athenaeum* that in that week alone they had received more than fifty new applications for membership.

# Kitchener Sinks

*My dear Hagberg,*
*Let me count then with joy on seeing you here Monday*
*evening the 18th at 8 o'clock. I shall be alone, for my*
*advantage – & heaven speed the day!*

*May 9th 1914*

*Yours all faithfully,*
*Henry James*

Most men would have contented themselves with destroying the
London Library and rebuilding it, or at least having it open again,
in three weeks. But all through the clanging of hammers on rivets as
Cubitt's fitted together Osborne Smith's cage of girders, all through
the more alarming demolition of the old house, Hagberg Wright
was coming in through the builders' dust with his waxed moustache and his clean white collar to work on the new author
catalogue.

Sometimes he managed with as little as four hours' sleep, sometimes he slept at the library. While the old building was still
standing he worked at the top in Bodham Donne's old 'precipice';
later, when they moved out, he shared with the rest of the staff the
cramped little house in Duke Street.

He meant to become master in his own library: he opened every
one of its 180,000 books, read the title, riffled through the pages,
and made a discreet pencil mark inside each flyleaf.

'*Everything* was scrapped: shelf-lists, marks etc,' he remembered
later. 'We started *de novo*.' All the existing catalogues and records
were set aside, everything begun again from scratch. It was finally
ready for the press in February 1902. Mr Cox was one of the clerks
who worked on it, and Hagberg offered small rewards, never more
than sixpence, for spotting mistakes.

All this work gave him an authority over the committee and the
members that no librarian had had before, and which none has
probably had since. He was also touchy, and Leslie Stephen, practically on his deathbed, had to write to him to say how sorry the
committee was that Hagberg's feelings had been hurt. Someone had
suggested he was spending too much money.

Stephen himself was one of those who infuriated Hagberg, by

absent-mindedly doodling monkeys in the margins of books he was reading – 'a species of automatic accompaniment to the workings of his mind' – and as Hagberg checked through the library's stock his rage increased.

Carlyle had begun the tradition, not only with his donkey's ears but with furious outbursts of expletive against the author – 'No!', 'Why?', 'Impossible!', 'Ignorant impertinence!', 'Was there ever such a *bête* of an editor before?' – and there is hardly a book in the library even today that is not underscored by subsequent members on one page or another with 'Rubbish!', or in one case, 'I don't think conversation agrees with Humphrey', scribbled in the margin. Hagberg decided to put his foot down.

> The essential function of the Library is the circulation of books for use at members' own houses. It is a grave misuse of this privilege when books are defaced by writing in them. Unfortunately the practice is common, and the offender not easily detected. Members are asked to refrain from the practice themselves, and to do what they can to put a stop to it by any means in their power.

It was in these years that Cox gained his extraordinary knowledge of the contents of the library: asked again and again in later life about some abstruse topic, he would scribble a note on a piece of paper, toss it into the little wooden lift behind his desk – still there, though his desk has gone – and in a few moments the best book on the subject would be sent down by an assistant who had found it on the shelves upstairs to the amazement of the member.

He also shared Hagberg's concern for the treatment of books, and surprised the young Lord Longford, then Frank Pakenham, who was returning a pile of books, in one of which he had turned down a page, by shouting, 'Right, you just wait there!' He then heaved himself off his stool and came back carrying a stack of books, all of them with pages turned down, banged them down on the desk, and roared, 'I've been lookin' for the culprit for some time!'

Hagberg also introduced a system of protecting the books by giving each individual volume a blue card. On this, at considerable expense, a staff of clerks at the end of each day wrote the name of the member who had borrowed it, and the date on which they had brought it back. The system was finally abolished in 1976, but from the last batch of blue cards which are still preserved it is possible, for instance, to establish that V. S. Naipaul borrowed *Sartor Resartus* on 2 September 1970, and returned it just over three weeks later.

Hagberg was by now a regular pen pal of many of the great writers of his day, some of whom he badgered unsuccessfully to join the committee, using Tolstoy's eightieth-birthday celebrations in some cases as an excuse for writing to them. He had met Tolstoy years before when he was briefly living in Russia, and had translated one of his essays. He rather preened himself on his Russian connections, and Henry James often addressed him in his letters as 'Dear Russophil'. James frequently had him down to stay at Lamb House in Rye, and even agreed to write something in honour of Tolstoy, 'though I fear you exaggerate the microscopic mass of one's name, cast to the howling winds of the snowy steppe'.

He had less success with charming some of the other authors, and if he hoped to publish his correspondence with Conan Doyle he was disappointed. One answer runs simply, 'Dear Sir, All right, Yours v. tly A Conan Doyle.' But H. G. Wells confided in him: 'I spend the best part of two years on a novel and then I have to listen to a damn fool of a publisher saying that the word "abortion" is a "little strong"'; he corresponded regularly with Galsworthy and Hardy, with Kipling and J. M. Barrie.

Hagberg was again raising money: gifts of books continued to come in, and one member offered to present the library with a bust of Carlyle by Sir Joseph Edgar Boehm, who taught sculpture to Queen Victoria's daughter, Princess Louise, that had come up for sale at Christie's. The bidding went higher than he expected, and Hagberg agreed to pay the difference, keen as always to focus in the public mind the literary traditions of the library.

He was still working very long hours. Having first examined the stock and put together an author catalogue, he set about entirely reclassifying and rearranging the books. By now they had 200,000, and he calculated that at a rate of 200 books a day this would take them 1,000 days. Allowing himself annually fifty-two Sundays off, fifty-two half days on Saturdays and thirty days for his holidays, he came to the conclusion that by stepping up their daily rate they could just finish it in four years and a bit.

All through the so-called Golden Age before the First World War, Hagberg had his black jacket off, hard at work. He recruited a younger assistant, Christopher Purnell from the Bodleian Library, and every book in the library, from tiny volumes of poetry to heavy dictionaries and atlases and encyclopedias, was carried up seventy-four steps to their cramped little Cataloguing Room high up under the roof in the new building.

There they sat opposite each other, attended by a team of Frederick Cox and another 'junior assistant', two typists, one boy clerk and a porter. Each book, according to Hagberg's own meticulous memoir, was logged by the team on two separate slips of paper, nine and a quarter inches long by two inches wide. One had the author's name at the top, the other the subject heading. The books were delivered in batches of fifty, each with their two slips of paper, and brought to the table where Hagberg and Purnell checked them and added any pencil notes they thought necessary. Wright and Purnell then double-checked each other's work.

In H. A. L. Fisher's obituary of Hagberg Wright he says there was a notice in the Cataloguing Room that said , 'No talking, no smoking, no thinking. Verify, verify!' Purnell has corrected this in the library's scrapbook: 'Notice was "No guessing, no thinking, Accuracy, accuracy, accuracy!"' Stiff collars and waistcoats, steel nibs and pots of ink, early typewriters clattering: it was the spirit that built industrial America and celebrated the vast economic power of the British Empire; the same spirit of grim determination to excel that was building battleships on either side of the North Sea.

But in Hagberg's Cataloguing Room there was a mood of industrious peace. He and Purnell occasionally exchanged a word about a particular book. Otherwise there was only the sound of feet on the metal stairs, the opening and closing of the door, the thump of books being set down in heaps, the scratch of pens, the sound of the typewriters. Like Adam naming the beasts, Hagberg was imposing his dominion on the library with his Headings. Following, but not too closely, the American Library Association List of Subject Headings drawn up in 1901, Hagberg produced his own very idiosyncratic definitions.

It is possible to trace the influence of Bodham Donne in the library's early theatre collections and in its acquisition of books about his pet subjects like the History of Roads, or Magic and Witchcraft. Harrison, too, with his knowledge of Russian and German literature, to some extent shaped the library. But Hagberg Wright, in addition to his passion for Russian and Scandinavian literature, did something a great deal more profound. He actually dictated a basic sequence of ideas, laid out like an inspired garden, through which the reader could find his way from idea to idea within a predetermined sequence, while still being free to follow his own instincts.

Housed in Osborne Smith's cage of steel stacks, in their day the very latest thing in utilitarian architecture, the confusion of books Hagberg had found in the last-century dwelling house became the modern London Library.

With their Piranesi perspectives of grilled walkways, intersected by diagonal iron stairways, the stacks are one of the wonders of the world: to sit there now on a winter's afternoon is strangely eerie. The strip of bluish-white fluorescent tubing flickering and puttering immediately overhead casts a limited local glow; at unexpected bearings, above and below, other readers sit engrossed, each isolated in their own circle of light, little galaxies hanging in space, remote and inaccessible in the diminishing vistas of books.

Raymond Mortimer felt it was like being 'inside the brain of mankind', but it is also like being inside the brain of Charles Hagberg Wright. It is one thing to search through the catalogue or the card index; it is another to wander along what one authority claims are twenty miles of shelves, particularly in Science and Miscellaneous, rambling, thanks to Hagberg's peculiarly practical imagination, from *Ballooning* to *Baths* and *Bee-Keeping* and *Beer*, then on to *Bells* and *Betting/See Gambling*: or from *Windmills* to *Witches* and *Women*.

When the final revision of the subject catalogue began the list was still far from complete: some books had been kept out by members and new books were still being bought or given to the library at a rate of 5,000 a year and could not be included. The printing took twelve months at a rate of forty pages a week. Correcting them even Hagberg Wright himself had to admit 'entailed great and protracted labour'. Frederic Harrison and Sir Frank Marzials, both vice-presidents, and six members of the committee, including Fred Pollock, helped with the work.

But Hagberg, when he wasn't working on the books or having dinner with Henry James, was dreaming of a bigger and better library. They were still repaying the loan they had raised to rebuild fifteen years before. More cautious members of the committee were asking for economies: Hagberg's answer was to borrow more and to expand. Despite his earlier talk of leaving the next stage of building to the next generation, he was now thinking a hundred years ahead, and realised that if they meant to stay in St James's Square they would have to expand westwards, towards Duke Street. They had bought Fortnum and Mason's old stables, and now owned most of the library's present site. The only obstacle was 8 Duke Street, which not only stood in their way but claimed the right of ancient lights, preventing any building on either side of it.

Hagberg, typically thought the best answer to that was to buy Number 8, pull it down, and sell a long lease to a tenant who would be more co-operative. He would then extend Osborne Smith's new bookstacks, making better accommodation for the staff as well as more room for books. He set a target this time of £15,000.

The first stage went exactly according to plan: the library bought the old house and demolished it, silencing any further talk about ancient lights. He sold the site on a fifty-year lease that would expire in 1963, and a block of flats was built on it called Dalmeny Court, where Isadora Duncan among others was to live during her time in London. Dalmeny Court was finally sold on a 99-year lease in 1978 for £530,000; money that became, under Lewis Golden's management, the basis of the library's late twentieth-century prosperity.

He then threw himself into another fund-raising scheme, dreaming this time of stacks not with grilled walkways but with green opaque glass floors. Once again he mobilised the press, and the *Manchester Guardian* came to his aid with all the puns it could muster.

> Alas! The republic of letters, it used to be said, was so named because authors could not muster a sovereign among them; and though that is not exactly the case today, they suffer like Falstaff from consumption of the purse. The secretary of the Library is Dr C. T. Hagberg Wright (St James'-square SW). etc. etc.

A. J. Balfour, who had been unanimously elected president on the death of Leslie Stephen, backed Hagberg. He, like Stephen, was an Apostle, but despite his commitment to the Education Act of 1902 his arguments did not have quite the same reforming fire as those of his nineteenth-century predecessors. Under Hagberg the library was becoming a comfortable club. When Balfour praised the library for its liberalism, he was talking about its 'relaxed rules', its readiness to remove 'small annoyances in the path of research'.

Even if you do not use the Library, the mere fact that you belong to it enables other people to use it. Therefore belong, in the interests of literature, of history, and of all branches of research, and you will be doing a great and honourable work in which this Library has led the way, in which this Library has proved an example to other cities and other nations, an example, hitherto, as I believe not equalled and not surpassed by those attempting to follow in our footsteps.

But Hagberg's opaque glass floors had to wait. Suddenly the country was at war with Germany, Carlyle's spiritual homeland, that had given them Goethe, hero of Carlyle, Lewes, George Eliot and so many more Victorians, whose *Theory of Colours* was the first book ever to be taken out of the library; at war with Prussia that had bred Count Bunsen of the first committee, and the philologists Alice Stopford Green was using in her work in reviving interest in early Irish literature.

Hagberg himself was in regular contact with German librarians, and perhaps the most interesting aspect of the London Library in the First World War was his determination to continue buying books from Germany. This, not surprisingly, was forbidden by the government. Hagberg pleaded for two years, and in 1916 he managed to convince the Home Office that German books were necessary to the war effort. He ordered a selection of new books that included philosophy, modern poetry and Professor Friedjung's *History of Austria 1848–1860*. They arrived, and Hagberg was ordered to lock them up: no members were allowed to see them, only government officials. Stumped, he argued as tactfully as he could that they were 'quite harmless to English readers', but they stayed in a locked room until the end of the war.

Despite that, Hagberg was emotionally patriotic. 'When a sleeper wakes from a long unbroken slumber', he wrote, 'to find himself in a strange environment, he is usually slow to realise his novel surroundings. So England, waking to a state of war and striving to meet the demands of unforeseen and terrible conditions, has blundered, stumbled, agonised, but still held on.'

Among his papers is an unpublished poem, provoked by an industrial dispute at Barrow-in-Furness that threatened to sabotage the war effort. It is called 'The Men and Masters of Barrow, who adopted an uncompromising attitude'; in the margin he has written 'Rotten crowd'.

> Engineers of Barrow, strikers grim,
> France's richest fields are red with strife,
> Sullen workers wasting time and limb
> Knaves to gamble thus with England's life!

Metrically it might not have been too even, but politically he did his best to maintain the impartiality he had displayed in answering the Lazarus question with the Bible and the book on Christian myths. After taking a tough line on 'ye strikers, loafing down the lane' he is equally stern with the bosses:

> Lords of Barrow, hearts ingrate!
> War enkindles love again;
> Share the profit; banish hate;
> Honour those who strive and strain!

Even Virginia Woolf was concerned when a bomb fell in Piccadilly in October 1917. 'Swan and Edgar has every window covered with sacking or planks. Windows are broken according to no rule; some intact, some this side, some that. Our London Library stands whole, however, and we found our books & came home in the tube, standing the whole way to Hammersmith.'

In 1918 all her old prejudices were again reinforced when a friend asked Mr Cox for *The Voyage Out*. 'By Virginia Woolf? Let me see; she was a Miss Stephen, daughter of Sir Leslie. Her sister is Mrs. Clive Bell I think. Ah, strange to see what's become of those two girls. Brought up in such a nice home, too. But then', Cox leaned forward authoritatively, 'they were never *baptised*.'

In November 1916 the committee had decided to take out insurance against bombing. The insurance salesman mentioned an annual premium of £50, but it turned out to be £162 10s 0d. Harry Yates Thompson voted against it, Edmund Gosse dithered and finally voted in favour, carrying the meeting. Yates Thompson, who had stood unflinching beside General Grant at Chattanooga, thought the expense of insuring the books against what he called 'Air-craft' was outrageous, particularly as Gosse had earlier argued 'in the contrary sense'. He asked for his letter of protest to be incorporated in the minutes, and it is still there. The library was never hit during the First War, though an anti-aircraft shell fell on the roof and a later librarian, Christopher Purnell, kept it in his cupboard as a souvenir. A First World War gas mask was not thrown away until 1950.

Other members were in the trenches, still entitled to their fifteen books as 'country members', and Maurice Baring, typing on his new Corona portable from an airfield somewhere in France in 1915, was very cross with Desmond McCarthy for not sending one on to him. 'You are a great Heygate not to send me a book from the London Lib. I have received such during a) Manchurian War b) Russian Revolution c) Balkan war & returned them.' Hagberg and the committee, often more concerned during the war with whether or not to sue their tenants at Dalmeny Court for failing to pay their ground rent, did not believe in carrying patriotism too far: all books sent to France required a deposit – Hilaire Belloc sent £3 – and Maurice Baring was mildly amused when his books finally arrived from St James's Square by the words 'To Be Kept Dry' printed on the side of the parcel. Many books were lost, and many readers, and the committee again and again coldly granted permission for a widow to 'use up the remainder of her husband's subscription'.

One set of books that was not kept dry was taken out by Kitchener, persuaded by the War Office that he might be less trouble to his country heading a diplomatic mission to Russia in 1916. He chose a selection of Conrad and Conan Doyle to read on the voyage, and set sail in the *Hampshire* from Scapa Flow in the Orkneys. Despite a very heavy sea he was observed to be 'reading quietly in his cabin'. About six miles out the ship hit a German mine. A lifeboat was launched, but he stayed on deck, waiting apparently for the *Hampshire* to be repaired or towed back. It sank very suddenly, drowning him and the remaining members of the crew.

Hagberg's war, by contrast, was astonishingly successful: twenty years of promoting the library had made him a familiar figure. According to the *Liverpool Daily Post* he was now 'one of the vitalising forces of the metropolis, and is on equally intimate terms with Mr Balfour and Lord Haldane, with Mr H. G. Wells and Mr Henry James, whilst he is a member of the Reform. In person, Dr Wright is handsome, looking quite a typical Norseman – as is appropriate since his mother was Scandinavian. His views on the suffrage question' – Mrs Green had just left the committee – 'are believed to be as strong as those of his brother, and he is still unmarried.'

He cultivated politicians in the same way he cultivated well-known writers, and reached the pinnacle of his fame in 1915, when the Home Secretary, Sir John Simon, was answering a question in the House of Commons. A story had appeared in a Russian newspaper from an unattributed source misrepresenting the British government's attitude. The passage, it transpired, had been found by Hagberg, who had volunteered at the outbreak of war to read and report on the Russian press. The Home Secretary flourished Hagberg's letter, and said that it was 'from a gentleman who' – unlike the Mysterious Leaker who had caused all the trouble – 'will be well known to many members: he is the Librarian of the London Library, Dr Hagberg Wright, whom everybody knows.' According to *Hansard* he was interrupted by cries of 'Hear Hear!'

In Russia itself, one of Hagberg's letters had an even more surprising effect. Arthur Ransome, asked by Russian guards for his papers, found that Hagberg's flamboyant signature on a letter from the London Library asking him to return some books got him through everywhere.

Hagberg was also making a name for himself with his war libraries. Two society ladies, Mrs Gaskell and Lady Battersea, had thought of the idea of a lending library to supply books for the wounded. Lady Battersea had offered her London home, Surrey House at Marble Arch. The scheme had been approved by Haldane, the war minister, and Sir Alfred Sloggett, head of the Royal Army Medical Corps. An announcement appeared in all the newspapers, it was the first appeal of the war, and van-loads of books arrived, filling Surrey House from floor to ceiling. This became the Red Cross Library.

Haldane was on the committee, and called in Hagberg. Initially he met with rebuffs. One member of a relief committee left him dumbfounded by asking, 'And what is the London Library?', and a serving officer told him that in wartime 'a hairdresser was more useful than a librarian'.

Bringing five assistants from St James's Square, Hagberg set about it with his characteristic thoroughness. He ordered a chain of lorries to pull up at the door of Surrey House, and tipped into them the enormous amount of junk that had arrived, sent by those who saw the appeal as a heaven-sent opportunity of clearing out their bookshelves. He also rescued any rare or valuable books, which he sold to buy 'standard authors' likely to appeal to the troops.

The first wounded arriving in empty hospitals found them already well stocked with books, all astonishingly clean. As the war went on Hagberg put advertisements in English-speaking newspapers all over the world. Books arrived from Madeira and the Canary Islands, New Zealand and South Africa. The British and Foreign Bible Society contributed 80,000 Gospels, bound in khaki, with the Red Cross or the Union Jack embossed on the front, and several publishers contributed special editions.

On his own initiative Hagberg started a separate library for the benefit of Russian prisoners of war in Germany. He made Edmund Gosse chairman, Purnell 'Secretary', and was himself the treasurer. It operated from the London Library, the staff doing the work in their spare time. By the end of the war they had sent eight tons of books to eighty-five camps all over Germany.

He got letters from schoolgirls in internment asking for books to learn English, from Russian soldiers wanting to brush up their Chinese, Russian officers interested in bee-keeping and the use of manure. He had met Lenin 'at luncheon' before the war and 'thought him dogmatic and mediocre', but he was thrilled that 'the highly-educated upper classes of Russia have given ear to the call of their peasant brothers, and the gulf fixed between the intellectuals and the illiterates is rapidly being solidly bridged over.'

Hagberg managed to turn even his war work to the benefit of the library and to building his new stacks with the green opaque glass floors. It all provided good copy. The value of the London Library, he told the *Observer* at the end of an interview about his work for the Red Cross, had been proved over and over again. 'Indeed it is not too much to say that the government would have found it difficult to get on without it.'

During the Conscription Debate in January 1916 Asquith had sent his private secretary across to the library: the Prime Minister had a dim recollection that at the time of the Battle of Agincourt something had been said about married and single men. After a considerable search they discovered the reference, which Asquith made use of in the House of Commons. Bonar Law made similar enquiries about the public reaction to the Conscription Act during the American Civil War.

Borrowing by government departments had been colossal: the Admiralty was using on average eighty books at a time, and the Russian map of Siberia had been out ever since the library had acquired it in the early days of the war. Dictionaries had been taken out, the Air Ministry for some reason had wanted a large-scale map of Prague, and the Foreign Office had borrowed a copy of *Das Grössere Deutschland* containing an article by Professor Rohrbach.

As a literary institution, Hagberg told them, the London Library had more than 'done its bit' during the war; to all intents and purposes it had become a government department.

These were the kind of requirements that were made week after week, month after month, and year after year, and the Library never failed to meet them, yet it has no grant from the government. It has received no official recognition for all the work it has done, and not a single department has expressed its official thanks to the Committee for the services it has rendered.

Hands in high places were already reaching in their pockets for the green opaque glass floors, and privately Haggy was still as popular as ever. His patron Harry Yates Thompson was now a very old man with a bushy white beard and a silk top hat, and among Hagberg's papers is an unsigned wartime invitation in his round black scrawl, asking him down to Oving, his country house near the village of Pilchcott, for a strenuous weekend of wood-cutting and cleaning out the lily pond. The spelling suggests a fairly cursory interest in contemporary politics.

*An Invitation to a certain Slavophil Librarian*

Come, Haggy, come! The elms and oaks
Are longing for your lusty strokes:
The shrubs are vastly overgrown,
The lawn is spoiling to be mown:
Pilchcott and Oving both are yearning
To hear your comments so discerning
On the ill-conduct of the war,
The tricks of Tino and the Czar,
Whether Kherensky's Washington,
Or Korhniloff Napoleon,
And whether Cossacks can be trusted
To save a nation that's been worsted.
Is Askwith very much to blame?
And Gray and Churchill just the same?
Or for unhappy Ireland's sake
Does feckless Birrel take the cake?
Come, Haggy, come! Resolve these doubts
On Friday next or thereabouts.

# A Green Box
# Tied With Strings

*Is there another Library in the world from which one could take out a copy of the 1612 edition of* Albion's England, *and read it, as I have suggested it should be read, in bed?*

Robert Birley, *Sunk Without Trace*

Raymond Mortimer joined the library in 1923, and one of Frances Partridge's first memories of the place is of seeing him with a bright red scarf round his neck walking down the steps into St James's Square with an armful of books.

'To general reviewers in London', he wrote, 'the London Library is a necessity. We have to brief ourselves with previous books by the author we are considering, and often also with books on the same subject. These cannot be borrowed elsewhere without delay.' When there was delay, the library staff remember Raymond Mortimer being extremely cross. 'When a book I need has been taken out by another member there is little hope of getting it back in less than ten days, and I have often had to unearth a copy in public as far afield as Chelsea, Pimlico, Maida Vale and Archway.'

The use of the term 'in public' speaks volumes, and there is no need to expand it, except to register the feeling of privacy still felt by members in their own London Library and their faint contempt for public libraries in general, where coarser tastes load the shelves with cheap novels and sex manuals, making *The Acts of the Saints* in Latin virtually unobtainable.

The public libraries had been launched in 1851 by William Ewart, the member of the London Library who had too many books out; the Royal Commission before that had listened to evidence from members like Bunbury, and to a large extent they had based their recommendations for the new municipal libraries on the running of the one in St James's Square.

Since then they had gradually spread to every town in the country and to every part of London. They represented competition, just as Mudie's did, and Virginia Woolf during the First World War used both Day's Subscription Library in Mount Street and Kingston

147

Public Library. 'I believe we shall find it more useful than the London Library, as no one, save ourselves, reads solid books.'

Solid books were what the London Library had been founded to provide, and Hagberg in his essay *The Soul's Dispensary*, published in 1922, tried to redefine its purpose. His brief preamble on the history of libraries in general is full of good Hagbergian quotes and turns of phrase: Pietro di Albano evades for many years 'the tentacles of the Dominican Inquisitors', and when the monastic libraries are dispersed 'the whirligig of Time' soon 'brings its revenges'.

It had never been the library's policy to 'expend its funds on ephemeral fiction and certain types of biographies'. This, 'despite heated remonstrances', had earned the gratitude of those for whom the institution was intended. If the library bought books according to demand, he often argued, it would go bankrupt. At the end of the war they had two thousand requests for a new life of Lord Roberts: he had no intention of buying two thousand copies.

Hagberg knew best. He had just spent nearly £3,000 on buying the Allan Library, 21,500 books left by a nineteenth-century bibliophile for the use of Methodist preachers. He also made it one of his 'golden rules' never to sell a book: there was talk, in the immediate postwar gloom, of auctioning unwanted stock, and Hagberg's only concession was to introduce what he called his 'Lethe Chamber'. When books went out of demand, all duplicates were put in the Lethe Chamber for seven years, and then if there was still no call for them, they were sent off to a library in the Seychelles. Edmund Gosse, now chairman of the committee, is reputed to have asked to see the Lethe Chamber, and found several copies of his own work *Father and Son*.

But there had never been any attempt, Hagberg claimed in *The Soul's Dispensary*, to compete with the British Museum 'in the possession of rarities such as abound in the great National collection'. 'The purpose of the London Library is to be a tool-house for writers, well stored with books of reference both ancient and modern. When by a lucky windfall, a gift or legacy, a rare and valuable work is acquired, however, it is welcomed and prized as it deserves.'

This is probably the most hypocritical line Hagberg ever wrote in his life. In the interests of the library he was ruthless: staying with aristocratic friends in the country he would embarrass fellow-guests by begging for rare books, and he was particularly proud of his success with Philip Cohen, who had given him a cheque towards the building fund, and asked him if he would like a book as well. Hagberg said he would, and chose Wilhelm von Bode's colossal work on Rembrandt, in eight huge volumes, costing £85.

It is possible that Hagberg learned these expensive tastes from his old patron. Harry Yates Thompson was the heir to a great Liverpool shipping fortune, and since his marriage to Dolly Smith, had inherited the publishing firm of Smith Elder. He was one of the greatest collectors of his day, keeping to a limit of 150 rare and beautiful manuscripts and disposing of one if he found another that was rarer or more beautiful. He left the British Museum what are now called the Yates Thompson Manuscripts, and to celebrate the end of the war he gave the London Library a perfectly preserved first issue Aldine *Theocritus*, printed in Venice in 1495, with a bookplate designed and painted in gold, deep blue and vermilion by Albrecht Dürer.

Hagberg encouraged others to compete, and the annual report year after year is full of long paragraphs of gratitude to members for their generosity. All these riches were put on display, often in little exhibitions in the Reading Room, supplemented by books rashly lent by members. The official openings became social events, sometimes with a guest lecturer. 'There are few libraries, if any,' Hagberg wrote in one of his puffs for the library, 'from which a reader can borrow so many costly and valuable historical artistic works, as for example, Sir Thomas More's *English Works*, 1557, Gould's famous book on *Birds of Great Britain*, Botticelli's Drawings for Dante's *Divina Commedia*, the Weimar edition of *Luther's Works* or the *Corpus inscriptionum latinarum*.'

Such gifts also made excellent advertising copy, and to supplement the roll-call of great literary figures who had used the library, Hagberg concentrated more and more in his interviews with the newspapers on listing these rare and valuable books that any member could in theory take down from the open shelves, tuck under his arm, and carry home with him on the bus.

If they could get them past Mr Cox. Mr Cox, already middle-aged, was still a bachelor. He travelled up every day from Kingston to Waterloo and took the Underground to Piccadilly. He had a brother who was librarian at the Carlton Club, and in earlier years he had sometimes taken walking holidays with a nephew in Brittany and Normandy. He had visited Paris, and did not like it. Otherwise his whole life was the library.

149

He was also fast establishing himself as a legend: he was already a Victorian institution, reminiscing about the days when Carlyle's visits were still a recent memory; when Gladstone – 'a fine, almost dandified figure in summer, frequently wearing the ultra-fashionable grey frock-coat' – came in to ask him for *Diana of the Crossways* and could still spot a shilling wrong in the accounts; when the Prime Minister Lord Rosebery's mother had ridden to the library on horseback with an umbrella up. Someone claimed he once mentioned Mrs Brookfield, who shared her husband's membership of the library, being a 'remarkably handsome woman'. The listener was amazed. 'You don't mean Thackeray's mistress?' Mr Cox looked conspiratorial, and dropped his voice to a whisper. 'Oh, so you've heard?'

Richard Aldington got past him, borrowing books for D. H. Lawrence, who was not a member. T. E. Lawrence who was, then languishing as Aircraftman Ross and known by his fellow airmen at Farnborough as 'Shortarse', may have upset Mr Cox by giving membership of the library to a friend in the ranks called Chambers. Cox was formidable, and relished the opportunity of upsetting Ford Madox Ford, who asked him about a book for the woman he had been living with for fifteen years, referring to her as Mrs Ford. Cox sniffed and said, 'I suppose you mean Miss Hunt?'

But even Cox was good copy for the press as the man who knew the answer to all the readers' questions, a 'character' who lent the library a solid, old-fashioned style, like a much-loved club butler.

The library came out of the war with its national stature if anything enhanced. While other institutions were on their beam-ends, the library raised the £22,000 it needed for Hagberg's new stacks within four years. They rose, with his long-dreamed-of opaque green glass floors, in seven storeys. He wrote:

> The shelves as well as their brackets are of metal. One floor is devoted to Science and Arts (and miscellaneous subjects), another to History, another to Topography, another to Theology. Two floors are given to literature, and three to periodicals and publications of societies.
>
> Each of these large subject groups is sub-divided into many subject divisions, arranged alphabetically, e.g., *History: Abyssinia, Afghanistan, Africa, Alexander the Great, Algeria, etc. Sciences and Arts: Aesthetics, Agriculture, Alchemy,*

*Anarchy, Anatomy.* This method of arrangement enables the members and the staff to find most books without reference to the catalogue, and there being no fixed shelf-marks, the book can be shifted when necessary without alteration of the catalogue.

He was also spending money on the staff, and in 1924 he persuaded the committee to put aside £1,000 to set up a Superannuation Fund that would for the first time provide retiring allowances for those members of the staff who had become too old or too ill to go on working there. By 1940, it had reached £23,217, and he asked them to bring it up to £25,000 – 'considered by the Actuaries sufficient to place the Fund on a sound basis'.

Balfour presented the library with an oil painting of Hagberg by Sir William Orpen. Hagberg had done his best to put the painter at his ease, and Sir William had to admit in answer to Hagberg's first letter about sittings that he was 'still just the same little thing as you saw playing (very bad) tennis at Fitzwilliam many years ago'.

The library was then offered something else: a work even further outside the range of tools for the writer it had been founded to provide.

Shortly before Christmas 1925, Hagberg got a letter from Horatio Brown, thanking the library for accepting 'a green cardboard box, tied with strings, measuring at most six inches by twelve inches by eighteen inches, and labelled "J.A. Symonds' Papers"'. The box contained the memoirs of John Addington Symonds, a member of the library who had died in Switzerland in 1896. He is probably best known even today for an extraordinary scandal in the middle of the last century involving the headmaster of Harrow, the Revd Dr C. J. Vaughan. Brown was his literary executor, and offered the manuscript to the library with the provision that it should not be published for fifty years.

Why it was accepted remains a mystery: they had never taken manuscripts in the past, much of the writing was highly indecent, and Hagberg was not noted for broadmindedness. A few years later he got into the newspapers, for the only time in his life without meaning to, by banning a book called *Ideal Marriage*, saying it had been published 'solely for members of the medical profession'. 'The London Library is not a library for medical and gynaecological books. Only one member asked for the book, and only one member, as far as I know, has resigned in consequence of its rejection.

Rejection of books outside the scope of the London Library does not imply Censorship.'

The green box was originally intended, according to Brown's will, for the British Museum. The museum has no record of any approach being made, and dismisses the idea that they might have turned down the memoirs of such a notorious homosexual: they had, after all, accepted the manuscript of Wilde's *De Profundis*.

In a letter to Brown from Davos in 1891 Symonds had explained that the autobiography was 'passionately, unconventionally set on paper'. 'Yet I think it is very singular book – perhaps unique, nay certainly unique, in the disclosure of a type of man who has not yet been classified. I am anxious therefore that the document should not perish.'

It is a life that is uncannily entangled with the life of the library. Symonds' father was a founder member in 1841 and a friend of F. D. Maurice; as a child he had stayed, like Monckton Milnes and Giacomo Lacaita, with Lord Lansdowne at Bowood, and he was a friend of W. J. Courthope, after whom Thornton Hunt had named his son.

He himself had joined the library in the 1860s, and appears in the list of subscribers printed in 1870 as living at 7 Victoria Square, Clifton, Bristol. He was married, had two small daughters, and was at the time giving a series of lectures on Greek art at Clifton College, the boys' public school. Shortly after that he had gone abroad, and had made his name as an art historian, compared to the Swiss Burckhardt.

He was, in many ways, a typical London Library reader. In the *Memoirs* he talks about his knack of pursuing his studies in hotels, in railway carriages, on steamboats, in lodging houses, in lonely Alpine chalets. 'The life of the spirit, a thin thread, it is true, but tough and elastic, was carried on continuously under conditions which would have appalled an armchair student or the habitué of a public library.'

The life of the flesh, too, was carried on in a way that would have appalled them even more. One of his sonnets in the manuscript describes a meeting with a young friend in Venice:

> . . . we had wine before us, and I said –
> 'Take gold: 'twill furnish forth some better cheer.'
> He was all clothed in white; a gondolier
> White trousers, white straw hat upon his head

A cream-white shirt loose-buttoned, a silk thread
Slung with a charm about his throat so clear.
Yes, he was here. Our four hands, laughing, made
Brief havoc of his belt, shirt, trousers, shoes . . .

But all that was written after he had struggled free of extraordinary and morbid inhibitions, and his story as told in the *Memoirs* is an agonising if at times unintentionally hilarious revelation of the other side of life in Victorian England. His difficulties with his wife can be imagined, but the tangled Pre-Raphaelite metaphors in which he describes them are hard to match:

18th June 1869. No one but she will know what burdens I have borne, imposed upon me by my temperament, and how I have been disciplined to the service of my congenital passion. I cannot write down what I have told her. And if I did, whom would it profit to know that this wretch, clasped from its cradle by a serpent, sought to elude its folds – that he ran to the waters of oblivion, but the stream dried up and the snake followed – that the thick leafage of close study was lightning-scathed, so that the glittering reptile-eyes shone through – that the high tree of marriage was hewn down beneath him, so that he fell into those serpent-jaws again . . .

The axe-wielding snake inevitably had its way in the end, but only after a long and highly operatic saga of self-loathing. It is also a terrible story of persecution, with Symonds as the persecutor, tormenting his old headmaster for acting out his own fantasies and then imitating his victim unpunished.

At Harrow Symonds was appalled by the antics of his fellow Harrovians who masturbated like apes – he was in a house, suitably enough, called 'Monkey's' – rolled about with each other on the floor of their dormitory, and cuffed and spat on younger boys, their rejected 'bitches', till they yelped off weeping. He himself hankered for a more ideal homosexual love, and was mocked as an intellectual. In 1857 he and a boy called Pretor won an internal scholarship, and were hurled down the steps of Great School by the head boy who had come third in the exam, falling in the mud in front of the whole school.

Against Pretor's wishes, Symonds insisted on complaining to their headmaster, Vaughan, threatening to tell the story to the newspapers unless the head boy apologised. Vaughan reluctantly agreed, and the head boy was duly forced to read a public apology. Shortly after that Vaughan fell in love with Pretor and began writing him passionate notes. At the height of this affair, Vaughan stroked the inside of Symonds' thigh during a private tutorial. Symonds was appalled, and for reasons he does not make clear, stole one of Vaughan's more steamy love letters to Pretor.

A year later, when he was at Oxford, he told the whole story to his father, who threatened Vaughan with exposure unless he resigned immediately. Mrs Vaughan travelled to Clifton and knelt before Dr Symonds, begging for mercy: Symonds found this all the more upsetting because she was of aristocratic birth and related to Lady Stanley of Alderley, but Vaughan had to go. He resigned from Harrow with the school still entirely in the dark as to why, and was given a moving farewell dinner.

Vaughan was invited to become bishop of Rochester, but Dr Symonds again wrote threatening to expose him if he accepted. When the story eventually got out, society sided entirely with Vaughan. Symonds, in the meantime, had gone to lecture at Clifton, where he had a tempestuous affair with a sixth-former he calls simply 'Norman', and then spent the remainder of his life abroad.

Looking at the green box in the Committee Room of the London Library seventy years after the scuffle on the steps of Great School, Harry Yates Thompson, then in his late eighties, must have felt conflicting emotions. He was the head boy who had thrown Symonds and Pretor down the steps. They had made it up before they left school, and he had given Symonds *The Ballad of Lenora*, with illustrations by Maclise. Perhaps it was he, as much as Gosse, who urged them to accept the manuscript.

Whatever the Victorian homosexual entanglements that linked the old men of the Jazz Age, Hagberg was no longer a bachelor. In 1919, at the age of fifty-six, he married a widow slightly younger than himself, Constance Tyrrell Lewis. Members old enough to remember her have no very clear recollection of how they met or what she was like, but the gossip in the library was that she 'gave him a terrible time'.

At weekend house parties, on holiday in France and Italy, Hagberg had been a happy bachelor. One friend remembered him as a 'playboy', swapping yarns with Kerry peasants, insisting on riding a stubborn mule during a fiesta at Palermo, or teaching urchins to turn somersaults at Blois. But those days were now over.

His new bride made two contributions to the life of the library: one was a crudish caricature of Hagberg, sitting under a tarpaulin and surrounded by heaps of books. The caption was 'Snowed Under', and it hung on the stairs among the pictures of side-whiskered early London Library worthies, an exhortation to support Hagberg's further building schemes.

Mrs Wright's second intervention in the affairs of the library was to extend her husband's old idea of exhibitions and lectures to asking people into the Reading Room after dinner for extravagant 'At Homes'.

In 1929 he launched what was to be his last great campaign. The staff accommodation he had promised before the war had still not materialised. The 'general staff rooms' were in the old basement kitchens of Beauchamp House, barely touched by the rebuilding work at the turn of the century, still with their early Victorian ovens where the porters brewed the tea. They had been inadequate, according to Hagberg, when the staff was half the present size. They had little or no daylight and were 'neither comfortable nor hygienic'.

The two cataloguing rooms were in the other old part of Beauchamp House under the roof, in what had originally been Mrs Trollope's bedroom in the days of Bodham Donne. There was no lift. The rooms were overcrowded and too small. At the back of the building, the accounts department were worse off. The chief cashier and two clerks worked in a tiny room ten feet by eleven, cluttered with desks, cupboards and shelves full of ledgers, at the bottom of a light-well with a window so high up that on dull days the electric light was left on all the time.

Finally, also on the Duke Street side, the Librarian's Room was dark and draughty. It had three doors, one of which opened on to the passage beside Dalmeny Court, and also needed electric light all day because of the high buildings all round it. On the floor above, the Committee Room was too small, and the whole of 9 Duke Street needed rebuilding. Many of the floors sagged and it would be dangerous to put any further strain on them. Extravagant promises were made: there would be a tearoom, where members could talk, and there was even a suggestion that there might be 'smoking cubicles'.

One of Mrs Wright's soirées to raise money for this fund featured an exhibition of recently published Russian books. Hagberg maintained close links with Russia and with Russian emigrés, and there was a famous occasion when, in the course of rescuing 'Nihilists', he received a parcel at the library containing a shirt. It had, so the story went, been worn by sixteen Russians in succession without being washed, and had a secret message written on it in code.

Invitations came on stiff cards from the Hagbergs' own home at 14 Gloucester Terrace, where guests were asked to send their replies. Mr and Mrs Charles Hagberg Wright would be At Home in the Reading Room, by permission of the Committee. Hagberg once listed his two greatest dislikes in middle age as taking exercise and listening to speeches, and it said on the card that there would be 'three speeches limited to seven minutes each', the first beginning at 9.45 p.m. Sometimes there were performances by folk singers or string quartets. Fortunately a South African visitor recorded his impressions of one of these evenings in considerable detail, and managed to catch a certain amount of period atmosphere.

St James's Square, apart from the Clerical, Medical and General next door and the Westminster Bank at Number 1, was still largely occupied by private houses. There were crocuses in the private garden in the middle of the square in spring, Lady Astor entertained opposite, and Mrs Wright was clearly damned if she was going to be outdone.

'A striped awning spanned the pavement as the guests began to arrive. Lordly motors, purring sedately, floated into St. James's Square. Broken-winded two-seaters made bad landings at the pavement side. Foot-people came in straggling succession.' The visitor was struck by the contrast between those who arrived in the lordly motors and those who came in the broken-winded two-seaters. 'This was going to be the most democratic party in all London.'

'Great names in literature were usually those with a word and smile for the attendants, who neatly packed away our hats and coats on bookshelves, swept and garnished for the occasion.' Mr Cox is not mentioned but can be imagined, in middle age, discreetly hissing instructions to the girls, bowing and preening as Lord Lansdowne, Lord Ilchester, Priscilla Lady Annesley, the Dowager Lady Foyle, Sir Frederick and Lady Pollock, the Dean of St Paul's and Mrs Inge, Commander and Mrs Stephen King-Hall, and Mrs Aubrey Le Blonde filed condescendingly by.

The only literary members spotted in the crowd that evening

were the young Rose Macaulay, the relation of Carlyle's old sparring partner, and Rebecca West. After them, in full Ruritanian costume, came the Estonian Minister, and Baron and Baroness Palmstierna, representing Sweden, Hagberg's motherland.

There would enter an ambassador, complete with sash, orders and benignity, and close behind a tall, peering student in brown suiting. Nor were the womenkind less varied. Witchery of Spanish shawls arrived amiably with the severest of neutral-tinted afternoon gowns. All were blended, however, by a certain serene mentality.

The London Library is not outwardly or inwardly impressive. There is nothing of the Cathedral about it, but the atmosphere is still distinctive. It is desperately alive, as though every one of these brown-jacketed books – there are miles and miles of them – had its millimetre of radium powerful enough, if rightly used, to move a mountain.

The guests chattered their way upstairs, past the picture of Carlyle looking like a mad peasant, past Gladstone and Monckton Milnes, past Mrs Hagberg's caricature of her husband 'Snowed Under', and standing rigidly to attention like an honour guard, 'rows of attendant Librarianesses, each with the impersonal look of their high calling'. These would have included the young Miss Manwaring, who was to rule her girls during the thirties and forties.

In the Reading Room, they were received by Hagberg and Mrs Hagberg, together with members of the committee, and coffee was brought round. 'Already,' the South African observer noticed, 'on the narrow balconies among the books, habituees had gone aloft to perch on stools and converse at ease near the shadowy ceiling.'

After the opening speech 'Our Predecessors at the London Library' by another member of the committee, Harry Duncan O'Neill rose to do the hard sell. O'Neill worked next door at the Clerical, Medical and General and was a bit of a wag. His favourite trick, as secretary of the insurance company, was to spread all the letters he had to sign at the end of the day in a fan-shape with only the foot of each page showing, and then sign them blindfold.

He told the guests that the Library had already spent £91,000 on the freehold of the buildings and the bookstores, and now intended to embark on a rebuilding programme which would cost something like £45,000. While fivers and tenners would be more than welcome, he urged the listeners to approach their 'Moneyed friends, those likely to confer good round sums like £40,000.'

Hamilton Fyfe, described by the South African visitor as 'a braw Scot from Frumes', then made a few jokes about the habits of book borrowers.

'The Library', said Mr Fyfe, 'saved many of us from being potential criminals, so strong was the urge to possess good books at all hazards. But for the London Library the prisons might be filled with literary folk!' He told the story of a man who owned a fine library, but would not lend a single book. 'Certainly not,' he would say, 'Borrowed books are never returned. I know something about that. All these are borrowed books!' There was loud laughter among the consciously guilty.

Sir Edward Parry then got up to make an unscheduled speech but the South African visitor did not think it worth while writing down what he said.

There were more speeches, more coffee, more gazing at treasured volumes, but I slipped away to the warehouses, which are solid buildings intersected with spidery staircases and alleyways like those around the engine shaft of a great liner. Thinly lighted, they yet revealed their world of books. Dainty ladies were tip-toeing about, fearful lest their high heels should catch and remain in the metal gratings. Their voices and laughter made music, and yet one wondered which were more alive – they or the endless noble ranks of dynamic books.

# The Manor Vanishes

*In a suburban train the passenger sitting opposite smiled companionably at the sight of the Library's label on the cover of my book and said 'The best library in the world'.*

An Older Member

His wife's love affair with Virginia Woolf over, Harold Nicolson turned in 1931 to a closer scrutiny of the London Library. He had been a member for years, and now joined the committee.

The first time he arrived late to find Hagberg in full flow, arguing about a bust of Samuel Richardson that had been offered to the library. Other people were saying it was a mistake to 'look a gift bust in the face', but Hagberg was adamant. Samuel Richardson had nothing to do with the library, and in any case they had no room for it. This allowed him to get back on to his favourite subject, enlarging the library.

The only other member of the committee Harold Nicolson thought worth mentioning in his typewritten diary was a man he spelt 'Riddle'. He thought he was 'a nice old bird, though I wish to goodness he was not the owner of the *News of the World*'. Lord Riddell was certainly a shrewd old bird, and the story of how the London Library in the thirties came to be largely subsidised by the *News of the World* is not one that figures large in the reminiscences of members or librarians.

Despite Mrs Hagberg's At Homes, O'Neill's appeals for 'a good round sum like £40,000', Mr Cox's wonderful character-acting and all the publicity, the library was mortgaged. During the twenties, Hagberg's extravagance had been eating away at the reserves, and his building fund reflected almost to the pound the amount they had been forced to borrow.

He was now nearly seventy, and it must have seemed to him that the days were finally gone when he had only to lift a finger for modern labyrinths of steel to rise all about him, peopled by great writers and intellectually inclined peers of the realm, many of them flourishing banknotes.

Then, in 1929, when everyone else was jumping out of windows, Hagberg thought he was saved. From out of the blue a relatively

159

rich member died, leaving almost his entire estate to the library. When the will was read, it turned out to be not quite so simple. Major William Prevost left all his money to the library itself, and Elfords, his country house in Kent, to the staff.

> So far as possible Elfords with the garden shall not be sold, but used by the Staff of the London Library, including the Secretary and the Trustees. If for any reason Elfords has to be sold it is my express wish that the proceeds of the sale shall not be used for the general purposes of the London Library but for such benevolent or charitable purposes for the benefit of the Secretary and Staff of that Institution as the Trustees of the Library shall from time to time determine.

For the staff of the institution this would have been nothing new: from Jane Carlyle's friendship with John Edward Jones to the present day the relationship between those who work at the London Library and those who use it has been one of generous interdependence. Joan Bailey remembers her amazed gratitude when Leslie Blanche, author of *The Wilder Shores of Love*, asked her and her mother to stay in her villa on the Mediterranean, or when she was given the use of a flat in the Albany for six months, but such experiences are by no means unique. It was therefore all the more shameful that Hagberg should have decided to divert such spontaneous generosity away from the staff and into his building fund.

At the next meeting of the committee he told them that 'the late Major Prevost had left the Library a legacy'. The committee were by now mostly very old men, some of them very deaf, and they agreed with Hagberg's suggestion that he and Harry O'Neill should be responsible for dealing with it and should have 'authority to consult the Library's solicitors when necessary'.

There is no excuse for Hagberg's behaviour, but he was an old man desperate to see his library as he wanted it in time for the centenary in 1941. Prevost's will already gave him nearly £32,000 in cash; if they sold the house and the rest of the estate he would have almost exactly the 'round £40,000' that O'Neill had been asking for at the time of the Russian exhibition. Hagberg set off for Hawkhurst, looked round the house for any furniture that could be used in St James's Square, and found a local estate agent.

Then came the first blow. Someone calling himself the Baron de

Hauteville appeared, claiming that Major Prevost had redrawn his will and left everything to him. The library could have taken it to court, but that meant every clause of the will being picked over in public and possibly even reported in the papers. They decided to try and settle privately. Hagberg chose a strong team capable of daunting any French baron, authentic or otherwise: it consisted of Lord Ilchester, a bluff red-faced man with a bald head who still shot pheasants in the park at Holland House, Lord Riddell and the ancient Fred Pollock, with Harry Duncan O'Neill in attendance, to try and reach a compromise. The Baron insisted on going to court.

The case was heard before Mr Justice Eve, and after much expensive talk about what had happened *in re* Badger (1905) or in the case of Cocks v. Manners (1901), the judge ruled that the will in favour of Mr Frederic Grand d'Hauteville was invalid. He also went on, at whose instigation it is not entirely clear, to discuss in detail the two clauses relating to the house and gardens being left to the staff of the library, which for technical reasons he found not to be legally binding.

The case, inevitably, was reported in full in the newspapers, and with the lights suddenly switched on Hagberg and his fellow conspirators looked extremely foolish. They began to argue that the house would have been a white elephant which they could never have afforded to keep up. Elfords had fifteen bedrooms, five and a half acres of garden, an orchard, woodland, a pond, what were described as 'two useful park-like enclosures of grass' covering a further twenty-two acres, and a lodge. In addition to this there was a home farm, let for about £50 a year, and consisting of a small farmhouse, farm buildings with an oast house, four cottages and about seventy acres of farmland.

Quite apart from having to pay Mrs Newell the housekeeper, maids and gardeners, there were responsibilities that lay beyond the grasp of most library committees, however widely qualified. Even during their brief possession of the house, they found themselves haggling with a local farmer over how much he ought to pay to graze his sheep, and having to answer letters from the Vicar of Hawkhurst asking for money for the new village cricket pitch, which they refused to give him.

Nevertheless the bitterness of the staff at the idea of Hagberg trying to swindle them was terrible, and twenty years later was still so bad that the committee was forced to go through the records to see whether their grievance was justified. The staff were angry not so much at the idea of losing a hugely expensive holiday home with acres of garden to look after, but at Hagberg's disregard for the second clause of the will that made them the beneficiaries if the house was sold.

It was in any case a bad time to sell, and the whole thing was mismanaged. Elfords was put up for sale at auction in October with a reserve price of £7,000, which it failed to reach. It was sold a month later to a local property developer, George Ticehurst of Heathfield, for £4,500; he cut the house in two and sold it off within the year, making a handsome profit. The rest of the estate was sold the same month, without any reserve, for £1,443.

Hagberg and the committee dealt with various minor bequests in the will, arranged for Prevost's gold watch to be given to a surviving relative who had otherwise been cut out entirely, and voted a 'gratuity' of £25 to Mrs Newell the housekeeper at Elfords. They then made a note in the minutes, explaining that as the property had been sold none of the other 'suggestions' contained in the will could be carried out.

Aware however of unrest below stairs, they made the gesture of offering every member of the staff an annual bonus of one month's wages, to be paid as soon as the Prevost money came in from a fund set aside on deposit. In Hagberg's typed minutes, this was recorded as £2,000. The only evidence of any heart-searching on Hagberg's part is that this has been crossed out, with an initialled stroke of the pen, and corrected to £3,000.

It was exactly half what the staff had a right to from the sale of the house. It was paid out on a scale of seniority to everyone working there at the time of the bequest, and continued until shortly after the war. By the time the last survivor retired, the scheme had cost the library £2,750.

Hagberg was unrepentant. His mind was on money, and Sydney Gedge's son John, now the library's lawyer, led him into further trouble, as he was going through the Prevost papers, when he discovered that William Prevost could have been worth more than they thought.

In 1868 a self-made Scottish-born brewer, banker and railway magnate, William Dow, had died in Montreal, leaving £300,000 to his sister-in-law, Dame Mary Brydie Dow. The Dame's granddaughter was Major Prevost's mother and, despite further bifurcations in the Dow family tree, Major Prevost, or so the lawyers calculated, could still have expected a further £15,000 from the original Dow Estate. Hagberg decided to lay claim to it.

Hagberg was determined to go on building, and some clue to his state of mind is given in an extraordinary essay he wrote for *The Empire Review* in 1931. He seems to have gone slightly mad. Politically he always tried to be fair, and he was one of the first to criticise anti-Semitism in Russia after the First World War, but his vision of the library transformed into the mystical hub of the British Empire is like a fascist painting of heroes meeting in Valhalla.

There is a memorable passage in the writings of Tolstoy in which he pictures the world 'as a vast temple in which the light falls from above in the very centre. To meet together all must go towards the light. There we shall find ourselves, gathered from many quarters, united with men we did not expect to see; therein is joy.' The simile, though framed to suit a cosmic theme, has certain points of similitude to our subject that suggest themselves. In the Reading Room of a great library there must often be surprising encounters.

People of the most diverse characters and occupations find themselves in unsuspected sympathy, with kindred interests of which they were unaware. The 'men we did not expect to see' are transformed into men to whom we are drawn by the bond of mutual aims and strivings, and by the ties of membership in a society ruled by a common purpose. And, beyond the walls of the Reading Room, extending to the farthest limits of our Empire, the rays stream out from the centre, strengthening the points of contact that distances tend to weaken, and minimising the sense of mental isolation which is the hardest penalty of exile.

He got his way. Harold Nicolson was at the meeting in 1932 when they decided to go ahead with Hagberg's last great scheme. His new building would create enough space, Hagberg claimed – unless a newspaper misprinted the date – *to hold all the new books they were likely to buy until the year 2081.*

Harold Nicolson at that time was seeing a good deal of Sir Oswald Mosley, and he may have overlooked Hagberg wiping the flecks of foam from his lips, but he was very intrigued by Fred

Pollock, now eighty-eight. Hagberg remembered that Pollock as a young man had proposed buying the freehold, and asked him now to propose the building of the extension, with Nicolson to speak second. Pollock told the meeting that the timid ones reminded him of the timid ones fifty years before. 'They blocked everything because it was something.'

Nicolson says they were all much impressed by this. He was embarrassed though by the fact that Fred Pollock, who was sitting next to him, instead of talking to the rest of the table, insisted on addressing all his remarks personally to him.

> He turns on me a fierce and myopic eye accusing me of the obscurantism of fifty years ago. As I am seconder of the motion I feel this to be unfair. I draw squares and triangles upon my blotting paper as an excuse for avoiding that denunciatory eye. 'In 1882', he says, 'an almost exactly similar situation arose. Then, as now, the older members of the Committee preached caution.' I look up. 'Caution' he hisses at me accusatorially. Yet I am the second, the partner, of his recklessness. Anyhow we get our point. The extension will be built. God bless it. But I wonder why Sir Frederick was so cross.

Behind his geriatric puppet it was Hagberg who was being reckless. With the new building announced, letters began to arrive from the lawyers in Montreal urging caution in pressing the Dow Estate. But Hagberg would not be deflected. He was running another of his press campaigns. Mr Cox, too, was wheeled out again to tell his Victorian stories.

But Hagberg's campaign was handicapped by the tired old committee. Balfour had died in 1930, and the new president H. A. L. Fisher was in charge of the appeal. John Masefield offered a poetry reading to raise funds, but there was no-one prepared to organise it.

Worse, there was bad news from Canada. Chief Justice Greenshields sounded English enough, even if the case was being heard in the Province of Quebec. But it soon became clear that to native Canadians the London Library, described as 'a Corporation with its head office in London, England', was the villain of the piece.

Hagberg, reading the report of the case in London, must have realised they were in trouble when the judge immediately meandered off into seventeenth-century French, recalling an ordinance of 1629 known as the '*Code Lichaud*', which covered '*les degrez desdites substitutions et fideicommis par toute notre royaume*'. The '*royaume*' in question was the kingdom of France, and even Greenshields himself realised he might be, as it were, flying a French Canadian kite.

'I am not unaware that there has been much difference of opinion as to whether this Ordinance was ever in force in Canada. The late Mr Justice Ramsay was of the opinion that it was not, because it had fallen into disuse in France.' He had, he told the court, 'read with much interest the very able article by the late Eugene Lafleur, K.C., in which in his usual able manner he discusses the whole question.' All this was costing the library a lot of money, and even Fred Pollock, a lawyer all his long life, when he was asked to run his myopic eye over the written judgment, had to confess that 'he did not begin to understand it'.

'This conclusion leads me to hold, as I do hold, that Major Prevost could not, by Will, bequeath anything' – of the Dow Estate, that is – ' to the London Library. The mis-en-cause, Miss Alice G. Prevost, the daughter of one of the institutes deceased, submits that the division should take place by roots and not by heads. The Defendants contend the contrary, that the division should be made by heads and not by roots.'

The fund had still only raised £1,300. Lawyers' fees in Canada were going to absorb most of that, but Pollock somehow succeeded in convincing Harold Nicolson and the committee that it was worth appealing. The only person who tried to persuade them against it was another old man, Sir Edward Parry, who Nicolson said was 'in a foul temper and very gaga'. The appeal failed.

With the architect's drawings to be paid for and the building about to begin, Lord Riddell stepped in and offered them a loan of £15,000 for ten years at $4^1/_2$ per cent. He also paid the expenses of applying for a royal charter for the library, which was granted in 1933. Fred Pollock had said in the past there was no point in their having a royal charter, and its practical benefits were limited. The library could now, for example, sue and be sued. But it appealed to Hagberg's idea of glory, and bearing in mind the shortage of money he had a pamphlet printed 'inexpensively' to commemorate it. The library became entitled to have its own seal, which it was decided should bear Carlyle's head.

It was probably Riddell too, as a close friend of Lloyd George who had made him first a knight, then a baronet and then a peer, who pulled the necessary strings to get Ramsay MacDonald to offer Hagberg a knighthood. He accepted, and Constance Tyrrell Lewis became Lady Wright.

The building went ahead behind a dustproof wall of canvas hung up in the Reading Room, which was extended westwards, as was the entrance hall immediately underneath. Hagberg got more floors of books, and there was a new Committee Room. The *Daily Telegraph* called the extension a 'fitting crown' to Hagberg's labours.

As a final irony the Committee Room, opened in 1934, and provided by Harry Yates Thompson's widow with a marble Adam fireplace in his memory, was christened the Prevost Room.

The morale of the staff had suffered. But the porters continued to wrap books for country members in a paper that according to one reader's affectionate memory of it was 'dark grey, almost black'; and the assistants went on in the old tradition of John Edward Jones, devoting their lives to answering the members' questions, writing issue slips, carrying books, and returning them to their shelves at the end of a long day when members left them littered about the Reading Room. They had no kind of representation except the occasional member of the committee who would listen to their complaints, and even then they were endangering their jobs. But there were resentments, and not all of them to do with the Prevost Bequest.

Walter de la Mare and John Masefield both wrote very appreciative letters to 'G. E.' Manwaring, thanking him for his help. He worked alongside Cox at the Issue Desk, but he was also a naval historian and a member of the committee for the preservation of HMS *Victory* at Portsmouth. He despised Hagberg, disliked Purnell, and couldn't stand Mr Cox. His son, Randle Manwaring, who worked next door for Harry Duncan O'Neill at the Clerical, Medical and General, describes his father as a handsome man, with long and sensitive fingers, black hair parted in the middle, and a wing collar. 'Despite a congenital heart condition he managed to be at the beck and call of members of the Library, and climbed innumerable stairs to find the books they asked for.'

He played table tennis with the boys on the staff in the lunch hour on a ping-pong table in the basement that was still there during the war. It was later moved up to the men's staff room on the fourth floor, and long tournaments were played without any reader hearing a sound.

He was frustrated, in his son's words, by the fact that 'his literary output and literary knowledge was infinitely superior to that of the men placed over him in the Library.' Hagberg, he felt, was not really a literary man, although he produced the occasional article or book review; Purnell was a narrow-minded member of the Plymouth Brethren; and Cox took what he considered to be 'an insensitive and intrusive interest' in the members' lives. Manwaring thought he was undervalued and unappreciated, and 'the set of his lips indicated resentment'.

His sister also worked at the Library all her life, and was in charge of all the girls on the Returns Desk until long after the war. Joan Bailey, who worked for her, remembers one of the girls pulling out and spilling a whole drawer full of blue cards: as she stooped to gather them up, Miss Manwaring approached unaware and at speed from the other side of the desk, keen to greet a favourite member with her booming 'Good after*noon*!', and went, as they said in those days, spats over collarstud.

Another time, Miss Cooper, the lifelong companion of Miss Bolton who worked throughout the thirties in the Reading Room – formality was always preserved: Miss Bolton would tolerate being called 'Blot' but never 'Ethel' – was larking about in the girls' staff room trying on Helen Manwaring's famous straw hat with cherries on it which she always wore in the summer. Another girl at the door shouted to warn her that Miss Manwaring was coming, she launched the hat frisbee-style towards the hatstand, and watched as it impaled itself on one of the pegs, the wooden coathook poking through the straw.

Miss Bolton herself tiptoed about the Reading Room, approaching Hilaire Belloc when he talked too loudly with a printed notice saying 'Silence is Requested' and regularly patrolling the armchairs by the fire on winter afternoons, giving the back of the chair a jolt if the snores were disturbing other members. Her most touching memory is of 'one lady who always used to come in and sit on the floor by the fire and rest her head against a gentleman's knees. I don't think they ever spoke.'

But it was not an easy life, and in the mid-thirties it was not made easier by Harry Duncan O'Neill displaying about the library various examples of his own light verse, all with a moral.

'*In the Book Stores.*'
If you leave up the lights when you've finished
It is surely the mark of the beast;
By as much as our light bill's diminished
– Our purchase of books is increased.

'*To dilatory readers.*'
If you won't send books back when requested
You are one of the Library's scamps,
Causing money, far better invested
In books, to be wasted on stamps.

'*To the careless reader.*'
When a page that is dog-eared confronts you
It may cause a sensation of shame
If your conscience confesses that once you
Were guilty yourself of the same.

'*To the worst reader of all.*'
Don't write in the margin, you divil!
All pencilled remarks are taboo,
For, however much authors may drivel,
We want to read them, and not you!

'*To overdue subscribers.*'
Fine wines, extravagant raiment
May seem more important to you
But to us it is 'Punctual Payment
The day your subscription is due.'

'*In the Lavatory.*'
Please leave, kindly member, this place in
The state that you found it before,
Neither leaving the soap in the basin
Nor tumbling the towels on the floor.

'*To moribund members.*'
When making your Will, please remember
The cats and the dogs have enough;
When your life has attained its December
Leave the Library some of your stuff.

He also liked to remind them that the building might be finished, but still wasn't paid for.

*'The Building Fund.'*
(For non-subscribers)

Our new building is finished! Inside it
You'll find all your dreams have come true
– But you – did you help to provide it?
Then let's have a subscription from you!

On the surface though, everything must have seemed to the members to be fine. Somerset Maugham even scored a victory over Cox, when he asked him for a book and Cox replied without looking up 'It's out', by calling him a 'B..b..bloody old fool!' But Cox, in the everyday life of the library, was gradually eclipsing Hagberg: much more in evidence, always at the Issue Desk, and growing for younger members into a kind of oracle. Nicko Henderson, later our ambassador in Paris and Washington, who began going to the library in the late thirties, remembers Mr Cox as 'our education'. 'He may have had a cockney voice, but you never noticed that: he knew everything. You asked him anything you wanted to know and he knew where you would find it, he'd get you the book.'

Meanwhile Hagberg was more and more detached from the staff. Miss Bolton never saw him there except when he came upstairs for the annual general meeting. He let himself in through the back door from Duke Street and sat in his new Librarian's Room. Most of the time none of the staff would have known if he was in the building.

Publicly, his triumph was complete. The building work had been finished on time, and the committee voted him three hundred guineas to be spent on a month's holiday. In a few more years he would celebrate the centenary of the library, and in 1943 he would have been there fifty years. Privately, he must have been anxious. The library was short of money and looked like becoming steadily poorer: the staff felt betrayed.

At that moment, John Edward Jones' ghost returned to haunt him. A clergyman called Martin wrote to tell them that Jones' son was in trouble, and asked if they could send him money. Hagberg, with the committee's approval, refused.

In 1937, when he was seventy-five, friends urged Hagberg to

retire; he told them the library would be his home until his end. A fortnight before he died, in February 1940, he invited a journalist from the *Daily Telegraph* to visit him. He was, he thought, recovering from bronchitis. His bedroom was full of books that had just been given to the library, a collection about the Caucasus.

# We Lose Our Religion

*Never again would he walk down the obscure and narrow lanes between the bookshelves in the London Library, sniffing the dusty perfume of good literature, peering at strange titles, exploring the fringes of vast domains of knowledge.*
                    Aldous Huxley, *The Gioconda Smile*

The Luftwaffe played rather a cat and mouse game with Hagberg's successor, Christopher Purnell. In the autumn of 1940 he was standing in his bedroom in Lewisham one night 'watching the fun' when a bomb fell two streets away, exploded and hurled what he estimated to be a seven-pound chunk of brickwork over the house in front and through his roof. He said it fell within a foot of him.

Shortly afterwards he came home from the library to find his home cordoned off. A bomb had fallen in the garden, and lay half buried in the earth, having failed to explode. He and his wife were allowed to go in and collect a change of clothes and their washing things, and were put up by a neighbour until the bomb had been defused. While they were there a second bomb fell, demolishing his house entirely.

The pattern at the library was rather similar, though the wait between the warning and the real thing was a good deal longer. In 1940 an incendiary bomb went through the roof, stamped its serial number on a brass rail and skidded away to a corner of the stacks, where it failed to ignite. The second, a high-explosive bomb, did not come for another four years.

Purnell, like his early predecessors, came to live at the library, with a bed in the basement and a gas ring in the Librarian's Room, though the old-fashioned ovens of Beauchamp House were still used by the porters during the day to boil kettles for their tea. Mrs Purnell came with him. A neighbour in Lewisham remembers her as being naturally curious, and caught her once reading her birthday cards. Whether or not with any success, Purnell had a green curtain fitted in the glass-fronted cupboard in the Librarian's Room to spare her the sight of titles like *Fanny Hill*.

His son, then in the RAF, remembers him as getting less prudish as he got older, and he eventually left tne Plymouth Brethren to

171

become churchwarden of an Anglican church in Kensington, but the girls in the library were always amused, whenever they had to collect a book from the librarian's cupboard, reserved for saucier works, when he wrapped it in brown paper before letting them carry the book the few yards to the Issue Desk.

Also inside the cupboard was the old anti-aircraft shell that had fallen on the library during the First World War without doing any damage, and two brown-paper parcels: one contained a bundle of rare pornography left to the library by Philip Cohen, only grudgingly accepted out of gratitude for his past generosity: the other John Addington Symonds' memoirs, still in their green box.

There had been a very solemn meeting of the committee in October 1939, overshadowing almost the outbreak of war, when Symonds' daughter had asked to see them. It was such a major event in the life of the library that Simon Nowell-Smith, who did not become librarian for another ten years, was convinced it happened in his time.

In his version the committee was appalled by the obscenity of the contents but felt that a typed copy should be made to protect the manuscript. They were then deeply embarrassed about approaching a secretarial agency. 'In the end, we managed to find an agency entirely run by young men, and *they* did it.' Symonds' daughter was then given permission to read them 'on the condition that a member of the library staff was in attendance'.

According to the records, they felt she 'might as well see them' in 1939 on the grounds that 'she was a tough woman, and knows very well that her father was a homosexual'. Tough she certainly was, and an inspiration to any child of unconventional parents. She had married young, was a keen mountaineer and skier, and was by then Dame Katherine Furse, international head of the Girl Guide movement. In the First World War she commanded the early WRNS, her sister the embryonic ATS.

Purnell was a natural second-in-command. He had all his life admired and modelled himself on Hagberg, and now, as it were, went on as his understudy. The son of an Oxford tailor, he was already in his late sixties, drier and more awkward, but in an interview he gave to the *Publishers' Circular* a month after Hagberg's death, all the old techniques for dealing with the press are still there.

He showed off Hagberg's old treasures, 'valuable historical and artistic works that any member could borrow and take home':

Sir Thomas More's *English Works* of 1557, Gould's *Birds of Great Britain*, Lepsius' *Denkmäler aus Aegypten*, 'and some eighty-two incunabula of great value and rarity.' These were all shortly to be evacuated to the country for their safety.

His interviewer suggested that the London Library was 'the aristocrat of its kind', and Purnell smiled appreciatively. Their recent indebtedness to the *News of the World* had not been widely publicised, and the voice of Mr Cox at the Issue Desk in his ash-spattered black jacket, a black band round his arm in mourning for Hagberg, shouting for what he called 'Prowst' clearly did not penetrate to where they were standing.

The man from the *Publishers' Circular* was impressed by the library's extent: behind the modest façade in St James's Square he found 'a brand-new, monster building, set up only a few years before, stretching backwards and upwards beyond the range of superficial eye: tier upon tier of books rising through steel-framed stories, designed upon a scientific and possibly unique principle.' There were 'reading rooms and lounges that would have graced an expensive club'. Members, he noticed, seemed to use it as if it actually were a club. He and Purnell talked about the war, and standing in the Reading Room agreed it seemed very remote.

Purnell even managed one of Hagberg's old 'surprises'. 'Come here and look at these booklists!' Of the newly acquired books few were related to the war; most were specialised works. The war did not seem to have stopped people reading serious books: some members who were civil servants had to consult military books in the course of their work, but otherwise the life of the library was not too seriously affected. 'We are carrying on. Not as if nothing had happened, but at least without appreciable dismay.'

Mr Cox was also very phlegmatic about the outbreak of war. Sought out by the press as a living symbol of continuity, he told them that if the last war was any guide, government departments would be making extensive use of the library. Whatever happened, people would be reading more.

This turned out to be true: with air raids and the blackout people wanted books to read in shelters and under the stairs as they listened to the uneven drone of German bombers and waited for the rising wail of the All Clear. Purnell noticed that there was a demand for Trollope as there had been during the First World War. 'The old chap has once more come into his own. You can call it an escapist tendency if you like. To read about small happenings in a placid

173

cathedral town is perhaps a welcome relief in these arduous days. Charlotte M. Yonge has also become suddenly popular.'

Several men on the library staff were called up. Others volunteered. They were replaced largely by girls, and both Joan Bailey and Elizabeth Ray joined Miss Manwaring's team. They had just left school, and found the library a glamorous place: both of them were very pretty, and it was full of officers in uniform. But Elizabeth Ray did not share the general enthusiasm for Mr Cox, whom she found a 'horrid old man', fawning on his grander customers, and being openly offensive to those he didn't approve of. Miss Bolton and Miss Cooper brought flowers for Purnell in summer from their garden in Merton to put on his table in the Librarian's Room.

One older member of the committee behaved with great heroism. Sir Arnold Wilson was fifty-five, a retired soldier who had met Hitler and been an admirer of Mussolini. He said he had become convinced that the issue between Germany and Britain had to be fought to a finish, refused 'to shelter behind the ramparts of the bodies of millions of our young men', and joined up as an air gunner. In June 1940 he was reported missing, and the following month, as a gesture of respect, was unanimously re-elected to the committee.

As the bombing began Purnell knew that any night one small incendiary bomb could turn Hagberg's stacks into hundred-foot walls of fire in minutes, and he supervised a regular team of fire-watchers. These were all volunteers, men and women ready with hand-operated stirrup pumps and buckets of water. On bad nights Purnell set up a camp-bed under Mr Cox's Issue Desk.

During the First World War Virginia Woolf had noticed the temporary wooden huts put up in St James's Square with the trees poking through their roofs: now the gardens were dug up to make way for reinforced concrete shelters, and the iron railings taken away for scrap. Purnell wrote a rather feeble letter of protest, saying 'part of their design is similar to that shown in prints in 1754'. There was a more robust letter from another resident of the square, G. R. Hall-Kean MP: 'I regard this ruthless tearing-up of the old iron railings, which opens up our ancient and historic London square, as a barbaric piece of Socialism.'

In 1941 the library, its windows criss-crossed with white sticky tape to limit the damage from flying glass in the event of blast, gloomily celebrated its centenary. Simon Nowell-Smith wrote a tribute in the *Times Literary Supplement*, and Mr Cox broadcast a short talk on the BBC.

The recording of Mr Cox's 'I Remember . . .' unhappily no longer exists, but a transcript survives, and it almost catches the tone of his voice. 'When I first went to the Library St James's Square used to be a nice quiet place. It was mainly inhabited by noblemen and bishops and bankers and of course there wasn't the traffic there is now. In the summer there was hardly anything doing at all. When Parliament rose in July all our members seemed to leave town, and they didn't come back till October. But that's all a thing of the past: we're as busy now in summer as at any other time.'

Professor Newbury presented the library with an armchair belonging to Carlyle, together with a small table, a number of books bearing his signature, and a large wooden-framed sofa. Newspapers celebrating the event quoted Jane Carlyle's letter to her husband at the time she bought it in 1835.

On that day I came, saw and bought – a sofa! It is my own purchase, but you shall share the possession. Indeed, so soon as you set eyes on it and behold its vastness, its simple greatness, you will perceive that the thought of you was actively at work in my choice. It was neither dear nor cheap, but a bargain nevertheless, being second-hand. Oh, it is so soft! so easy! and one of us, or both, may sleep in it, should occasion require – I mean for all night.

Professor Newbury insisted the sofa should not be treated as a museum piece, but should be used. One of the fire-watchers took him at his word and slept on it. She said it smelt disgusting.

Purnell's promotion to librarian had left his own old job empty, and the new assistant librarian was a bird of another feather. Lionel Bradley was a bearlike bearded homosexual from Manchester with large, rather naughty eyes behind horn-rimmed spectacles. He was known to many ballet dancers, and to the boys at the library, as 'Uncle Leo'. He had a passion for the ballet, some private means, and lived during his time at the library in South Kensington, looked after by a loyal housekeeper called Mrs Whittaker. He had, earlier, been chief librarian at Liverpool University Library before being obliged to leave in a scandal concerning an undergraduate.

'Bradley took music, opera and ballet', one friend remembered, 'the way other people take opium: he could not have enough.'

When Richard Buckle had brought out the first number of his magazine *Ballet* shortly before the war he got a twelve-page letter from Bradley listing its inaccuracies and misprints. Very sensibly, Buckle enrolled Bradley as a regular contributor, delighted by his 'ant-like industry and perseverance'.

Soon after he joined the library he was given permission to keep his ballet notes in a room in the basement. True to form as an assistant librarian, he took an obsessive interest in the more curious byways of dance, and after the war he had his own column in *Ballet* called 'News from Abroad'. Sacheverell Sitwell said he always turned to it first to see which girls' school had been staging *Scheherazade* in Bechuanaland. He was an unusually acerbic critic, and like many critics thought it unfair if a colleague came under attack. Caryl Brahms, later to write lyrics for the BBC's satirical programme *That Was The Week That Was* in the sixties, was then ballet critic of *The Times*.

Among Bradley's unpublished papers is an entry he received to a competition for readers' 'three worst ballets'. It is from J. M. C. Bernard, and suggests 'a ballet on a theme suggested to Caryl Brahms by a young man who prefers to remain anonymous. The entire action takes place in Miss Brahms's flat. Choreography by Miss Brahms, whose hats are all original models.'

'Mr Bernard's attempt to be funny', Bradley wrote in the magazine, 'is so illegible that I find it difficult to decipher. What I can read strikes me as rather cheap.'

In one of her books with S. J. Simon, *No Nightingales*, Caryl Brahms was quite funny herself at the expense of the library. The Duchesse de la Bazouche is talking to a younger librarian.

> 'You are an imbecile', she screamed, 'I ask for a nottee book by that Miss Austen and you, you bring me ze wishy-washy *Decameron*.'
>
> The learned librarian wiped his brow. 'Madame', he said stiffly, 'the library does not undertake to supply new works of fiction. We have already written to you to that effect. Twice', he added.
>
> 'Fiddles-di-dee!' said the old lady, 'I write to Miss Austen, and zen she will be angry with you and refuse to sell you her nottee books, none of zem.'
>
> The learned librarian attempted a sniff.
>
> 'These light works,' he said, 'Evanescent. No one will ask

for it in six months' time. Really, we are little concerned with this type of writing.'

With the temporary suspension of the entrance fee – membership was four guineas – there was soon a waiting list. There was an influx of academics, in London to do war work. Kathleen Tillotson and her husband found themselves in London together for the first time, and both became members of the library. 'Until then, as working academics, my husband and I had felt really that the London Library was "not for the likes of us".'

The new president would probably have stuck to that view. H. A. L. Fisher had died soon after Hagberg in 1940, and had been succeeded by Lord Ilchester. He was not a natural democrat – 'Communist' fire-watchers were accused when Holland House was hit of letting it burn for some time before they called the fire brigade – and with the old men dead, the committee was dwindling into an insecure little clique of upper-class clubmen who felt threatened by a changing world.

With Purnell almost literally a caretaker librarian, stoking the boilers himself every night in the winter, the inner momentum of the library was already slowing, stunned by the war, before disaster struck.

A member of the library found Purnell sitting on a bench in St James's Park one summer evening in wartime. They walked round the lake together, talking about Purnell's son in the RAF, and the way in which rosebay willowherb had colonised all the bomb sites. Anything was a relief that helped to hide the scars.

Purnell had been to a lecture by Professor Salisbury on 'The Flora of Bombed Areas', and had learned that after the Great Fire of London in 1666 the ruins round St Paul's had become overgrown with London rocket. This plant had now become extremely rare. Rosebay willowherb, on the other hand, was on the increase, having come to the attention of botanists before the war taking over areas of burned heath, 'which had become more frequent since the cigarette and the motor-car'. It was therefore already associated with areas devastated by fire.

Purnell was intrigued by the Professor's having drawn a parallel between the aerial devastation of 'our fair city', and nature's covering the bomb damage by means of the willowherb's airborne seed pods, 'each about a millimetre in length, and carried on a little parachute of seventy long silky hairs that open out in dry air but close when the air is moist'. If the Professor mentioned the willow-herb's more sinister way of spreading underground along its roots Purnell did not talk about it.

They discussed the ragwort, a close runner-up to the willowherb, a native of Sicily. It flourished in the volcanic ash around Mount Etna, and found a sympathetic terrain in our burnt-out London buildings. It first came to Britain in 1794, where it was seen growing on the walls in and around Oxford.

Then they sat on a bench facing Duck Island, and Purnell pointed out the nests of the coots, whose children wore red hats that turned to white as they grew older. 'We watched the diving ducks and the Abyssinian geese, and when I asked Mr Purnell how he had learned all the species by name he said he took good note of any bird that seemed strange to him and then looked it up at the Library.'

An old admiral walked by, greeting Purnell. He was a regular reader, with his wife, in the Reading Room. One evening recently he had been out for a stroll and come back to find his house bombed, his wife dead.

On the evening of 28 February 1944, Lionel Bradley was out reviewing a ballet at Sadler's Wells, and Harold Nicolson described the air raid later that night as 'amazingly beautiful'. During it, a stick of five-hundred-pound high-explosive bombs was released somewhere over Bloomsbury. The first hit the London Library, the last exploded in the road outside St James's Palace, blowing out all the ancient glass, and destroying the windows of the Chapel Royal.

Early next morning Joan Bailey arrived at the corner of Duke of York Street, on the north side of St James's Square, and found it cordoned off by air-raid wardens. A fireman asked her where she was going. She said the London Library, and he shook his head. The library had had a direct hit.

Her first thought was not for the books but for 'poor Mr Purnell'. Allowed through the cordon, she was at first reassured. The façade was still intact, and apart from broken glass and rubble lying on the pavement outside there did not seem to be any very extensive damage. When she walked up the steps through the broken glass and felt the grey dust hanging in the air, she saw that above the entrance hall the library was open to the sky.

Christopher Purnell's daughter Ruth reached the square a few moments later, on her way to work at the Clerical, Medical and General. The first thing she saw was her mother, waving to her from behind a broken window.

The Purnells had been in the basement, and 'a large bit of the ceiling' had fallen on them, but they and the fire-watchers had somehow escaped injury. If it had been released a split second earlier, the bomb would have entirely destroyed the library: a split second later and it would have missed. It had caught the roof at the back of the 1898 stacks and exploded, leaving a tangle of Osborne Smith's steel girders. They stuck out, bare and bent, some of them still supporting bookcases that hung in space above floors littered with plaster, rubble and torn books. The grey dust was everywhere.

Everyone who saw it that morning remembered the twisted steel – one poet imagined the moment of impact, 'books flying like bats past the bent daffodil-stalk of a girder' – and almost immediately everyone began to work. Rain could ruin more books even than had been damaged by the bomb.

Staff and members climbed up and down through the grey dust, stacking books in those parts of the building that still had a roof. Joan Bailey worked with James Lees-Milne and Rose Macaulay, climbing as high as they dared, lifting books out of the hanging shelves and bringing them down. Rose Macaulay was bravest, telling them to hang on to her legs as she leant out into space. One member organised a chain of passers-by, including American servicemen, to hand books down to safety.

Harold Nicolson got there soon afterwards and describes the entrance hall with books dumped everywhere, the counters filled with dust. Purnell took him up to the Reading Room and showed him the hole in the roof, part of a wall hanging sideways and steel bookshelves jagged against the sky. 'All the books in the top store were flung out of their shelves and it will take months to sort them again.'

Then Mr Cox arrived from Wimbledon, wearing a soft black hat and a white silk scarf, looking, as someone said, 'as if he were going to the opera'. The girls found him an armchair and made him a cup of tea. According to one story he went upstairs, and a member met him coming down from the burned-out stacks at the top saying, 'We've lost our Religion!' Another, repeated by more than one witness, was that he sat flabbergasted in his chair, dust everywhere, the grey daylight coming in through the roof, and said, 'It's not what we're used to, you see!'

Something like 16,000 books were destroyed, either in the explosion, by fire, or by the water used to put it out. Purnell showed visitors a memento of 'the most exciting night of his life': a copy of

George Adam Smith's *Modern System and Preaching of the Old Testament* with a piece of shrapnel embedded in it.

Harry Yates Thompson's Aldine *Theocritus* with the Dürer bookplate, given to celebrate peace in 1918, had been evacuated with Hagberg's other treasures at the beginning of the war. Purnell was delighted to find that 'the *Gentleman's Magazine* with Mitford's famous and eloquent review of Nyrene's *Cricketers of my Time* is more or less intact'.

Most of the Biography department had been destroyed, and *The Sunday Times* was particularly distressed about the damage to Theology. 'The contemporary bindings of many of the religious works of the Reformation are spoilt beyond recovery, and some German editions of the early fathers will hardly be used again.'

A notice appeared in *The Times*: 'The London Library – Members are Requested not to ask for Books or Return them until Further Notice.' A printed notice to the same effect was hung on the front door of the library.

Elizabeth Ray remembers two unexpected benefits of the bombing: one was the sudden warmth and friendliness of many of the members who had until then seemed rather cold and stand-offish; the second was that a copy of *Fanny Hill*, entirely undamaged and with charming coloured engravings, was blown from the seclusion of the librarian's cupboard. The girls fell on it, hiding it behind the radiator in the ladies' staff room, and taking turns to read it throughout the lunch hour.

More damage was done during the emergency repairs. An oxyacetylene welder cutting through one of the twisted girders started a fire in the Art Room, and the fire brigade ruined more books putting it out. The rain came, and there was not enough dry space.

Sir Henry Hake, curator of the National Portrait Gallery and a member of the library committee, offered their cellars, and Joan Bailey remembers riding on the back of a cart, her head wrapped in a turban and her clothes grey with dust, as a very old carthorse drew them and the books up into Trafalgar Square. Her most vivid memory, though, is of carrying books past the open door of the office of Sir Henry Hake, 'old fishface', and of his refusing even to say good morning to her.

Committee meetings were held at the National Portrait Gallery until the Prevost Room was repaired. The ceiling had come down and the window had been blown out, but Harry Yates Thompson's marble fireplace was undamaged. Purnell turned up to the first meeting there looking shaken, and they sent him away for a fortnight's holiday.

The library offered the girls a grant of 30/- for clothes they ruined moving the books, and claimed over £8,000 in war damage. The library re-opened in July 1944.

The annual general meeting was postponed until October, and there is a bleak description in a contemporary newspaper report of the scholarly rows of grey heads and bald heads sitting in the semi-darkness of the Reading Room with the windows boarded up, listening to Ilchester's gloomy musings.

'There was a general feeling of justifiable resentment at the infliction of such indignities. £3,000 had been spent on emergency repairs, but with the beginning of the Flying Bomb raids in the early autumn all work had stopped and one heavy rainstorm was reckoned to have done £100 worth of damage.'

In November the committee was back in the Prevost Room, and Harold Nicolson noted in his diary that 'old Mr Deacon', who had worked at the library since 1897, came in to say goodbye. 'Ilchester is charming to him, and he weeps.'

# Buzzard's Ghost

*It must have been about 1960 when, climbing the stairs beyond the Reading Room, I saw a man, book in hand, run down a short flight; pause; throw his head back; gleefully smile; run down that next short flight; again pause, throw back his head, gleefully smile. He was not too tall, well dressed, with hair sleeked back, quite sallow, wearing spectacles and his eyes were rather big, nearly popping. Instantly I identified an American academic enjoying temporary membership. But over the years supposition has strengthened almost to conviction that I watched the frisky T. S. Eliot.*

An Older Member

'Darling Blondy, please accept my congratulations on your election to the London Library,' Evelyn Waugh wrote in November 1946 to Lady Mary Lygon, whose family had sold Beauchamp House to Foster the auctioneer exactly a hundred years before.

I hope you will always remember to behave with suitable decorum in these grave precincts. Always go to the closet appointed for the purpose if you wish to make water. Far too many female members have taken to squatting behind the Genealogy section.

Never write 'balls' with an indelible pencil on the margins of the books provided. Do not solicit the female librarians to acts of unnatural vice. When very drunk it is permissible to fall into a light doze but not to sing. Fireworks are always welcome in the reading-room but they should be of a kind likely to divert the older members rather than to cause permanent damage to the structure.

By observing a few simple rules such as the foregoing you will find yourself perfectly acceptable to the more amorous scholars who abound in the darkened bays.

He also told her that there is a 'very beautiful character' at the library called Mr Cox, but said she should not make jokes about his name.

Jokes were one of the many things the library was short of after the war. The lift was out of action for eight years, books lost in the bombing were hard to replace, and as late as 1949 they were unable to publish a new catalogue because the printers were short of staff. For the first time Russian, Greek, Arabic and Armenian titles were transcribed into their approximate English spelling.

Class warfare had also finally broken out on the committee. When Lady Moray applied for membership she was told, like everyone else, that there was a waiting list. She was very cross: they must understand it was urgent, she had to educate her daughter. Obediently, as Hagberg would have done, Purnell moved her name to the top of the list. A new man, Professor Willoughby, said this was outrageous. Harold Nicolson backed Purnell, and 'much to my amusement a certain heat was generated in that placid Committee'.

Placid it remained most of the time, but the reactionaries were determined to put up a fight, and when Evelyn Waugh talked, in more sober mood, at the annual general meeting, he managed to link the import of bad American films with controls on the supply of paper that were stifling English literature.

A hundred years before, in 1848, the Year of Revolutions, when Chartists were massing in the capital, Panizzi expected the Museum to be sacked, and withdrew to the roof with armed constables, amusing them no end as he chanted in his quaint Italian accent, 'England expect' every man thissa day will a-do his duty!'

Arthur Helps had volunteered to help keep order in the streets, and wrote a pamphlet afterwards, *A Letter from one of the Special Constables*. He imagines his Brother Special confronting a Chartist, and his message is printed in bold italics. '*The evils of the day are not to be met by giving up power but by making more use of it.*' 'If he begins with his Liberty, Equality and Fraternity, tell him *that there is here neither time nor space for such things!*'

He then becomes more conciliatory. 'There is', he says, 'such a thing as civilisation' and the poor stand to lose as much as the rich if it breaks down. No-one who has 'studied the life of the poorer classes' will pretend that they cannot be raised 'many degrees in thought, refinement, and enjoyment'.

'If they were so raised, we might say to the revolutionaries – revolve if you like: in your course you will bring nothing uppermost which we should much fear to see!'

In the past hundred years something at least of this had been achieved, in many cases through the work of writers and politicians who took a leading role in the life of the library. Now, finally, there was a strong Labour Government, and the heirs of the liberal-minded Apostles who had advocated slow organic change were to face the consequences.

There was a ground swell of acceptance: in 1973, for instance, the library began to participate in the national interlending system, so that an unemployed member of any municipal library in the poorest part of the country can get a book, if it is available nowhere else, from St James's Square.

But there were many who were as alarmed as Arthur Helps, and the more obvious effect was to make the library more snobbish, more exclusive and more defensive. This was clear when Purnell had to go.

Cochrane, Bodham Donne, Harrison or Hagberg were chosen from hundreds of candidates. But Purnell's successor as librarian was appointed virtually behind closed doors on the recommendation of Henry Hake. Simon Nowell-Smith was thirty years younger than Hake, and they had struck up a friendship when they were both staying at the Travellers' Club during the Blitz. He was assistant editor of the *Times Literary Supplement*.

Nowell-Smith was a book-lover, an authority on Henry James and later became president of the Bibliographical Society; he had no experience of librarianship. But as he himself pointed out in his notes on the history of the library, he was, like Bodham Donne, a gentleman. This was what the committee wanted. Purnell, according to Nowell-Smith, 'burst into tears whenever they talked about it.' He was worried about money, the pension was not large, and was in the end supplemented by allowing him to stay on for an extra year to work on the catalogue. The atmosphere at Nowell-Smith's appointment in 1950 is well caught by Harold Nicolson.

> Nowell-Smith is introduced to the general committee. We discuss whether we should have a contract, but feel that in a place like the London Library we do not want to reduce our relations to purely legal and commercial ones. We therefore agree that we shall write a minute in which we embody all the conditions and then get Nowell-Smith to write a letter saying he approves of the minutes.

Nowell-Smith himself had decided exactly what their relationship was going to be. 'A Library is either run by the Committee or it is run by the Librarian, and I was determined the London Library was going to be run by the Librarian.'

The committee were very happy at the arrangement, and his short reign at the library was clearly a very agreeable one. He not only revitalised the library's book-buying policy, but he had a fund of entertaining stories, and lectured amusingly about the library all over America. His favourite joke was a letter to the librarian from a member saying, 'Dear Sir, Kindly re-enter Dante's *Inferno*.' The staff had orders that if a particular lady asked to see him in the Librarian's Room he was not thereafter to be disturbed.

He also, regrettably, turned out a great deal of what he considered to be old lumber to do with the history of the library. His rule was to preserve 'one letter' from each of their eminent past members. In many cases these are of no more interest than an autograph book. He and the committee did think, on the other hand, that it was worth preserving a collection of signatures of obscure eighteenth- and nineteenth-century dukes, none of whom had anything to do with the library, each supported by a reproduction of his coat of arms.

In 1951 T. S. Eliot was asked whether he would like to be president, and accepted, according to Harold Nicolson, 'in a curiously stiff note' which he thought 'sounded ungracious'. But at the annual general meeting the following year he was on his feet in the Reading Room arguing in defence of the library under the threat of Socialism.

There was certainly a slightly left-of-centre tone in the account of his speech in the *Evening Standard*. 'While the occasional rattle of the booklift was heard bringing volumes down to the ground floor,' it reported, 'members listened to an address from Mr. Thomas Stearnes Eliot, the American-born poet, who after settling in this country, has made a considerable name for himself. On this occasion Mr. Eliot kept to prose as he delivered in the slightly strangled tone of the English upper class his "testament of faith" in the London Library.'

He had joined many years before, he told them, 'under the sponsorship of the late Sir Sydney Waterlow, one of his many kindnesses to me'. Working in a bank in the City he could only go to libraries on Saturday afternoons, and at the British Museum 'it often happened that I had hardly opened the essential volume for which I had been waiting, when there sounded the familiar warning which corresponds to the phrase "Hurry up, please, it's time." '

He came instead to the London Library. 'I could at my leisure, after lunch on Saturday, rummage the stacks, and emerge with nine or ten volumes to take home with me. Without the London Library, many of my early essays could never have been written.'

He talked very modestly and engagingly, too, about his own library at home in Kensington.

> It includes books which I reviewed years ago and have never consulted since (some of them still containing the label for returning them to *The Times* after the review was written); it includes books which I have bought to read and never opened; it includes books presented by their authors – which I keep, some in the hope of reading them, some out of personal regard for the author, and some out of politeness or prudence. It includes some books which ought to have found their way to Foyle's outdoor bin years ago. I have an accumulation of books so various, so recalcitrant of order, that when I want to consult some book I know I possess, I cannot find it, and have to borrow it from the London Library.

Most of us living in London lived in 'boxes too tight for us'. When he was sitting in the vast smoking room of some large club he could imagine himself the proprietor of a palace: when he came to the London Library he had a better library than the library he would like to own himself. The library took the place of the 'gentleman's library'; it was the private library of every one of its members.

But sooner or later, he said, 'given current tendencies of opinion', someone was going to try either to abolish it or to bring it into the state system. It was very short of money. Could it survive, Eliot asked, and *ought* it to survive?

It was not like the British Museum, obliged to accept, store and catalogue every book that appeared, in danger of being 'buried under an increasing weight of words'. Circulating libraries served a different public. What the London Library most resembled was a municipal public library. Should it therefore become part of the public library system? Many people argue that 'to exclude people from something they cannot pay for is contrary to social justice'. Should St James's Square be thrown open to everyone?

'I do not propose to enlarge my subject to include general affirmations about liberty, equality and privilege: a region of discourse in which passionate prejudice obfuscates counsel and eclipses reason. I am only concerning myself with the special case of libraries.'

It was the very fact that it was not 'thrown open to everyone', Eliot believed, that made the London Library unique. It had what he called 'a certain homogeneity of membership'. 'If this is "privilege", then it is privilege which I defend with complete conviction.'

In what this homogeneity consists would be hard to define: but with great diversity of interests, our membership has always represented the high level of culture and of what I may call serious readership. And without such a membership, the assembling of this collection of books would have been impossible. The Committee, when they buy a book, know, in a sense, for whom they are buying it. I do not believe that there is another library of this size which contains so many of the books which I *might* want, and so few of the books which I cannot imagine anyone wanting; and in saying this I believe that I am speaking simply as a representative member.

These were not the private thoughts of a private man. It was a political statement. Carlyle had imagined the London Library reader as Hero; Hagberg, in his wilder flights of marketing, had imagined the committee as a British Academy. Now all five thousand members were presented to the press as a British Elite, defending Culture against Socialism.

In the Prevost Room the reactionaries held firm. When Walter Besant raised the staff's long-standing grudge about the country house at Elfords, Nowell-Smith was reported to be furious, as was Sir Andrew Rowell from the Clerical, Medical and General next door. Rowell and Harold Nicolson grudgingly agreed to look into it. They decided that the library had been quite right to sell the house, though neither of them seems to have considered what its value would have been as an investment. On the question of the money raised by the sale they were less convincing, but said that taking into consideration the amount of money paid in since to staff pension funds 'no serious fault could be found with the Library'. Nicolson noted: 'We lay the ghost of the Prevost Bequest. Rowell's memorandum is accepted without comment or discussion.'

The year after Eliot's address, Nowell-Smith gave a dinner at the Athenaeum to celebrate the completion of the new catalogue, with Purnell as guest of honour. Harold Nicolson attended it, and was very distressed when 'poor Bradley', still assistant librarian, was taken ill and had to go home. On New Year's Eve, Bradley failed to appear at a party for the staff, and was found by the police dead in his bed on New Year's morning.

In March 1954 Stanley Gillam was appointed in his place. He was a professional librarian, and just what the committee needed to back up Nowell-Smith as the kind of gentleman figurehead Christie had envisaged when the library started. But Nowell-Smith was getting bored and decided to resign.

The committee was still placid: Harold Nicolson complained of his deafness and amnesia; on one occasion he suggested as a possible candidate for the committee, though not in particularly flattering terms, a man who was sitting beside him at the table. Walter Besant finally resigned at the age of eighty-seven. They interviewed one possible candidate for Nowell-Smith's post, but the simplest thing seemed to be to let the deputy take over. So within a year of his appointment as Nowell-Smith's assistant, Gillam found himself, much to his own surprise, librarian of the London Library. Nowell-Smith agreed to come in occasionally 'to advise'.

Then, on April Fools' Day 1957, and without warning, the library got a bill through the letter box from Westminster City Council, asking for £5,000.

They had not paid rates since the Philological and Statistical Societies had moved out eighty years before, claiming exemption under the Learned Societies Act of 1843. Now Section 7 of the Rating and Valuation (Miscellaneous Provisions) Act of 1955 had tightened up exemptions. Mr Buzzard, the long-dead parish clerk of St James's, Piccadilly, was back.

There was immediately outrage in the shires. 'I say, Rupert, the London Library!' George Lyttelton wrote to his literary correspondent Rupert Hart-Davis, now an active member of the committee. 'Have you, as it is, *any* spare five minutes in the week – and at this moment when the poor old institution is under fire from those marble-hearted fiends of the Inland Revenue.' He was particularly cross with lefties who criticised the library for being 'a sanctum for the well-to-do', and failing to 'bring Shakespeare to the costermongers'.

I have never belonged, as I never lived in London, but my grandfather was one of Carlyle's first associates in it. I once met old Hagberg Wright, who struck me as the rudest man I had ever seen – till I met his brother Almroth who easily dead-heated. How I do hate the recurrent evidences of a general trend to diminish, to pare away, destroy all standards save those of the damned 'common man'.

*The Times* agreed, though not in so many words. The library was being asked 'to pay its way or go to the wall', Westminster City Council was motivated by 'naked materialism', and would be quite happy to see it turned into another office block if it brought in more money. Unexpectedly, from a paper then selling itself on the slogan that Top People Took *The Times*, the leader writer adopted a certain amount of egalitarian camouflage: 'scholars and research workers' relied on the library, as Hagberg had said, for the 'tools of their trade'; such craftsmen were 'seldom in easy circumstances'.

Somehow the turn was too sudden: Hagberg, admittedly, had used that kind of language in an essay for limited circulation, but all his life at the library he had emphasised in his sales campaigns the Men of Eminence Caressing the Rare Incunabula aspect of life in St James's Square. Eliot if anything had given it an extra charge of Cultural Elitism. Now the spectacle of members wringing their hands in the tumbril inevitably produced a few cruel chuckles, and more importantly influenced the ideas of some very stupid lawyers who knew the library only by repute.

The real problem was not rates but money, and an offer from George Lyttelton to talk to Sir C. Fison – 'if only the L.L. dealt in chemical manure rather than books, hopes might be bright' – was not much help. The committee decided to appeal. They paid £1,000 into court, and engaged a barrister, Geoffrey Lawrence QC, then fresh from his triumph in what Gillam remembered as 'that awful doctor case', when he had defended Dr John Bodkin Adams, accused of murdering rich old ladies in Eastbourne.

Lawrence offered his services free of charge, although Gillam felt some sympathy for his junior, Frank Stockdale. 'He would normally have got a rake-off. I think we made Lawrence an honorary Life Member, which was all right for him, but his poor old Number Two didn't get anything at all.'

Stockdale none the less opened the case, quoting from Christie's original prospectus for the library in 1841, and summarised the original Act under which exemption could be claimed for any land, house or building belonging to any society instituted for the purpose of science, literature, or fine arts, provided it was supported wholly or in part by annual voluntary subscriptions.

Gillam then went into the box, and, prompted by Stockdale, told the court that the library spent about £6,000 a year on buying about six thousand books. Another thousand books a year were donated to the library. There were about five thousand members, and some commercial subscribers.

Mr Rougier, for Westminster City Council, Buzzard reincarnate, asked Gillam to confirm that the literature accumulated by the library was not available 'to the whole world' but only to members. Gillam agreed. It would also be true to say, Mr Rougier argued, that a large number of members took out books to read 'for their own satisfaction'. Gillam had to admit that this was true. The hearing was adjourned for nearly three weeks, then the appeal was rejected.

Under a headline IN DARKEST WESTMINSTER, *The Times* said that Westminster City Council and the Inland Revenue were making a 'shocking mess' of the case, criticised Rougier, and asked in a kind of stage-Victorian apostrophe whether 'the dregs of forensic sophistry had ever been drained in a more impudent fashion'.

There was now war between the private and the public libraries, and the spectre raised by Eliot, of St James's Square becoming a branch of the Westminster City Library, began to look alarmingly real.

Shaw-Kennedy, chairman of Westminster's finance committee, understandably needled by the press coverage, wrote to the papers pointing out that Westminster City Council was spending £148,000 a year on their own public libraries, and that letting the London Library off paying its rates would mean them dipping even deeper into other ratepayers' pockets.

Meanwhile debts were accumulating. Harold Nicolson, having finally accepted that he was too deaf to know what was going on any more, gave up the chairmanship and Rupert Hart-Davis took over. One of the committee wrote to him, he told George Lyttelton, to say, 'Thank God we've got a Chairman at last!' He announced that they would appeal again, this time to the Lands Tribunal. The appeal would be well publicised, and they would produce as their star witness T. S. Eliot himself.

Rupert Hart-Davis was questioned first. What did he mean when

190

he called it a 'specialised library'? Were 'steps taken on application forms' to ensure that its members were specialists? The tribunal had the impression that anyone could join, 'whether they were interested in literature or not'. Hart-Davis thought about this, and said that if they applied for membership of a library the assumption was that they were.

The tribunal then moved on to the question of whether or not the library was maintained wholly by voluntary contributions. Simon Nowell-Smith was asked why it was that members seemed to prefer giving books to giving money. His answer did not please those trying to present the library as a proletarian hire shop. 'There is a kind of snobbery about it. I myself have never given the library any money, but I am rather proud of having given it some books.' Then, to use a phrase of his own, 'dropping a few names', Nowell-Smith told them that Carlyle had given the library all the books he had bought in connection with his work on *The French Revolution*, and that Edmund Gosse presented them with his collection of Scandinavian works.

Giving books, the tribunal decided, did not count as 'supporting the Library by voluntary contributions', whoever might have given them.

T. S. Eliot then went into the box. He had warned Hart-Davis that he was having trouble with his false teeth, 'which did not allow him to eat raspberries in public', but he did his best. Jeremy Hutchinson, who had the opportunity of calling him in the *Lady Chatterley* case, had decided he would be 'a disaster', and so it proved.

He gave them an almost exact re-run of his address to the library. He told them about his troubles at the British Museum, his rummaging in the stacks at St James's Square on Saturday afternoons, his emerging with his arms full of books. He then moved on to the attack. The members were 'the elite of culture'. 'The life of literature in a country depends on three groups of people: the few great writers, the secondary authors, and the cultivated readers. The last group is that core of the public that encourages good literature, and through whom good taste in literature is indirectly spread.'

The tribunal put their heads together, clearly aware that they did not belong to that core of the public through whom good taste was indirectly spread, and reserved their decision.

The annual general meeting that summer was the shortest on record, lasting less than half an hour: the tribunal had still not given its verdict, and the mood was gloomy in the extreme. An elderly member called Waley-Cohen complained that he had found a book in the library that was full of anti-French propaganda and demanded it be sent back to the publishers.

Then Eliot stood up. He spoke despairingly of 'all the forces making for the deterioration of culture, all the mass media of entertainment which are in danger of becoming agents for the diffusion of illiteracy'. As the population relentlessly increased, so the proportion of people of culture who supported and maintained the civilisation of a country was dwindling. The disappearance of the library would be a catastrophe, the consequences of which could hardly be measured.

Rupert Hart-Davis turned up in a Brigade of Guards tie and spoke, according to one observer, in a voice that would have done credit to any sergeant-major at Wellington Barracks. He told them that the rates remained unpaid, that the library was running at a loss. They needed an extra £13,000 a year to meet their commitments, the annual subscription should be raised to eight guineas. There was a vote, and the members agreed almost unanimously that it should not.

Less than a week later, the tribunal ruled that the London Library was not instituted exclusively for the purpose of science, literature or the fine arts, but 'for the personal convenience and gratification of its members'. George Lyttelton wrote to say that he was 'black with sympathetic rage', and quoted Housman:

> The signal-fires of warning
> They blaze, but none regard;
> And on through night to morning
> The world runs ruinward.

Now in desperate straits, Rupert Hart-Davis and the committee took the appeal to the High Court, where it was heard by three judges.

Lawrence did his best. The tribunal's interpretation of the old statute was absurd and illiberal, no-one could doubt that Carlyle and the founders had the welfare of the general public at heart, that the library should be actively encouraged as a place of learning. Members of the library were 'making themselves better members of the community'.

The tribunal had claimed there was 'a personal gratification enjoyed by a limited class of persons known as members and therefore that the Library was instituted for the collateral purpose of entertaining its members'. Lawrence conceded that this might have been a collateral or incidental intention of the founders, but insisted that the library had an essential purpose which was more serious. Would it, he asked, verging on irony, be a collateral objective not exclusively literary if padded chairs were provided in the Reading Room? If central heating were supplied in the library during the cold months?

He tried, reasonably enough, to establish a distinction between what he called 'the sincere and disinterested pursuit of literature', and 'personal recreation and amusement'. Lord Justice Hodson did not think it 'assisted' to talk about amusement, 'since some people might be more amused than others'. Lawrence persisted. There was a difference between passing the time with a book and pursuing serious literature. Hodson said he didn't know what the difference was, but he thought nobody would 'do it at all' – pursue literature – if it wasn't for pleasure, 'unless you were very highly paid for it'.

Lawrence made a final sentimental appeal. 'A library is not a sterile collection of leather, paper and cloth-covering but something that can be translated into living substances by those who read and enjoy the books.' No-one quite knew what he meant by 'living substances', but there was a thin echo of the old Tree Igdrasil. He claimed that all the readers' privileges, including the right to 'read books, to take them down from a shelf and handle them lovingly', were subsidiary to the main purpose of the library, for which it had been founded, and for which it had for nearly a century been declared exempt from paying rates.

Widgery, for the enemy, went back to W. D. Christie's original proposal 'to supply the great want in London of a library embracing every part of literature and philosophy, and from which books might be taken for use by members to their own homes'. Nobody could read into those words 'an exclusive desire to promote literature'. If the founders of the library had intended to provide rare books which might otherwise be lost to posterity, or to encourage authors, or to teach literature, that would have been another kettle of fish. But these were not the main, let alone the exclusive objects of the library. It had obviously always been intended from the outset to be a members' library, not for the benefit of the public or even a substantial section of it.

Their lordships conferred, and Lord Justice Hodson gave their judgment. The case rested on the purposes for which the library had been founded. It had been founded, they decided, not primarily for the promotion and advancement of literature, but to enable persons interested in reading to indulge that interest. They therefore rejected the appeal.

The next morning *The Times* had a headline PHILISTINES REJOICE. The library was £20,000 in debt.

# Under the Hammer

*It would be a sad thing if the gates of this paradise, which owes its existence to a man of letters who suffered from a shortage of books, should now be closed to his successors.*

*The Times*

Mr Cox had finally retired in the early fifties after being at the library, incredibly, for nearly seventy years. He still affected a wing collar, and talked about the days when he fetched books for Lord Albemarle who had fought at Waterloo. Walter Pater's gloves changed colour from lemon-yellow to lilac in his memory, and more details of Bryan Hunt's suicide came back to him: Carlyle now 'burst in on the Librarian in a fine rage', shouting, 'Nice to think I can't get my papers just because some confounded relative of Leigh Hunt has gone and shot himself.'

The old snob eventually got his reward. When Queen Mary wanted books from the library it was Cox who found them for her, and in his last years a Daimler would occasionally arrive at the library to take him to tea at Clarence House.

The new librarian Gillam, too, had worked in a library since he was a boy: his father took him into the Bodleian, he was fascinated by the manuscripts displayed under glass, the bustle and the atmosphere, and wanted nothing more than to be one of the boys carrying books about. 'I remember thinking "This is the place for me!"' He joined what he still calls 'Bodley' when he was sixteen.

St James's Square was, as Mr Cox would have said, not what he was used to. 'One of the things at Bodley was that all the books were counted every year, all the shelf-marks checked and so forth. At the London Library there are no shelf-marks. I asked them, "How do you check the shelves?" and they said, "We can't."' But he was a natural conservative, and he loved the atmosphere. 'There was a marvellous old Head Porter, Jim Hyde. He stoked the boiler, packed the books, swept the floor. He'd do anything, Hyde would.'

There was still, in winter, a fire in the Reading Room for Hyde to stoke, and downstairs the old iron kitchen range was kept alight all through the winter. Gillam particularly liked the mood in the entrance hall, with Cox, before his retirement, wheezing away at

the Issue Desk on the right as you went in, with his little booklift
rattling up and down behind him, and the girls taking Returns
behind the counter on the left. 'It was so nice when you swept out
and swept in, quite regally, up the front stairs. That was before they
put the fire doors in.'

He got on relatively well with the committee, and liked Harold
Nicolson 'enormously' – as chairman, Nicolson took him out to
lunch – though he found Sir Andrew Rowell 'a strong character'.
Rowell resigned from the committee shortly after Gillam got there
when the library refused to let the Clerical, Medical and General
buy part of their property in Duke Street.

Gillam also enjoyed ordering the new books with very little
interference from the committee. 'Publishers' reps would call in;
that had been going on since Hagberg's day. Sometimes we got
books at reduced rates, sometimes for nothing. There were no
university faculties breathing down your neck as there were at
Bodley. I had totally free rein. The Committee enjoyed their meetings as a social occasion, but they never seemed to offer anything
terribly constructive.'

Gillam was slightly overwhelmed, as Bodham Donne had been,
by the tone of some of the members. Raymond Mortimer seemed to
take it as a personal insult if a book he wanted was out, and many
were 'a bit crusty'. The job of greeting members in the entrance hall
he left very happily to the assistant librarian, Oliver Stallybrass.
Stallybrass looked like an eccentric young professor, with a bushy
beard that Nowell-Smith had tried unsuccessfully to make him
shave off when he first arrived, saying he didn't mind beards on
himself but he didn't like them on other people. Stallybrass was a
keen cyclist and mountaineer, and came to the library in sandals
and strange homespun tunics found for him by his Norwegian wife
Gunnvor.

As a boy at Winchester he wanted to be a schoolmaster, but
found trying to keep order at Portsmouth Grammar School too
much for him and joined the library. He was colourful and out-
going, and gave musical evenings at his home in Sydenham Hill
where he sat happily playing the piano – 'appallingly' according to
one friend – accompanying singers and dispensing small glasses of
brown sherry. Thirty years later people's faces still brighten when
they talk about him.

He was a favourite of writers who used the library, and
Masefield wrote him a parody in gratitude:

If we were in a pavender,
A pavender or pub,
I'd pledge you in a javender,
A javender or jubbe,
Or orange-juicy shravender,
Rum-shravender or shrub,
For taking so much travender,
Such travender or troub.

In his correspondence with John Betjeman, it was Stallybrass who wrote the parody:

Sir J. Betjeman, Sir J. Betjeman
Disarming and charming with verses that scan
What ingenuous, tenuous jingles are these
That I strike from my portable Underwood's keys

Like Jones he longed to run the library. He was, it is true, impulsive and impractical: his wife describes a dinner party at their home at which he and five old friends from Winchester were trying without success to do his son's eleven-plus exam. Suddenly they discovered a skylight was leaking, and cheered on by his friends Stallybrass climbed out on to the roof. When she at last persuaded him to come in out of the rain he had already put his foot through the skylight, and was about to test his mountaineering skills by roping himself to some precarious lead pipes which would certainly have come away from the wall and killed him.

In such a stable institution as the library he was valued for his flair and theatrical dash: when an American visitor once asked him if he was a celebrity, his answer was, 'Not yet!'

Most journalists thought the library was a Good Thing. Lawyers might think it was a stuck-up institution that needed taking down a peg but journalists had always been charmed into printing Hagberg's stories, and the more literary ones had been using the library since it opened as an ordinary place of work.

All the serious newspapers were sympathetic, and the *Manchester Guardian* managed a lament.

The last appeal is lodged in vain,
    And justice deems it fit and fair
That now Westminster may distrain
    On Number One, St James's Square.

The battle of the books is lost,
  No quality of mercy shown;
The Library to meet the cost
  Henceforth on charity is thrown.

One ancient tenant in the square
  Served with the city council's writ,
While Chatham House, next door they spare
  And the Arts Council, opposite.

Why send the bailiffs to the door
  Of this old haunt of learned men?
They never knock at Number Four,
  Or ring the bell at Number Ten.

St James's Square sends out a call
  The fight for life is now begun.
Westminster Council never shall
  Put out the light at Number One!

This produced a letter the next day from the Arts Council at Number Four, pointing out that they had never been exempt from paying rates, and another from the library, explaining that they lived at Number Fourteen. But the *Manchester Guardian*'s heart was in the right place, and they printed an appeal for money to be sent to the correct address.

Writers, obviously, supported the library. John Masefield, by now a very old man, had written Stallybrass about a hundred and fifty letters in the last two years asking for information about everything from windmills to the rigging of sailing ships, and was now persuaded by Hart-Davis to write to *The Times*: 'What the London Library has been to writers this century is beyond telling. I have met with nothing like it elsewhere in the world and hope that so glorious a generous thing may meet with the generosity that is so often this country's glory.' Eliot himself was asked to launch a disaster fund, promising that once the debt of £20,000 had been settled, the Library's future could be secured.

Hart-Davis worked extraordinarily hard. Having given up drinking, he agreed to have dinner at the House of Commons with Leslie Hale, MP for Oldham West, 'a vigorous, frank, engaging fellow – a country solicitor from Leicestershire who has the reputation of speaking faster than any other M.P.' and thirty-six other MPs who were members of the library. He woke next morning with a split-ting hangover.

Harold Nicolson suggested they rope in Winston Churchill, who had been a member for sixty years; Hart-Davis talked to Lady Churchill, and a letter was drafted for him to consider. 'The debt of those', Churchill finally wrote, 'who have benefited over the years from the services of this famous institution is great. The closing of this most worthy foundation would be a tragedy. I earnestly hope that the appeal will be generously answered.' It was.

BBC researchers had been using the library for years. When a first edition of *The Rubáiyát of Omar Khayyám* was shown on television, it was the library's copy, and the corporation agreed to give £1,000. They asked Hart-Davis if the library would mind if they told the newspapers. He said on the contrary, it might encourage other people. The fund soon reached £7,000.

Christie's offered their saleroom for a charity auction, and on Nowell-Smith's old principle that there was a kind of snobbery about giving things rather than money, establishment artists as well as collectors were soon queuing up to compete.

Despite Cox's rudeness in the past, J. B. Priestley gave them the typescript of his play *Eden End*, Edith Sitwell *A Song of the Cold*, and Somerset Maugham the manuscript of his novel *Up at the Villa*. Aldous Huxley, L. P. Hartley, Graham Greene, Robert Graves, Lawrence Durrell, Vita Sackville-West, Edmund Blunden, Raymond Mortimer and H. E. Bates all presented manu-scripts.

John Betjeman gave them 'A Subaltern's Love Song', Evelyn Waugh a manuscript of *Scott-King's Modern Europe*, Stephen Spender offered fifty-seven pages of 'Scraps', including sketches for *Trial of a Judge*, Arthur Waley his pen and pencil drafts of three poems translated from the Chinese. Stracheys and Wilberforces came forward with manuscripts by their distinguished ancestors, as well as Samuel Butler's portable inkstand and soap dish.

There were rare books and manuscripts from individuals and antiquarian bookshops; Robert Birley, headmaster of Eton, gave a volume of Herodotus, and there was even a book given by Cambridge University Library. Most of the expensive galleries spared an old master, and there were pictures from Augustus John and Barbara Hepworth; from Vanessa Bell, Mark Gertler and Duncan Grant; from Graham Sutherland and John Piper. Henry Moore brought along a bronze.

What Gillam called 'the stars of the show' were the manuscript of E. M. Forster's *A Passage to India*, Eliot's *The Waste Land*, the original manuscript of which had been lost, and which Eliot had spent his holiday in Morocco copying out specially for the sale, and a Sheffield-plate wine cooler circa 1820 presented by the Queen Mother. The Queen herself sent a book from Queen Victoria's library about Benvenuto Cellini published in Paris in 1884 and stamped with the royal cipher. 'This was Harold Nicolson's doing', Hart-Davis told Lyttelton, 'and the publicity value should be considerable.'

The Queen Mother, who had succeeded George VI as patron of the library, had, like everyone else, been approached directly, and said in a letter from her private secretary that she had been 'following the difficulties and tribulations of the Library of which she and her family had made such real use'. It was, whatever the more questionable motives of some individual donors, an astonishing vindication of Hagberg's marketing, even of Eliot's belief in the library as representative of the Elite.

Stallybrass was asked to prepare the Forster *A Passage to India* manuscript for the sale and he was a natural choice to deal with the press in their time of trouble. 'When we have what appears to be the only copy of a book we let *anyone* see it. That must surely remove all tags of snobbishness.' The complexity of Forster's manuscript, its corrections and the evidence of green ink or pencil that he used to date its different stages made it an ideal story for the columnists.

Stallybrass explained how the papers arrived at the library, 'a jigsaw puzzle of some five hundred pieces', which Forster told him 'he might feel tempted to lose'. Piety, as he put it, prevailed. 'Only two blank pieces of paper and a few rusty paper clips have been discarded, and a pattern had finally emerged.'

Forster had begun the book in 1913 when he got home from India, and had taken it up again, after a second visit, in 1923. It was written on paper of different sizes, and there were a great many lines crossed out and corrected. As Forster himself put it, 'Scriggles surge up from the margin, they extend tentacles, they interbreed.' Forster called his own handwriting 'cacography, if there is such a word'. Stallybrass confirmed that there was such a word, and laboured through it, identifying spelling mistakes, and noting improvements.

The sale was to take place at Christie's in June at nine o'clock in the evening, and the idea was to make it a spectacular social event. Invitations were sent out, and hearts in the librarian's office sank as the replies were opened. The American Ambassador, together with his wife Mrs Whitney, 'regretted exceedingly' that he could not be there. The Duke of Wellington 'much regretted that he was unable to have the pleasure of accepting their kind invitation.' Peter Calvocoressi, now chairman, wrote to thank his own committee for their invitation but regretted he was unable to accept it. Sir Kenneth and Lady Clark had a previous engagement. So had the Gaitskells, the Churchills, L. P. Hartley, Rosamund Lehmann, Sir Compton and Lady Mackenzie, Dame Edith Sitwell, J. B. Priestley, Vita Sackville-West, Leonard Woolf and Vanessa Bell. Evelyn Waugh wrote to Nancy Mitford to say he 'rather longed to go, but shan't. I think the prices will cause much jealousy among our confrères and consoeurs.'

But Graham Greene came, and there were enough grandees to make it worth while for the gossip columnists. Probably more important there were enough dealers, including two from New York, Lew David Feldman and Philip Duschnes, to set the committee's pulses beating a little faster.

Even Stanley Gillam, normally shy, enjoyed it. 'Dinner jackets were worn', he remembers, 'and refreshments provided.' There was free champagne. Unmanned by Harold Nicolson's preamble to the catalogue – if the library closed 'educated opinion throughout the world would regard such a catastrophe as a reproach to British Learning' – and rendered unsteady by the champagne, buyers were expected to spend freely. The week before, there had been a sale in the same room in aid of the National Libraries Appeal, which raised £5,218. Hart-Davis and the committee were hoping for a little more than that.

The Queen Mother's wine cooler went for £30, the Queen's monogrammed Benvenuto Cellini for £70. Lew David Feldman of New York, staying at the Westbury Hotel specially for the sale, soon showed his hand. When they got to Eliot's handwritten copy of *The Waste Land*, the bidding rose to £1,000 in ten seconds. When it finished at £2,800, knocked down to Mr Feldman, Eliot was observed to smile at his young wife, apparently satisfied. 'The audience clapped', Hart-Davis reported, 'and the old boy beamed modestly.'

There were disappointments. Robert Birley's Herodotus was knocked down for £10, Vanessa Bell's *Snow in the Garden* for £30, and Duncan Grant's *Peaklets in Summer* for £35. A first edition of James Joyce's *Pomes Penyeach*, given by Janet Adam Smith, made only £5.

John Betjeman's 'A Subaltern's Love Song' – 'Miss Joan Hunter Dunn, Miss Joan Hunter Dunn' – fetched £130. Graham Greene watched his manuscript and corrected typescript of *The Complaisant Lover* go for £350, with the consolation that Priestley's *Eden End* only raised £60. The Somerset Maugham made £1,100, Lytton Strachey's manuscript of *Queen Victoria* £1,800. Evelyn Waugh was probably wise not to come as his original handwritten draft of *Scott-King's Modern Europe* went for only £160.

Feldman was beaten to a collection of manuscript notes by T. E. Lawrence, which went to his New York rival Philip Duschnes for £3,800, but came back to win by paying the highest price ever recorded for the work of a living writer when he successfully bid £6,500 for Forster's manuscript of *A Passage to India*.

The sale made £25,632. Hart-Davis announced the result to George Lyttelton with four exclamation marks, and Lyttelton said he deserved a knighthood. It was enough to pay off the library's debts and arrears of rates, and to invest £10,000 for the future.

The Christie's sale, very indirectly, produced a tragedy. Oliver Stallybrass, having prepared the Forster manuscript, became increasingly obsessed with Forster and his work. Initially, as he himself told the story, he had made an arrangement with Joan Bailey that when they were called to assist members she could have Laurence Olivier if he could have E. M. Forster. Joan Bailey still remembers with a thrill the gentle pressure of the great actor's hand on her back as she guided him round the stacks. The first encounter between Stallybrass and E. M. Forster was nothing like as successful. They talked about the relative merits of living authors, and Stallybrass, always impulsive, told Forster that in his opinion the greatest writer alive was Joyce Cary. Forster noted the occasion only briefly in his diary, describing him as a 'silly young man'.

But in preparing the manuscript for sale he had made his mark as an editor, and he was soon flying to Texas to work on more Forster papers. He continued to work at the library, but in 1962 it became clear to him that he would never be librarian: Gillam was still a relatively young man and showed no sign of leaving. Stallybrass told his wife that he was fed up with filing books away; he wanted to make them.

His time at the library had not been as easy as it might have seemed. When he first arrived he found himself working for Lionel Bradley, who had been sacked from his job in Liverpool following a complaint from Stallybrass's father. Nor had he got on well with the librarian, who had a reputation for remoteness and tactlessness, and it was only after Gillam had what amounted to a nervous breakdown – he was a keen Scoutmaster, and two of his Scouts were drowned – that he began to take Stallybrass in any way into his confidence, and appointed him his deputy.

Alan Secker of Secker & Warburg had been trying to seduce him away from the library for some time, and Stallybrass now gave in. Life outside the library was obviously draughty and unprotected. Colleagues who worked with him at Secker said he was badly treated: his enthusiasms were often impractical and unlikely to make a lot of money, and after two years he left to become a freelance editor.

He had continued to work on his Forster research, and edited the Festschrift for his ninetieth birthday, *Aspects of E. M. Forster*, to which he contributed a detailed study of variations in the texts of *A Passage to India*. His agent, Andrew Best of Curtis Brown, suggested him to King's College, Cambridge, as editor of the Abinger Edition. It was a vast undertaking, and Stallybrass took it very seriously, feeling it was his duty to read every word that Forster had ever written.

He had also taken on another immense task, for Alan Bullock, of editing his *Dictionary of Philosophical Ideas*. It was a job that frequently reduced him to despair, trying to put together the systems of thought of two hundred and fifty individuals in some kind of unified style as a work of reference. He promised it in three years, and took seven.

Andrew Best was with him when Stallybrass finally took the completed *Dictionary* to Collins, his publishers. There were a dozen huge folders of typescript, and he delivered it in a wheelbarrow. They were greeted by Billy Collins. He appeared not to notice the wheelbarrow but flourished in one hand a slim manuscript. 'A new book by Mother Teresa – straight from Calcutta!' Collins then sat on the book for three months without writing to him, all of which contributed to Stallybrass's gloom.

He had suffered from depression all his life, an introvert, as

Andrew Best remembers him, 'with an extrovert's manner'. What happened as he became more and more involved at Cambridge with the Forster edition is still not entirely clear. Best is convinced they all underestimated how hard he was working. 'I don't think any of us appreciated how much detail, how much fine labour went into editing a manuscript like *Howard's End*.' Gunnvor, his wife, remembers that four people were engaged to take over his work.

In 1978 he left home in Sydenham Hill with nothing but a knapsack. He had fallen in love, and his friends thought he had gone slightly mad. Andrew Best remembers that 'without Gunnvor he seemed completely rudderless'.

A few months later a package was left at Curtis Brown's offices in Craven Hill, Paddington, addressed in his own handwriting. It was his manuscript translations of Knut Hamsun, but without any note. Andrew Best and his secretary were alarmed. Shortly afterwards Best got a letter from Oliver Stallybrass staying that by the time he received it, he would be dead. He had put his head on a railway line at Paddington Station. At his funeral in a crowded crematorium chapel Andrew Best read a poem by D. H. Lawrence that might provide a fitting epitaph for all librarians.

> Not I, not I
> But the wind that blows through me . . .

Nearly twenty years later his widow, looking out over the quiet garden of their beautiful Edwardian house on Sydenham Hill, was still bewildered by it. 'Oliver had to try everything for himself. His nanny said to him once, "Don't touch the iron, it's hot!" Oliver touched it; he swallowed his tears and hid his hand. He was vulnerable, gullible, he was working very hard: Oliver confused himself. A lesser man would have survived.' Then, after a long silence, she said, 'I think Forster understood the problem, Oliver did not.'

Then she took down two folded sheets from behind a jar on the kitchen shelf, and read from a photostat copy of a letter Forster wrote to Naomi Mitchison about her story 'Maiden Castle': 'If we have once given our heart to a person, or a hope, it matters very much if we withdraw it, the barbarians say. Whereas to the civilised man life is full of justifiable treacheries.'

A less well-publicised sale was to follow six years later. The money from Christie's was already fast disappearing: books were getting more and more expensive, and Gillam admits that they were constantly having to dip into what capital there was left even to pay the wages. 'It did look pretty grim.'

Poking through the library's safe one morning Gillam came across the library's treasures. The Aldine *Theocritus* given by Harry Yates Thompson, the Fourth Folio Shakespeare given by Philip Cohen, Henry the Eighth's *Assertio Septem Sacramentorum adversus Martin Lutherum*, which earned him the title of Defender of the Faith, published in London in July 1521, bound in the original calf and stamped with the King's arms. There were altogether eighty-eight early printed books, including bibles printed at Basel in 1474, Venice in 1475 and Nuremberg in 1477, and a single hand-copied volume of the Chinese encyclopedia, the *Yung Lo Ta Tien*.

The encyclopedia originally ran to almost a million pages, and was commissioned during the Ming Dynasty. Only three copies ever existed, and two of these were destroyed on the fall of the dynasty in 1643. This single volume belonged to a third set which was kept in a building next to the British Legation in Peking. During the Boxer Rising in 1900 the house was set on fire, and nearly five hundred volumes were lost in the flames: thirteen volumes were saved. Five are in the British Museum, seven in the Bodleian Library at Oxford. The London Library's copy still bore traces of fire and water.

'They were covered in dust. Nobody ever looked at them. A man from Sotheby's came round. I suggested to the Committee that they sold them.' The committee, described by Rupert Hart-Davis at the time as being 'like lumps of driftwood, moving sluggishly with the current,' agreed.

The Aldine *Theocritus* returned to Nuremberg. Harry Yates Thompson had bought it for £260 at the same auction rooms at the end of the First World War; now it sold for £26,000. Many of the bibles went to Texas, and the entire sale raised £65,000. It was, as Gillam said, 'quite a morning'.

# Friends in Need

*Here one roams at will about grilled galleries, reading what one chooses, removing books by armfuls and leaving them scattered on tables to find their own way back, or taking them away, either after being entered in ledgers if one is a person of probity or concealed in despatch cases if one is a thief . . .*

Rose Macaulay

In 1962 Graham Greene resigned from the library. He was in the habit of sending his secretary in to collect books, and Gillam had forbidden her to roam about the stacks as she was not a member. Nor, it turned out when his resignation came to be entered in the books, was Graham Greene. His first wife had taken out membership early in the war and he had used it ever since.

Gillam was trying to protect the books from thieves and vandals. This was not in itself a new problem. In Harrison's time there was one member who found a particular book too heavy and tore it up into more convenient twenty-page instalments. Another, according to Hagberg, disgusted by its contents, hurled the library's copy of *Mein Kampf* into the Atlantic. A third, more seriously unhinged, made a point whenever he finished a London Library book of throwing it in the Thames.

Hagberg took a long view of the problem, and liked to quote an inscription found on a clay tablet belonging to an early Assyrian library, cursing any thief with destruction by Ashur and Belit. He listed the things that happened to books: they fell down behind bookcases, they were left on trains and in taxis, forgotten in gardens and foreign hotels, or damaged by smokers. But most were 'taken out unentered', which usually meant stolen. 'Thus this inanimate object in which human thought – that precious life blood of the master spirit – is carried down from one century to another runs a number of dangers before it returns, if ever, to its owner.'

But the dangers were now far greater. Gillam's first idea when he took over was to put a turnstile in the entrance hall: this incurred universal fury. 'I suppose people felt the London Library would be a less welcoming place with a turnstile.' He then started asking members for their membership cards, and was bellowed at by several purple-faced old members who told him they'd been coming to the library before he was born. After that he seems to have withdrawn into his little office upstairs in a mood of baffled fatalism.

Some of his difficulties were of a very traditional kind. He wrote repeatedly to an old and famously vague Jesuit, Father Anthony Stephenson, who taught theology at Exeter, asking for books to be returned, and eventually telephoned the university to leave a message. He dictated the list of books that were overdue, a secretary noted them down, and knowing Father Stephenson was coming in to celebrate Mass, left the list on top of his prayer book. As a result the old Jesuit surprised the congregation by announcing that 'their prayers today were asked for the London Library, and for the return of the following books . . . '

Even when books came back, they were sometimes bulging with matchsticks or hairpins that had been used as bookmarks. In one book Rose Macaulay left a very private letter, half-written, apparently breaking off a relationship; Joan Bailey found it after her death, and on her own initiative burned it.

When June Knox-Mawer, interviewing Joan Bailey for a recent BBC radio programme about the library, asked her whether she had found other letters in books Joan replied, 'Oh yes, and sometimes *French* letters!' This exchange did not form part of the edited broadcast.

But by Gillam's time, with very little control of who got into the building and hypodermic syringes being left in the lavatories, there was a feeling, as one member of the committee put it, 'that things had got terribly bad, that another kind of world had caught up with us'.

The staff found themselves doing detective work. Joan Bailey noticed there were a lot of books missing to do with the Ionian Islands, and wrote to local second-hand booksellers asking if they had replacements. An ominously complete list arrived from a shop in Charing Cross Road. All the library's labels had been skilfully removed and the page-stamps steamed out, but Douglas Matthews managed to identify them from the faint impression of the stamp on a subsequent page.

They had been stolen by an expert, a young man who worked in a bookshop in Norwich. He had also looted the Norfolk and Norwich Library, taking only books he knew to be valuable, and his entire haul had brought him £25,000. Of these, nearly three-quarters were recovered from a rented villa in Corfu. Sentencing him to eighteen months' imprisonment the judge said it was 'incredibly distressing' that a young man of his talent, ability and education should have to go to prison, and that he had no doubt he would do well in life.

Two years later, in 1978, Joan Bailey was going round turning off lights in the stacks, and sensed she had left someone in the dark. It was a young man who had taken out temporary membership, which did not allow him to use the open shelves. He had, as she remembered it, 'a funny flat oblong shape in the front of his sweater'. He told her he had lost his cheque book, and she suggested they go to the front desk to report it. He reluctantly agreed, no cheque book had been found, and he left the library.

When she went back to the shelves she found several volumes of prints and early photographs stuffed down behind the books, all torn apart and with little more than the covers remaining. She told Gillam she wished she had 'looked up his jumper'. He laughed, seemed at first disinclined to do anything about it, but in the end agreed to tell the police, who traced some of the prints to a dealer in Islington.

'It became clear they had a lot of our prints,' Gillam remembers, 'and I think the print dealer was put in jug overnight. One Saturday morning I was asked to go along to the shop in mufti. If the suspect came in I was to blow my nose and the police would descend. Unfortunately he came into the shop, recognised me and ran off.'

The thief, they discovered later, went to Yugoslavia on a forged passport and was only arrested on the way back when he started shouting at immigration officials in Dover making trouble about his young Yugoslav companion, who in the heat of the moment called him by his real name. He too got eighteen months. The damage he had done to the library's books was estimated at over £100,000.

Gillam's troubles were not confined to the books. On one occasion the central heating burst. 'I think a workman must have stood on one of the pipes in the top floor of Periodicals. All the water started gushing out over those glass floors towards the lift, and it just cascaded down floor by floor until there was really quite a deep pool of black, horrid water in the basement. It was some time before we could find the stop-cock.'

The girls lifted the books out of the oily water, and set to work with hairdryers. 'What they do nowadays, of course, is to freeze them, and dry them out very gradually, but in those days the London Library didn't possess a deep-freeze.'

Innovations were never Gillam's strong point: he describes, quite happily, how he was the first victim of the new rolling cases in the basement. They are made of steel, mounted on tracks, and despite their considerable weight when they are loaded with books, they can be shunted together to save space. Before the retaining rails were properly fitted at the top, the end case overturned on top of him, burying him in books on archery.

He was also by nature a conservative. The girls had always traditionally worn black dresses. One morning Miss Cooper, by then the senior woman on the staff, strolled up to him and asked, 'Would you mind if some of us wore trousers?' 'After that, of course,' he reminisces ruefully, 'the rot set in.'

He is still surprised, looking back, at 'how adventurous a librarian's life could be'. One night he and his wife were asleep in bed in Orpington when the telephone rang. It was Vine Street police station, to say the fire alarm was ringing in St James's Square. They arrived, expecting to find the square full of fire engines. There were no lights showing in the library, but the bells were still ringing. Inside they found a window had been forced. There was a trail of matches, and someone had tried to start a fire of paper on Douglas Matthews' desk. 'By the grace of God, the paper had gone out.'

A recorded message should have been passed to the fire brigade but the apparatus had failed to work. 'We sent for the firm who had installed the machine, and it turned out they had forgotten to put the tape in. I wrote them a very strong letter and I think after that they reduced their rental.'

The most bizarre story was to do with a new porter he had taken on. 'He seemed extraordinarily efficient, extraordinarily nice. We thought, We've got a good egg here!' This turned out to be a misapprehension.

Early one Sunday morning Gillam and his son arrived without warning in St James's Square. 'I went into the library, and this chap appeared from the Porters' Room. I thought, This is very odd! There was a strong smell of bacon frying. I said, "What is the smell of bacon frying?" and he said, "It's the café at the back, I think they're giving someone breakfast." '

His son suggested afterwards that they drive past the Café Bonbonniere in Duke Street, and it was closed. 'I knew then that he had been lying. He was a wrong 'un. Sure enough, we found a pile of blankets in the Porters' Room. But there was more to it than that. He turned out to be a homosexual who had boyfriends sleeping there.' Joan Bailey surprised him in the ladies' staff room one Friday evening, loading into the refrigerator several pounds of pork sausages.

It is impossible not to feel sympathy for Gillam. It was an old-fashioned library: it had survived into a world its founders could never have imagined, governed by a traditionally inefficient amateur committee. But if he felt, as he said, that he 'wasn't so much Librarian as an Administrator: if the roof leaked or if the lavatory overflowed I was the one who had to deal with it,' he really only had himself to blame. By withdrawing to his old office upstairs he was surrendering power, and the balance between the librarian and the committee was about to swing back to what it had been in Carlyle's day, when the librarian was a 'guidable quadruped'.

Libraries in general were in a bad way. With the growth of television and the paperback trade, W. H. Smith's lending library collapsed in the sixties, closely followed by Boot's Booklovers' Library with its familiar shield-shaped label. Between 1967 and 1972 the price of new books almost doubled, and libraries all over the country were making economies, cutting staff, and buying as little as possible.

One of the oldest in the same league was the Hull Subscription Library, founded at the time of the first London Library at the end of the eighteenth century. It closed in 1975. In Manchester the Portico Library in Mosley Street, where De Quincey, Roget and other luminaries had once played backgammon and enjoyed 'coffee, soups, and other refreshments, excepting spirituous liquors' in the oil-lit newspaper room, was fighting off a property developer, and reduced to 'a little lady who did Oxo and sandwiches' in the reading room.

Despite the Christie's sale and the money from Hagberg's treasures, the library was still living from hand to mouth. The old lift had to be replaced. Another Labour Government introduced Selective Employment Tax (SET) to be paid by employers on every individual worker. Those in agriculture got it back with a bonus, those in manufacturing got it back without a bonus, and those in less socially useful jobs like librarianship did not get it back at all. But the London Library had cried 'wolf' too many times, and Rupert Hart-Davis's complaints about the iniquity of SET were rightly interpreted by many as evidence of bad management. The old committee meanwhile considered ending the open-shelf system, and there was even vague talk of moving to somewhere beyond Acton. Help was on the way, but it was to throw the library into a constitutional crisis.

First, the whole absurd muddle of the rates was cleared up. According to Gillam, the first approach came through one of the library's lawyers. 'He was called Keeling, he was a very good lawyer, and he knew a man at the Inland Revenue. The man from the Inland Revenue said, "Bring your Rules to me, and I will look through them, and I will tell you what alterations you will have to make in order to turn yourselves into a charity." ' With heavier taxation, this was a device being adopted by a great many of the older-established institutions. Legacies, donations and investment income were free of tax, the library could reclaim SET, and Westminster Council halved the rates. In exchange, the library had to accept that anyone could join, without being recommended by an existing member.

In the same year, the Arts Council was persuaded to look com-passionately at the library. Jenny Lee was now Minister for the Arts, and as Nye Bevan's widow represented the soul of the old Labour Party. As Lord Goodman remembers, 'She was an excellent Minister of Culture: she didn't enjoy it much herself but she was sure it was good for everyone else.' She was also determined to dispel the impression created by Eliot and others that Socialists were against Culture. The London Library was given a grant of £5,000. But more importantly, this marked the beginning of an extraordinary alliance, mirroring the politics of its founders, that was to put the library firmly in the black for the first time in nearly a hundred and fifty years.

It was at this juncture that the Labour Establishment's lumbering and many-chinned Mr Fixit came to take an interest in the troubles of the library. If it had not been for Arnold Goodman, it is unlikely that the library would have survived. His allies and clients stretched far beyond the confines of the Labour Party, and he selected as the unlikely saviour of the library a dilettante with a reputation for tiring of anything faster than Toad of Toad Hall, consumer of an enormous family fortune, patron of the arts and discreet supporter of many individual artists, a fastidious man with large china-blue eyes, an engaging sense of humour and a terrible temper. He was the Hon. Michael Astor, son of Nancy, and brother of Bill Astor who came unstuck in the Profumo Scandal.

Arnold Goodman brought him in initially to help with the appeal fund. This was launched in 1972 with the declared objective of raising £500,000. Goodman's idea was that a rich man would be less likely to alarm other rich men when he came to ask them for money. Astor himself saw the point of this; as he said to Goodman: 'There are only three people on the committee capable of raising large sums of money, and you are two of them.'

The Appeal Committee fielded a strong cast of personalities, graced by Sir Kenneth Clark as president of the library, and led by Roy Jenkins. Clark, never very dynamic, was then at the height of his international fame as presenter of the BBC's series *Civilisation*, for which he was relentlessly mocked in *Private Eye* as an effete figure draping himself in well-made suits in front of the great works of European art and architecture and proclaiming them to be 'very agreeable'.

Addressing the press from behind a long table in the Reading Room, Roy Jenkins told them that the money was needed 'partly to extend the facilities of the Library, and partly to put the Library on a secure financial basis for the future without a continual piecemeal approach.' Half would be spent on building four new floors of bookstack, and replacing the old vaults in the basement with the famous rolling cases. 'The rest would be invested to secure the future of the world's largest and most distinguished private library.'

Jenkins, then deputy leader of the Opposition under Harold Wilson, was at pains to insist that the library was 'no elitist body, and certainly not the preserve' – one imagines the curious circular motion of the left hand – 'of the rich, middle-aged, well-established literary gentleman.' This did not prevent Michael Astor from entertaining his colleagues fairly lavishly, and Roy Jenkins remembers them returning from lunch at the old Ritz Grill, and saying as they climbed the steps – the famous 'r' rolling in appreciation at the memory of it – 'We may not save the London Library, but we've certainly rescued the Ritz Grill!'

Foyle's gave, or rather promoted, a literary luncheon at the Dorchester, tickets costing £3 a head. The guests of honour included His Excellency the Luxembourg and Robert Morley. Christie's held another sale, and both Graham Sutherland and Francis Bacon contributed pictures. *The New York Times* devoted the best part of half a page to 'An Old Friend in Peril', and in the *Daily Telegraph* magazine fourteen distinguished members of the library, including Edna O'Brien, Sir Bernard Miles, Christopher

Logue, Frank Muir, Lady Antonia Fraser and her mother Lady Longford agreed to have a group photograph taken. At the last moment it became fifteen when they were joined, at his own request, by Lord Longford, author of *Humility*.

*The Times* gave £5,000. Contributions from members of the library ranged from £5 to £1,000. Lord Goodman bullied institutions, but as he had foreseen when he engaged the help of Michael Astor, £100,000 came from five large anonymous donations from private individuals. Astor himself gave £10,000 for immediate roof repairs, and probably more in commissioning a sculptress to make seven busts of Lord Goodman, to be sold in aid of the fund. These were bought by various rich friends, and can still be seen today, usually crowned with a straw hat, brooding from the top of a cupboard or a hall table in a country house.

Astor, never having had a job except for a brief period as an MP – he decided the House of Commons was 'too boring' – threw himself into it with terrifying energy, having found a role he thoroughly enjoyed. In the course of the campaign, however, he made various approaches which gave rise to rumour and wild surmise, including one to a property developer. Some members of the committee were alarmed, news quickly spread to the staff, and in no time there was talk of asset-stripping, the building being sold and vast profits being made, little or none of which would find their way into the coffers of the library.

This story was revived when Astor brought in Max Rayne, also a property developer, as one of four vice-presidents. Rayne was born in the slums of the East End, had made an immense fortune, married Lady Jane Vane-Tempest-Stewart, sister of Lord Londonderry, and had been a generous supporter of the Royal Opera House and the National Theatre. Within four months, the appeal was halfway to its target with £250,000 and this was then matched by an anonymous single donation of £250,000.

Other donations continued to come in, and when the fund closed in October 1973 it was well over its original target, at £593,000.

Astor now turned his attention to the committee. A member at the time describes it as going through 'a rather shambling period'. Conversation was dilatory, turning in the main on gossip about mutual acquaintances, only some of them writers, and discussion of recently published books, only some of which ever reached the shelves of the library. Nobody had any experience of administration or business outside publishing, Peter Calvocoressi had never wanted to be chairman, and when he resigned Astor was the only person prepared to put himself forward to succeed him. He was elected in 1974, and began to run the library in a way that no chairman had ever run it before.

He immediately brought in two professionals who were not even members of the library. Cyril Sweett would advise on investments, and Lewis Golden would take overall control of the money. He also formed what amounted to a secret inner committee with Bamber Gascoigne and Nicholas Barker of the British Library, which made all the real decisions over pheasant and good claret at Wilton's in Jermyn Street.

Astor took an almost instant dislike to Gillam, treating him according to one witness 'like a member of the lower orders'. Douglas Matthews he liked, and determined to promote.

Librarians in the past had always prepared the minutes of committee meetings, exercising a degree of control. Astor insisted on writing these himself, and demanded immediate reforms. Despite the success of the fund, the budgets for the next three years, based on Lewis Golden's gloomy estimates, envisaged deficits of £29,000, £42,000 and £57,000.

The staff would be reduced by a process of 'natural wastage', those who retired would not be replaced, and this would lose eight jobs out of forty-seven in under two years. The blue card system would be abolished, and Bamber Gascoigne was credited with a proposal, not accepted, for a surcharge on country membership and a single central enquiry desk. The climax of the horror was the demolition of the entrance hall, part of which was closed off as a new Cataloguing Room, with Issues and Returns amalgamated behind one counter on the left, and fire doors in front of the stairs. Older members of the staff were reduced to tears, and it was no great consolation to Joan Bailey as she sat looking unhappily at the wreckage of Mr Cox's old desk, when Lord Clark himself laid his hand on her shoulder. 'There,' he said, 'it's not so bad, is it?'

Publicly, Clark tried to distance himself from what was happening. 'The president is wheeled out every year like an idol and takes no part in executive details. If he did it would be resented.' Privately, even he was alarmed. The committee, he confided in a friend, 'did not seem to have asked the staff (still less the President) before making all their recent changes.'

The staff found their champion in an extraordinary figure, then working there, Keith Harling. A young but donnish figure in pebble spectacles, he was admired by younger members of the library for his waspish wit. He took a particular dislike to Douglas Matthews as Astor's man, and denounced him to *The Sunday Times*. He was not a qualified librarian, Harling told them, he was an ex-palmist and Butlin's Red Coat. This had a basis of fact. Before embarking on his virtuous career at the India Office Library and the Royal Library in Stockholm, Douglas Matthews had spent one Long Vacation working at a Butlin's holiday camp and spent an afternoon sitting in for the palmist.

Harling's behaviour was however considered to be not that of a gentleman. This was unlikely to deter a man who boasted he had offered himself to University College Hospital as a case of tertiary syphilis, and who was eventually sacked by Gillam who was afraid he might pass the infection to members 'on the pages of the books'.

Harling organised meetings in a local pub. Staff talked to members, among them Philip Bovey, subsequently under-secretary at the Department of Trade and Industry, and Christopher Booker, then one of the editors of *Private Eye*, an investigative journalist who specialised in property developers and the destruction of our architectural heritage.

The first story appeared in *Private Eye* as Astor took over: Astor had never read a book in his life, he upset staff at the library by sending out for smoked-salmon sandwiches and shouting at them if the crusts weren't cut off, he was bringing in Max Rayne. The library's money troubles would be solved if it could sell its beautiful and historic building at 14 St James's Square, and it would be interesting to see how long Sir Max would wait before proposing this course of action. This was picked up by the *Daily Telegraph*. Michael Astor said he appeared to be dealing with a group of people who were 'vastly misinformed'. Booker's answer was that if they were vastly misinformed it was because they couldn't get any information.

They called themselves initially the Committee for the Preservation of the London Library, then the Friends of the London Library, to which Astor's response was that they didn't seem very friendly.

Philip Bovey, an experienced civil servant with particular expertise in company law, was then a junior solicitor at Slaughter and May, and claims he had their permission to use the firm's writing paper when he worked for the Friends in his spare time. Slaughter and May's name certainly added weight to a letter he wrote to the library, claiming members had not been properly warned in writing about elections to the committee. All the reforms Astor had pushed through were therefore illegal.

Astor was shaken enough to ring Goodman, and acted on his advice. It being laid down in the rules that three constituted a quorum, Lord Clark as president summoned the other vice-presidents, all appointed for life, and re-elected the existing committee, who in turn ratified all their previous decisions. Michael Astor also persuaded Booker to come and have lunch at his home in Swan Walk, Chelsea. Douglas Matthews was in attendance. By the end of lunch they agreed that the staff 'might have displayed some of the characteristics of Balaam's Ass' in their reaction to the reforms, and Booker dropped out of the battle.

Not so Philip Bovey, who reported the library to the Charity Commissioners, demanded new elections, and still using his Slaughter and May paper, terrified the committee with the idea that they might all be individually responsible for any debts the library had incurred under their management. The London Library Committee found that much reality hard to bear, and never forgave him for it.

Astor and Goodman now discovered that Bovey was not a partner of Slaughter and May. From then on, according to Bovey, official permission to use their paper was withdrawn, and he is 'fairly certain' that his papers were somehow read by the lawyers representing the committee.

It had been agreed, however, that the Friends could put up their own candidate for the committee. This really got Kenneth Clark's goat. 'Dissidents make their way onto a Trust', he complained in a letter to an old friend, 'and then proceed to try and destroy it from within. I suppose it is an extension of Trade Union practice, and that it will end by meaning that no decent person will serve in public life.' Astor, while publicly conceding that 'certain forces did seem to be trying to erode what they saw as establishment organisation', alerted his allies.

For the first time since it had moved to its present premises, the London Library had to find more space than the Reading Room could provide to accommodate the expected crowd. The 134th Annual General Meeting took place in the John Power Hall at the Royal Institute of International Affairs, Chatham House, at 10 St James's Square. Three hundred and fifty members turned up,

216

more than had ever attended an annual general meeting in the history of the library. The hall was so full that Joan Bailey and other members of the staff had to stand at the back. Lord Clark was on the platform, as were Astor, Golden and Gillam.

Clark opened the meeting in his most agreeable manner, recalling the library in his undergraduate days as 'a haven of peace and order'. He praised the committee, he praised the staff, he even praised Stanley Gillam, about whom he was privately extremely rude. The committee had been accused of being a set of 'self-perpetuating old men'. In fact they had been thinking for some time about having a rule that nobody should serve on the committee for more than four years, and should stand down for at least twelve months before being re-elected. He hoped this would now become official policy.

Michael Astor then called for a motion of confidence in the administration of the library, backed by Kingsley Amis, Robert Kee, Sir Edward Playfair and Dame Veronica Wedgwood. A forest of hands rose in support.

Looking round the room at Michael Astor's friends from White's and from the shires, Philip Bovey realised he was in trouble. 'I knew the constitutional point about the Committee was dynamite, and I imagined that we had only to produce it to bring the walls tumbling down. I underestimated the importance of gaining political support.' When he got up someone called him a Communist. He began to explain that they were raising a serious question of principle, and added, unwisely, that 'they had tried to remain as friendly and helpful as possible'. Michael Astor said he did not think it was very friendly or helpful to report the library to the Charity Commissioners, and the rest of Bovey's speech was shouted down. One of his supporters thought they were going to be lynched.

When it came to the elections for the committee the Friends' candidates, including Philip Bovey and Elizabeth Ray, were rejected by a majority of five to one.

Looking back, Bovey admits that he was 'politically outmanoeuvred'. 'I had never experienced anything quite like it before. In such cases the law alone is not enough.' But the committee had learned some important lessons, and the library moved more cautiously into its Golden Age.

# Still Possessed

*I do not think that the rules of the London Library are to be taken very seriously. I never paid a fine in my life, and once when I kept a book three years it provoked no more than a mild remonstrance.*

A. E. Housman

By the time you read this the London Library may no longer exist. Its books may be scattered through second-hand shops up and down the Charing Cross Road, its old home in St James's Square pulled down and redeveloped as the headquarters of some international communications company. It is more probable that the London Library will be muddling on.

In the year of the library's 150th anniversary, under Douglas Matthews and his deputy, the Russian expert Michael Higgins, there is a happier balance of power: Matthews is very tolerant of the committee, and the committee relatively respectful to Matthews while preserving much of the uncomfortable drive it had under Michael Astor. The treasurer, Lewis Golden, continues to keep a shrewd eye on expenses, and John Grigg still irritates the librarian's secretary by 'wanting everything yesterday'.

'We should thank God every morning', one member has written in the Suggestions Book, 'that we have a Librarian strong enough and wise enough to resist the senseless and destructive mania for change which afflicts us so grievously on all sides. The pressures on him must be enormous; our debt to him is incalculable. *Mais après lui le Déluge!*'

'I would not want it thought that I am opposed to change *per se*,' Douglas has written on the opposite page, 'and please do not be pessimistic about the future. As things stand it is rather *après moi l'inconnu.*'

Like Bodham Donne, the librarian still litters his comments with French and Latin tags, and like Cochrane or Harrison, Hagberg or Nowell-Smith he still happily gossips away to his favourite members as if he had all the time in the world. Books are still kept out for years, and I recently overheard him at a party in the country being quite firm with a lady member who was swearing she would bring some books back immediately: 'No, don't do that for goodness' sake. If everybody brought their books back we wouldn't have room for them on the shelves.'

The library, together with its familiar dusty perfume of good literature, still has the same mysterious air of mid-Victorian confidence, its open shelves witnessing to the same patrician trust as when the library was used exclusively by country gentlemen and ladies, clergymen and members of the House of Lords, and when London was still a village. Even today the staff still manage to give the impression they are there to serve rather than to supervise.

Efforts to prevent thefts have been steadily resisted. 'Is it in the tradition of the Library', someone else asks in the Suggestions Book, 'that the bulk of members should be inconvenienced as the only means of confounding the knavery of the few?' For the last few years, all bags and briefcases have had to be left in the hall. This stops thieves from filling cases in the stacks, but also means that honest members have to leave their bags unguarded within ten feet of the door to a busy London pavement.

Inevitably thefts continue. Douglas Matthews once plucked up the courage to ask an American research student to open the portfolio he was carrying out of the Art Room.

He seemed perfectly ready to do so, and inside we found several illustrations, all with jagged edges, that had clearly been cut out of books. I asked him to step into the Librarian's Room, which he did, and I sent someone into the Art Room to see if they could match the jagged edges of these cut-out illustrations with the equivalent edges in our books. I couldn't very well accuse him without proof.

Well, as you can imagine, that was very difficult. All they could do was look for books of roughly the right size, and there are a great many books in there. When it came to closing time, I felt I had to let this young man go, asked him to leave his portfolio behind overnight, which he agreed to do, and asked him for his name and address, all of which he provided. Then, next morning, of course, we found one that matched. I rang the police, gave them the address, and the bird had flown. And the police said, 'You bloody fool, why didn't you call us round last night?'

Since then a valuable clock has disappeared from the Prevost Room while workmen were putting up scaffolding at the back of the building next door, and an eighteenth-century mirror has vanished from the downstairs Gents.

Should the library ever be dispersed, the Suggestions Book will provide a vivid record of its daily life. Traditionally, suggestions for new books were written on a piece of paper and handed over the counter. Since the Great Rumpus of 1975 the Suggestions Book has been in the hall for anyone to write in, and often it reveals more about the members than it does about the books.

The lavatories continue to figure large. Very occasionally, there is an unsolicited tribute: 'Whoever is responsible for the Ladies, I know no better anywhere.' But most of the time there are complaints. Can obscene graffiti be removed – 'though exuberant, the penis is poorly drawn and the Library surely has enough character already without needing such attempts to add to it' – or can the Librarian supply better-quality lavatory paper. His answer to this is that he has been 'falling back on old stock'. This in turn leads to a humorous exchange in which various books are suggested as an alternative, and certain authors encouraged to present their works for this purpose free of charge.

But the suggestions are largely high-minded and responsible. There are the kinds of request that make clear how nightmarish the life of a working librarian must be. 'Page fifteen of *The Times* of 19 November 1936 has been removed. Is it possible to get a duplicate replacement?' Some, for new books, are mildly surprising, like a suggestion in the seventies that the library should buy *Confessions of a Long-Distance Acid Head*. A note opposite says this will be considered. *Facing Reality*, published by Springer-Verlag Berlin the same year, is rejected on the grounds that 'it is not within the fields we cover'.

There is the predictable range of batty interests: *Monopsychism, Mysticism, Metaconsciousness, The Art of Rock*, J. Mordaunt Crook's *The Dilemma of Style*, *A Carver of Coal* by Eona Macnicoll, *Sex Songs of the Ancient Letts*, *Rubbish Theory*, *The Grand Duke's Woman – the Life of Countess Brassoff*, *A Stress Analysis of the Strapless Evening Gown*, *Why is British architecture so lousy?*, as well as *Pornography and Silence*.

Almost all the suggestions are accepted; it is after all, as Carlyle intended, a private library for the benefit of its members. Where a book belongs to the library, it is marked 'already possessed', a phrase first used by Gillam and carried on by Douglas Matthews. When it was recently queried, as a too-cumbersome alternative to

220

'got it', Matthews defended it on the grounds that it had 'a fine Dostoievskian ambiguity'.

But a large proportion of the Suggestions Book is devoted to physical life in the library. Readers who have been using the place for years ask for maps in the upstairs floors; they have to come back to the Issue Hall every time they want to find their way to another part of the building. Older members with slipped discs complain they cannot use the lower drawer of the card index without experiencing a sharp pain – 'anyone in such a condition should try consulting "J" ' – and ask for 'shallower card-indexes'. 'Not only shallower but *lower*. If one is *short*, apart from having a slipped disc, one can only see the back of the cards in the drawers on the top rank with the greatest difficulty.'

On the opposite page the librarian says he is sorry, and wishes they could afford to replace the catalogue stands. But members are always full of ideas. 'M. C. Rintoul. In connection with the index catalogues – could not an inch or two be sawn off the legs of their supporting tables, or would this cause more inconvenience to giants than is at present suffered by dwarfs?' As a compromise, stools are provided, and a few pages later someone else complains they have tripped over one of them in the half-darkness.

The lighting is constantly criticised, theories bandied to and fro over a period of twenty years as to whether it costs more to turn fluorescent lighting on and off or to leave it burning all day. The electrical equipment gives off 'an unpleasant whine'. 'Gervase Jackson-Stops: Fuse box at the entrance to the history floor has for many months (years) been building up to a massive crescendo. Is *Götterdämmerung* now at hand?'

On almost every page, year after year, there is some fresh account of members electrocuting themselves on the metal shelves in the stacks.

The static electricity shocks on the Societies floors were particularly unpleasant today and my feeling of discomfort lasted the better part of thirty minutes afterwards.

Is there any scientific explanation for the fact that I continually experience electric shocks when touching the metal shelves? One today caused me to yelp, thus disturbing the sepulchral silence.

N. Tolstoy: Is there a cure for the electric shocks I receive in the iron galleries? Perhaps I am exceptionally susceptible but it is an unnerving experience.

Would it be possible for the library to purchase James Reynold's *Irish Ghost Stores* – a classic of its kind – published c. 1946? *Also* I still receive electric shocks from the light switches in the Occult section.

Remedies are put forward: the floors should be sprayed every morning with water – the librarian explains that this 'would not be practicable in the Library', all members should be issued with rubber galoshes, readers should touch the shelves first with a key or other metal object. Someone tries this, and reports that his biro exploded.

There are sudden outbursts of rage, covering sometimes two or three pages, at the cataloguing system, with Lord Strabolgi wanting to know why Stendhal is listed under B for Beyle, or Gerard de Nerval under G for Gerard. This mutter of conservative irritability is very occasionally interrupted by a more strident radical voice. 'Z. Leader: Do you think Mary Wollstonecraft would like to be catalogued under *Godwin, Mary M.*? Aren't you worried about the feminist reaction?' 'Mr Leader: No. S.G.'

From Douglas Matthews the feminists get slightly longer shrift, but no real concessions.

Has the time not come for the Library to reconsider its classification of books pertaining to women? Given that we accept that we form a separate category – and do we? – it seems inappropriate and somewhat insulting to list the majority sex under the Miscellaneous end of Science – after *Witchcraft* and before *Wool* and *Wrestling*! It makes it very difficult to seek out serious studies on Feminism when you have to fumble through all the Victorian and later misogynist rambling. Incidentally '*Women*' have disappeared in the subject catalogue. The tab has gone.

Matthews makes some sort of apology, but explains that the alphabetical position of the word *women* 'is something we cannot alter'.

Innovations are always being suggested, but unlike the requests for books, not often acceded to. Some are reasonable – 'The Groucho Club has a card phone. May we have one please?' – although having a public telephone in the entrance hall at all is a touchy question: 'Box up the public telephone!! If one has a bad line, one has to shout. This causes embarrassment to the caller and inconvenience to those trying to make themselves heard by the staff.' Some are outrageous, like a demand to be allowed to smoke in the Reading Room.

But the longest runner of all is the Great Tearoom Debate. This twists and turns over the years, at times degenerating into demands for a coffee machine, at others rising to satire. The library staff are envisaged by one humorist bringing trays to the desks and handing round fairy cakes, and Benedict Nightingale and Alan Brien propose a 'discreet and tasteful licensed bar'.

Stanley Gillam argued that even a coffee machine would endanger the library's charitable status. Virginia Surtees protests in block capitals 'Coffee ON NO ACCOUNT', but one historian of the library assures his fellow-members that 'in the thirties, under the Librarianship of a Mr. Cox, tea was provided, *and toast*!'

Someone else suggests that members would be better off drinking water. 'Yes, *please* make a drinking-height water tap available.' A supporter foresees trouble. 'I am aware that for some of the Library's members, "American" equals "anathema" but it seems to me that the provision of drinking water in places of this kind is one of the inestimable benefits conferred upon the literary public in the USA – so why not here?' 'A.M.H. Bale: And a hot dog's (*sic*) stall?' 'No – don't be impertinent!'

Not that gracious old Americans don't still drop in, as Henry James's father or Longfellow did before them: 'A. Spater: The Century Club in New York has a table in its Library where member's books, recently received, are displayed. A similar arrangement at the London Library, plus a note at the time annual dues are solicited should produce some books for the Library at no cost.'

Members frequently irritate each other: they still scribble in books, they still snore in the Reading Room, and one unnamed offender is denounced for clumping about the metal gangways in wooden-soled shoes. But usually it is the library that is at fault. Doors marked 'Push' are said to be locked, and then discovered to be 'merely stiff', the lift makes extraordinary noises 'like an old tram' and breaks down so frequently that a member of the staff risks the sack by suggesting that a card should be hung on the door when it is working.

Even the library's most sacred traditions come in for abuse. 'Must that awful bell ring (a) at all (b) as early as 5.15?' '(a) Yes

(b) it should start at 17.20.' The air is dry: windows are never opened in the summer, and in winter the heating is turned up too high. 'Members come in their outdoor clothes, and it is awful looking for dusty books in an over-heated cul-de-sac.'

Wearers of high-heeled shoes and sufferers from vertigo beg for 'some kind of cheap carpeting' to cover the grilled floors in the bookstacks, always with unsympathetic comments from other members telling them not to wear high-heeled shoes and defending our 'lovely grilles'.

But whether the debate is about carpeting in the stacks, the lighting – 'the relentless vulgarity of fluorescent bulbs' – or a proposal to leave dust-jackets on the books and to cover them with plastic, aesthetic considerations are never far away, and the question of good taste is paramount. 'Will the Library harden its heart and not listen to the suggestions being made about *Dust covers*? One earnestly prays and hopes that the time-honoured custom will continue of ripping these vulgar things off the books as soon as they arrive. All the library's charm exists in one's being able to stroll among cases of fading bindings without having to stare at a lot of hideous glaring trade puffs which, moreover, can only be affixed if expensively encased in ghastly plastic.'

So the old London Library Society, for the time being, survives. 'Nothing has changed,' says Frances Partridge, looking back over seventy years: 'absolutely nothing. The same smell, the same atmosphere, the same clanking noise as you walk through those long passages at the back, and you always seem to meet someone you want to meet. I have always liked the way you suddenly come nose to nose with an old friend.'

Such encounters are part of the library's mysterious appeal, but so are encounters with books. Under the heading 'The Library Angel' in his contribution to a collection called *The Challenge of Chance*, Arthur Koestler described how he was commissioned by *The Sunday Times* in 1972 to write about the Spassky–Fischer chess championship in Iceland. He went to the London Library to look for books on chess and on Iceland.

I hesitated for a moment whether to go to the 'C' for chess section first, or the 'I' for Iceland section, but chose the former, because it was nearer. There were about twenty to thirty books on chess on the shelves, and the first that caught my eye was a bulky volume with the title: *Chess in Iceland*

*and Icelandic Literature* by Williard Friske, published in 1905 by the Florentine Typographical Society, Florence, Italy.

But for all the crackle of dark creative electricity in the Occult department, all the energy the library has created, the social revolutions set turning in its faded Edwardian Reading Room, the library's most endearing and enduring quality is its respect for leisure. Its current president, Lord Annan, like his predecessors Leslie Stephen and Arthur Balfour, is an Apostle, and he calls it creative laziness.

People forget how important it is to be lazy in libraries. Not of course idle: idleness means day-dreaming. Laziness means reading the books one ought not to be reading, and becoming so absorbed in them and following the trails along which they lead you, so that at the end of the day you still have most of the reading to do that you had before that morning. Creative laziness broadens the mind.

But there is also an uncreative idleness of a kind unique to the library, described by the author Jonathan Gathorne-Hardy in the same year that Arthur Koestler was rummaging in the stacks for books on Iceland. The library, he said, was 'very, very peaceful'.

There's a sort of university atmosphere, a vaguely studious air of people trying to read and mostly falling asleep. In August it reaches a pitch where you're no sooner in the library than you pass out. You relax completely. You go up to the Reading Room and sit in those huge leather chairs and open the window and sort of vaguely listen to London drowsing and droning on outside and quietly pass out. I suppose the knowledge that people are sweating in the streets a few yards away makes your own relaxation very much more pleasant.

The other people at the London Library are very, very charming. About two people go there to work: John Julius Norwich goes there *not* to work, actually, and I should think Antonia Byatt is one of the only people who does work. The people who *do* work are all the assistants who are for ever scurrying about doing no-one quite knows what – repositioning books, answering letters – and they provide the essential background for true relaxation, which is the sound of other people working.

\* \* \*

The closer you get to the idea of the London Library, the more it recedes into infinity: thousands of millions of words, housed in so many storeys, or as the *Oxford English Dictionary* prefers it, stories. Children, for all I know, may have been conceived there, and certainly, in the way books mysteriously reproduce themselves, millions more words, and many more stories. Many remain untold.

There is something tantalising and miraculous about the place, a working model of ideal societies: a mystical Carlylean dictatorship under Hagberg, a centre of Christian enlightenment, a Positivist tool-shop, a refuge for T. S. Eliot's embattled Elite, or simply a charming anachronism within five hundred yards of Piccadilly Circus, in the middle of Clubland. Other high-minded early Victorian institutions near by have atrophied into mere drinking clubs, dining rooms and day-care centres for the elderly: the London Library still fulfills the purpose of its founders, breathing the same air of nineteenth-century leisure, when members of the library were in the habit of having their shoes made, their clothes made, cooks to cook for them and servants to serve for them, and where even today their descendants who want a good book to read at the weekend and can't face making the choice, can still ask the kind librarian to make it for them.

# Sources

The author and publishers would like to express their gratitude to the following who have very kindly given permission for use of copyright materials:

Valerie Eliot for excerpts from T. S. Eliot's Address to the library;

The Ardizzone Estate for the cartoon 'Half a million books';

Alan Clark for access to the unpublished letters by Sir Kenneth Clark;

Andrew Barrow for an interview with Jonathan Gathorne-Hardy in *Harpers & Queen*;

*The Adam International Review 1976–77* for an article by Lord Annan;

The British Library Board for permission to quote from Carlyle's letters;

The Dean and Chapter of Westminster for the Coroner's Report on Bryan Courthope Leigh Hunt;

HarperCollins for excerpts from Harold Nicolson's *Diaries*;

John Murray Publishers for excerpts from *The Lyttelton/ Hart-Davis Letters*;

The Society of Authors as the literary representative of the Estate of John Masefield for his doggerel verse 'If we were in a pavender . . .';

Weidenfeld and Nicolson for permission to quote from *Evelyn Waugh's Letters*, edited by Mark Amory.

The 1952 drawing by Mays is reproduced by permission of *Punch*.

Every effort has been made to trace all copyright holders but if any has been inadvertently overlooked, the author and publishers will be pleased to make the necessary arrangement at the first opportunity.

# Index